A HANDBOOK FOR "HELP YOURSELF" SHANGHAI TOURS

SHANGHAI MUNICIPAL TOURISM
ADMINISTRATIVE COMMISSION

SHANGHAI SCIENTIFIC & TECHNICAL PUBLISHERS

FOREWORD

Shanghai is situated in the middle of China's south-north coastline and a gate to the beautiful and fertile Changjiang River valley. Since China's reform and opening to the outside world this brilliant pearl in the East has been shining ever so bright with greater vitality; its magnifying spirit and tremendous changes with every passing day have attracted world attention. Tourists, businessmen, students from home and abroad come in crowds in an endless stream.

In rendering convenience and ease to domestic and foreign visitors and giving them more freedom in visiting Shanghai's historical sites, appreciating its culture and folk customs, the cosmopolitan atmosphere of its prosperous commerce and trade, we have collected a large amount of up-to-date material, and compiled this "Handbook for 'Help Yourself' Shanghai Tours" to dedicate to our readers. The principle of compiling this handbook is "novelty, practicability, self-help and convenience" developed along the six main lines of tourism: catering, accommodation, travel, sightseeing, shopping and amusement". It contains a large amount of information, practical, popular and easy to understand. We sincerely hope that this handbook will provide visitors to Shanghai with convenience and be a faithful guide to new visitors.

Limited by editing standard and time, plus the rapid changes in development of Shanghai, the handbook has much room for improvement. Your comments are welcome.

The editor

CONTENTS

IV. AMUSEMENT

V. CATERING

VI. ACCOMMODATION

VII. TRAVELING

VIII. SURROUNDING AREAS

IX. Service

SHANGHAI IN BRIEF

GEOGRAPHICAL LOCATION

Shanghai, situated at 31°14" north latitude and 121°29" east longitude. is China's largest city. It is in the middle of China's east coastline and a gate to the Changjiang River valley, with a very favorable geographical location.

AREA AND POPULATION

Shanghai occupies an area of 6,341 sq.km. consisting of 16 districts and 4 counties, of which the city proper occupies an area of 2,642.6 sq.km. Shanghai has a permanent resident population of over 14.6 million, of which 9.48 million live in the urban areas. The average life span is 77 years.

CLIMATE

Shanghai has a sub-tropical monsoon climate, warm and humid, with an average annual temperature of 16℃. The annual precipitation is 1,100 mm. Shanghai has four distinct seasons: spring, summer, autumn and winter. The hottest month is July with an average temperature of 28℃ and the coldest month is January with an average temperature of 3℃. The climate is favorable for making tours all year round.

HISTORY

Shanghai has much influence on China's history for several hundred years. From textual research we have found that 5,000 years ago during the period of the Songze culture, Shanghai already took the shape of a plain in the Changjiang River Delta. Our ancestors had left their footprints here. During the Spring and Autumn Period, Shanghai belonged to the Wu State. During the Period of the Warring States, Shanghai first belonged to the Yue State and then to the Chu State. King Lie of the Chu State appointed Huang Xie as his prime minister and bestowed him the title of Lord Chunshen. Shanghai was part of his feoff. The other name of Shanghai"Shen" was derived from this. Shanghai has another name "Hu", which came from "hu du". In ancient times, the fishermen in Shanghai invented a bamboo fishing device called "hu". ("Du" in Chinese means "creek".) This area was called "Hu Du" before it became known as Shanghai. The name "Shanghai" actually came into being during the Song Dynasty, when Shanghai was then becoming a new rising trading port. There were then in Shanghai 18 creeks, one of which was called Shanghai Creek, a section of the Huangpu River from the Bund to Shiliupu. On its western bank was a Shanghai Town; the name "Shanghai" was derived from this. During the Yuan Dynasty, Shanghai Town had greatly developed and set up a shipping administration. Later on, the town was promoted to a county, which consisted of today's urban areas, Shanghai, Qingpu, Nanhui and Chuansha Counties. By the Ming Dynasty, Shanghai had already become China's largest textile center and business was developing fast. In the 24th year of Qing Emperor Kangxi's reign (1685), the Qing government set up in Shanghai the customs. During the reigns of Qing Emperor Qianlong and Jiaqing, Shanghai gradually became China's major trading port and water transportation center for grains. It was then known as "A place accessible by sea and rivers; a capital in the southeast".

In 1843, after the Opium War, Shanghai was forced to become an open port by the colonialists. In 1845, Britain first set up its concession in Shanghai. In 1848, the United States set up its concession, then followed by France in 1849. In 1863, the British and American concessions amalgamated into the International Settlement. Shanghai was actually partitioned into the Chinese Section, the International Settlement and the French Concession. In the 100 years since 1943, Shanghai had become an important port for the foreign colonialists to dump their goods, ravaged raw materials and money. Shanghai was thus known as "A Paradise of the Adventurers".

On July 7, 1927, Shanghai was proclaimed as a special municipality. In 1945, after the victory of the Anti-Japanese War, the concessions were reclaimed. On May 27, 1949, Shanghai was really liberated. Through the continual and long-term reform and construction by the successive municipal governments and the people, Shanghai has become an important industrial and commercial base in new China. In the 20 years of reform and opening to the outside world (1978-1998), especially after Deng Xiaoping, the chief designer of our reform and opening policy, made his speech on his inspection tour of the south, Shanghai has been developing and changing with every passing day and has become China's center of economy, finance, science and technology, information and culture, an international modernized metropolis.

A BRIEF INTRODUCTION TO THE CITY

Shanghai, situated in the watery regions in the south of the Changjiang River, is fertile in soil, crisscrossed by rivers and canals. Its main agricultural products are rice, cotton, wheat, edible oil crops and vegetables, with prosperous livestock and poultry breeding farms and abundant agricultural and non-staple produce.

Shanghai is the largest industrial base in China. As industry is the mainstay of the city's national economy, its industry, complete in systems, strong in its material and technical foundation, with highly qualified technical professionals and famous brands, have attracted world attention.Today,Shanghai has become a comprehensive industrial city with 6 leading manufacturing industries of automobiles, electronic communication equipment. complete sets of power plants and large-scale electric and machinery equipment, petro-chemical and refined chemicals, iron and steel and household electrical appliances, accompanied by such traditional and newly developed industries as metallurgy, chemicals, machinery, ship building, electronics, meters and instruments, textile,light industry,new-type metals, pharmaceuticals, high polymer synthetics, computers, precisionary machine tools and space technology.

Shanghai is one of the largest commercial centers in the country. It is also an important hub for collecting and distributing goods in the Changjiang River Delta. Shanghai's financial business has a history of more than 200 years. In the '30s and '40s of the century, Shanghai was already China's largest financial center and an international financial center in the Far East. Shanghai's financial market is developing, gathering the domestic and oversea banking, stock and insurance business talents to paint a brilliant picture. Shanghai's foreign trade has a long history; it is complete in all branches, with specialized import and export companies dealing in all kinds of commodities; there are industrial and trade combined import and export companies and factories directly dealing in import and export, together with a complete system for the service of foreign trade in oversea transportation, storage, packing, advertisement and insurance.

Shanghai is one of China's centers of science, technology and culture. There are now 40 general institutions of higher learning with a student and graduate student body of a hundred thousand. There are over 1,000 research and development institutions with a million technical professionals, among whom 500,000 are professionals in natural sciences. Shanghai's science and technical undertakings are developing fast and have achieved and developed many new techniques and results and scientific exchanges are very active. Shanghai's cultural, press, publishing, broadcasting and TV businesses are well developed.

Shanghai is the hub of our country's water, land and air transportation. Shanghai Port is one of the leading ports in the world. Domestic shipping is also well developed. International shipping can reach 400 ports in 160 countries and regions in the world. There are two trunk railway lines - the Beijing-Shanghai and Shanghai-Hangzhou lines - linking all the trunk lines in the country. Shanghai Railway Station dispatches every day 80 pairs of trains to different parts of the country. The Shanghai-Nanjing and Shanghai-Hangzhou freeways have already opened to traffic, rendering more convenience and accessibility among the areas in the Changjiang Delta. The building of Shanghai-Beijing express railway is underway. Shanghai International Airport dispatches planes on more than 300 air routes from Shanghai and the annual civil air transport volume is 13,000,000 person/times. Shanghai's largest airport underway, the Pudong International Airport, will open to traffic in 1999. After the completion of the first phase of the project the passenger volume will be 20,000,000 person/times and cargo freight, 750,000 tons. The project will greatly facilitate the entry and exit of domestic and foreign travelers.

Shanghai is one of the principal hubs of international and domestic postal, telecommunication. It is equipped with up-to-date international programmed exchange system with IDD and DDD automatic telephone lines. There is also an advanced mobile telephone communication system and international internet to meet the needs of domestic and overseas customers in exchanging information.

SIGHTSEETING

(I) NEW SCENIC SIGHTS IN THE CITY

In the '90s, when "There is change every year and great changes in three years", many new scenic spots have come into being and are much appreciated by people. In 1995, when Shanghai Tourism Administration sponsored the appraisal of 10 new scenic spots in Shanghai, and voted by Shanghai citizens, the "10 new great scenic spots of the '90s" were chosen. They are typical of the achievements of city construction.By the last year of the century, more high-standard new architecture will rise at every corner of the city. These will fully express the vitality of the ever changing development of Shanghai. They also indicate, on the other hand, the tremendous changes brought about by reform and opening to the outside world. Shanghai is growing taller, bigger, more beautiful, and glowing with unprecedented vigor and vitality.

THE NEW BUND

The Bund has been a symbol of Shanghai since a hundred years. It begins with the Waibaidu Bridge at the estuary of Suzhou Creek in the north and ends at Jinling Road, East, in the south, with a total length of 1,500 m. On the east of the Bund is the vast Huangpu River and the beautiful new embankment. Here tourists can enjoy the beauty of Shanghai's mother river-the Huangpu-and the new looks of Lujiazui in Pudong on the opposite bank. Here visitors can take a walk amidst luxuriant plants and blooming flowers, appreciating the landscaping of a garden in a bustling metropolis and enjoy the fresh air and bright sunshine rarely found amidst the hustle and bustle of a city. The section extending from the new Bund to Nanpu Bridge is called the Southern Bund, which will be built into a new financial and business zone. On the Bund is group of buildings known as "a Gallery of world architecture." These buildings were built respectively during the '20s and '40s of the 20th century with different architectural styles but were well harmonized.The buildings are all decorated with floodlights. At night, the Bund is brightly lit, glittering and dazzling to the eye. It is the symbol and mark of Shanghai.

Time of lights on: 19:00-22:00

Add: Zhongshan Rd, E 1

Means of communication: Public buses 20, 22, 37, 55, 65, 42, 126, 135 and 145

ORIENTAL PEARL TV TOWER

Shanghai Oriental Pearl TV Tower was completed on Oct. 1, 1994. It is 468 m high, being the highest in Asia and the third highest in the world, only next to the TV towers in Toronto in Canada and Moscow in Russia. It stands opposite to the bund on the west bank. The architectural modeling of the tower is unique, expressing the flavor of oriental culture. The structure of the tower consists of 11 spheres, different in sizes and arranged at different levels, hanging from the sky down to the green lawns. It expresses the artistic concept of "pearls, big and small, dropping on a jade plate". The body of the tower is formed of two huge glittering spheres and one small delicate sphere; the sightseeing level in the upper sphere is 45 m in circumference, 263 m high, offering a bird's-eye view of the city. In the upper sphere at the 267-m level, there is a revolving restaurant, with one revolution every hour, a disco ball, a piano accompanied bar and at the 271-m level

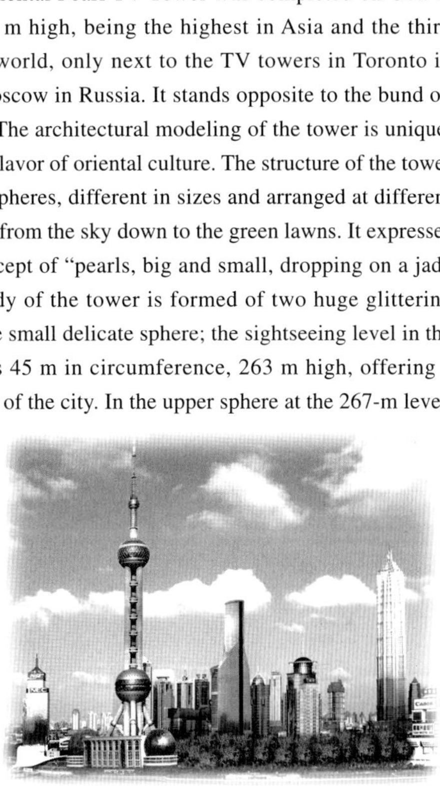

there are 20 KTV private rooms. The space cabin is at a level of 350 m, containing a sightseeing terrace, a meeting hall and a coffee room. Hotel in the Air is in the five smaller sphere with 20 guest rooms. The lower sphere contains a space city. There is a science fiction city inside the tower pedestal. The Oriental Pearl TV Tower combines sightseeing, catering, shopping, recreation, accommodation, broadcasting and TV transmission into one body. It has become a symbolic architecture and a favorable spot for tourists in Shanghai.

Visiting hours: 8:00-21:30

Entrance ticket: 50 yuan

Add: 1 new century highway, Pudong

Tel.: 58791888

Means of communications: Public buses 81, 82, 870, 871, 872, Tunnel lines 3, 4, 5 and 6

SHANGHAI INTERNATIONAL CONVENTION CENTRE

Shanghai International Convention Center is located on Riverside Promenade in Pudong opposite to the Bund on the other side of the river. Together with the Oriental Pearl TV Tower it has formed a popular tourist sight in the Lujiazui area. It has a total floor space of 110,000 sq.m. with 73,000 sq.m. aboveground and 37,000 sq.m. underground. It consists of up-to-date convention halls and meeting rooms, a multi-functional hall of 4,300 sq.m., able to accommodate 3,000 diners or 4,000 meeting attendants and can also be used as an exhibition hall. There is a news center and an exhibition room, each of 3,600 sq.m., a meeting hall for 800 people and two meeting rooms each for 200 people and 30 meeting rooms of different sizes for 100 and 50 people. The center has 270 guest rooms, including presidential suites, executive suites and standard rooms. It is complete with high-class catering facilities, including Chinese and Western restaurants, a special cuisine restaurant, a coffee room, comfortable recreation and rest areas like a ball room, a show room, a gym, a swimming pool, a bowling room, a billiard room, a sauna bath and a shopping arcade. There is a parking lot for 600 cars. The convention center is another new scenic sight in Shanghai.

Add: 2727 Riverside Highway, Pudong

Tel.: 50370000

Means of communications: Public buses 81,82, 870, 871, 872, Tunnel lines 3, 4, 5 and 6

CITY GOD TEMPLE (YUYUAN COMMERCIAL CITY)

The City God Temple in Shanghai was built during the year Yongle (after 1403) of the Ming Dynasty. In the temple were enshrined the statues of City God Qin Yubo (granted the title of city god of Shanghai County

by the first emperor of the Ming Dynasty), and Huo Guang (a Han Dynasty general). During the Qing Dynasty there were many worshippers. The temple is popular among the Shanghai people. Since Shanghai was made an open port, merchants have flocked to the surrounding areas of the temple and market is prosperous; people go to the temple bazaar to buy articles for their daily lives, especially small articles of daily use. In 1991, the city government began to rebuild the temple market into a large-scaled, modernized shopping center with traditional national characteristics — the Yuyuan Shopping Market. There used to be narrow streets in the market and most of the buildings were built before 1911, the last year of the Qing Dynasty. They have the feature and style of ancient Chinese architecture. In the market little shops stand in rows with beautiful collections of merchandise of special feature, keeping the appearance of ancient town markets. It has become a must for the majority of visitors to Shanghai, Chinese and foreigner. In the market there is a collection of local snack bars. The Mid-lake Pavilion, built in 1784, is now a popular tea house in Shanghai. Sitting there and enjoying a cup of tea one can admire the scenery outside from the window. It is really appealing! Here, one can get special Shanghai local commodities and foodstuff like the pear syrup candy, effective for curing coughs, reducing phlegm, soothing the throat and stimulating the appetite and the five-flavored broad beans with a curing history of 60 years, much appreciated by domestic and foreign visitors. The area for business has expanded from the former 18,000 sq.m. to 75,000 sq.m. One can see before him in today's Yuyuan Commercial City a group of Ming and Qing Dynasty imitation ancient buildings. Every building has upturned eaves and protruding corners, carved pillars and painted beams, all in national style. The new buildings though typical of Ming and Qing Dynasty architectural style but house modern shops inside. The "antique exterior and modern interior" is a feature that harmonizes with the original scenic sight. It has become a tourist shopping center, combining shopping, tourism, catering and recreation into one.

Add: Fuyou Road-Anren Street-Yuyuan Old Street-Jiujiaochang Road

Tel.: 63554831

Communications: Public buses 11, 42, 64. 66, 126 and 926

SHANGHAI OLD STREET

Looking back to the old days and exploring old Shanghai you will be brought by "Shanghai Old Street" through the times-times back to 100 years ago. The rebuilt Shanghai Old Street is 825 m long from Renmin Road to Henan Road, divided into the eastern and western sections. The eastern section runs from Renmin Road to Guanyi Street; the western section runs from Henan Road to Guanyi Street. Shanghai Old Street is an important east-west passageway for sightseeing in the Yuyuan commercial and tourist area. Back in the old days, it was called the Great Street Before the Temple. There gathered a group of Shanghai's earliest old-style private banks, gold shops, silverware shops, wine shops, teahouses, theatres and firms, a passageway for a passenger flow linking Shiliupu, the City God Temple and Yuyuan area. It was an old street gathering all the 360 trades of old Shanghai. It now presents to visitors the almost extinct trades, like the private banks, shops with mahogany furniture, pawn shops, old-fashioned teahouses, old-fashioned wine shops, and embroidery stores. In the eastern section of the street after "remodeling and restoration to antique feature" the folding screen doors and aluminum windows of many shops are no longer there but replaced with latticed windows, wooden door-boards and swing-doors typical of decorations of last Qing Dynasty residences. Besides, the patterned drip-pipes, upturned eaves, protruding corners and horse-head walls make visitors feel as if they have gone back to the old days. The western section is mainly laid out with Ming Dynasty imitation buildings with black tiles and white-washed walls, red pillars and upturned eaves, typical of the architectural style of old towns in the Ming and Qing Dynasties. Here one will find rows of antique-featured shops, such as the water pipe store, pottery art workshop, bean curd workshop, embroidery store, glutinous dumplings store, roasted nuts shop, teahouses, Dingniang little cotton store, and hot water boiler teahouses. A visitor here will find the different trades of business and travel and a hundred different features of the town market.

Add: Fangpang Rd, M

Tel.: 63281796

Means of communications: Public buses 11, 42,64, 66, 126 and 926

PEOPLE'S SQUARE

Located in downtown Shanghai the People's Square is the largest public square in Shanghai with a total area of 140,000 sq.m. In the concession days, together with the People's Park next door it was a race course. After liberation, the northern part of the race course was built into today's People's Park and the southern part, into the People's Square. The square is a public place for people to hold festival activities and spend their leisure time in rest or recreation. In the early '90s, the municipal government rebuilt the square and there before the visitors stands a new and more magnificent square. The new city hall is at the northern side of the square and opposite to it at the southern side is the new Shanghai Museum. Next to the city hall is Shanghai Grand Theater. To the left of the city hall, Shanghai City Planning Exhibition Hall is underway. No 1 Subway People's Square stop is underground and connected to the subway stop are two shopping malls — Hong Kong Famous Brand Shopping Street and Dimei Underground Shopping Arcade. The People's Highway, paved with granite, 600-m long and 32-m wide, runs from east to west through the square in front of the city hall.

In the southern part of the square underground are three large-scale structures: a multi-functional commercial city connecting the subway stop, an underground transformer house, the largest city transformer in Asia and a parking lot of 20,000 sq.m., the largest in Shanghai. The square aboveground is covered with lawns and planted with trees and flowers. Amidst the green lawns and flower beds are fountains, sculptures, artistic lantern posts and stone chairs and stools. The People's Square today is Shanghai's political and cultural centre and, at the same time, a new metropolitan scenic sight of the '90s.

Add: People's Avenue

Means of communications: No 1 Subway People Square stop; public buses 17, 18, 20, 23, 37, 46, 48, 49, 123, 145, 916, Tunnel lines 3 and 6

NANPU BRIDGE

Completed and opened to traffic on Dec. 1, 1991 Nanpu Bridge is 8,346-m long, with the main body 846-m long, 30.36-m wide and a span of 423 m and a net height of 46 m, accessible for ships up to 55,000 tons. It is the fourth largest double-tower and double-cable slant-drawn bridges in the world. The "H" shape bridge tower is 150 m on which is inscribed by Comrade Deng Xiaoping the four Chinese characters "南浦大桥"(Nanpu Bridge). On the surface of the main bridge are 6 lanes for automobiles and a sidewalk on each side. Visitors can take the elevator up the bridge for enjoying the scenery on both sides of the bridge. Nanpu Bridge is the first large bridge over the Huangpu River.

Visiting hours: 8:30-16:30

Add: 1410 Nanma Road

Tel.: 63763155 × sightseeing office

Means of communications: Public buses 43, 65, 82, 83, 89, 109 and 868

YANGPU BRIDGE

Yangpu Bridge, overlooking the Nanpu Bridge in the distance, is the second largest bridge over the Huangpu River. It was completed and opened to traffic in October 1993. It is 7,654-m long, joining the Inner-ring Road on the west bank to Pudong. The main bridge is 1,172-m long, 30.35-m wide, with a span of 602 m and 6 lanes for automobiles. It is a double-tower, double-cable, overlapped slant-drawn bridge with the largest span in the world. The "Y" shape main bridge tower is 203-m high with the name of the bridge inscribed by Comrade Deng Xiaoping inside the triangle of the tower. The designed daily passage flow is 45,000 automobiles. The bridge is 48 m above the river, available for ships above 10,000 tons to pass through. There are also sidewalks on both sides of the bridge. Visitors can take the elevator up to the bridge for sightseeing. The building of Nanpu and Yangpu Bridges, followed by Xupu and Fengpu Bridges, have contributed to the development and opening of Pudong.

Visiting hours: 8:30–16:00

Add: 88 lane 2175 Pudong Avenue

Tel.: 58854701 × sightseeing office

Means of communications: Public buses 81, 85, 870, 522, 574, 571, 592, bridge lines 3 and 4

XUPU BRIDGE

The cable slant-drawn Xupu Bridge is another bridge linking both banks of the Huangpu River in the southern part of Shanghai. It is 1,072-m long, 35.95-m wide, with 8 lanes for automobiles. The main tower is "A" shaped, 217 m high. The cables are arranged in a plane of a fan, with 240 strands in 30 pairs. It is a bridge at the southern end of the Outer-ring Road in crossing the river, directly linking the Shanghai-Nanjing and Shanghai-Hangzhou freeways. It is also the fastest and most convenient thorough-way between Hongqiao International Airport and Pudong International Airport.

HONGQIAO ECONOMIC DEVELOPMENT ZONE AND GUBEI NEW RESIDENTIAL AREA

Hongqiao area, a vast farmland 10 years ago, has now become an important window of Shanghai in opening to the outside world, with rows of high-risers, crisscrossed by roads and bustling with people and cars. Hongqiao Economic Development Area is located in the western part of the city covering an area of 65 hectares. In Auguest 1986, the Hongqiao Economic Development Area was set up, with a planned floor space of 1,500,000 sq.m. to be a center for foreign trade, plus the functions for foreign affairs. There were 4 projects approved by the government, with a total investment of 1.521 billion US dollars, of which 1.14 billion US dollars were foreign funds. Projects completed are the New Town Mansion, Shanghai China International Trade Center, Shartex plaza Yangtze New World Hotel, The Westin Taipingyang Hotel, Rainbow Hotel, New Town Club, Hongqiao Friendship Shopping Center with New Age Plaza, Sun plaza and Tianhong Building. These buildings express the wisdom of many architects from different countries, different in styles, each with its own characteristics; it is also an exposition of world architecture.

Gubei New Residential Area covers an area of 136.6 hectares and a total floor space of 3,000,000 sq.m. The area is divided into 3 sub-areas and 24 neighborhoods. No 1 Sub-area is a comprehensive area with high-rise apartments, office buildings and exhibition halls; No 2 is a residential area and No 3 consists of consulates, villas, and commodity housing. This is mainly a residential area and, in the meantime, provides service for foreign affairs and trade. Here live a large number of foreigners, compatriots from Hong Kong, Macao and Taiwan, who have come to Shanghai to work and to live. This is a window of Shanghai opened to the outside world in the western part of Shanghai. Many of the apartments and mansions were designed by famous European architects with alternating arched exteriors, decorated with artistic sculpture, fountains, flower-beds, lawns, iron railings, courtyards with lanterns, finding expression in European continental style and romantic sentiments. The building of Gubei New Area, forecasts the prospects of the development of Shanghai's residential areas. It has become a tourist attraction.

Means of communication: Public buses 48, 57, 591, 911 and 925

VIADUCTS

Completed in Shanghai are the Inner-ring Viaduct, the South-North Viaduct, Yanan Road Viaduct and Yixian Road Viaduct. These viaducts have provided the thorough passage for traffic in urban Shanghai and played a great role in the development of the city.

The Inner-ring Road is 47.66-km long, with an average width of 18 m and 4 two-way automobile lanes partitioned by protection barriers and breakers and sound-insulating walls and a designed speed of 80 km/hr. The road consists of 3 parts. The 8-km Pudong section connects the two bridges. The ring road is the largest in scale of public works in Shanghai since its opening up. Along the road are 6 overpasses and 37 entry and exit passes, linking the viaducts with the surface roads below and the South-North Viaduct, forming a three-dimensional traffic network in the city. The Inner-ring Road is equipped with advanced monitoring, communication, photoelectric indicator and light source lighting systems. There are 28 television screens monitoring the 24-hour operation on the road. It is most advanced in modern city communications.

The South-North Viaduct begins at Laohutai Road, links the inner-ring road and ends at Zhongshan Road, East 1, and Luban Road in the south. It is 8.45-km long with 6 two-way automobile lanes. It cuts the city proper from the south to the north and has improved the traffic conditions in Shanghai from south to north.

Yixian Road Viaduct crosses with Zhongshan Road, North 1, and Guangling Road, West, links with the Inner-ring Road, passes Dabaishu to end in the south of Wusong Bridge with a total length of 9.5 km. The road has been widened from its original 4 lanes to

6 fast and 2 slow lanes, part of the fast lanes are two-way 4 lanes and part, 6 two-way. There are altogether 15 passes for entry and exit.

Yanan Road Viaduct, 6.2-km long, extends from the Inner-ring Road towards the west, traversing the bustling business area of Hongqiao and Gubei areas, reaching the Hongqiao International Airport, to connect the Outer-ring Road now underway. The viaduct is 25.5-m. wide, with 6 driving lanes and a designed driving speed of 80 km per hour. There are altogether 4 pairs of passes to the ground and a special pass to the Hongqiao International Airport. This section of the viaduct will connect with the middle section and the eastern section of Yanan Road Viaduct to form a complete Yanan Road Viaduct system and together with the Inner-ring Road and the South-North Viaduct to complete the elevated expressway in the city in the shape of a Chinese character " 申 ", ("shen" is Shanghai in short).

SHANGHAI NO 1 SUBWAY AND NO 2 SUBWAY

Shanghai No 1 Subway is 21.51 km long, running from Xingzhuang to the Railway Station with 16 stops, i.e., Xingzhuang, Waihuan Road, Lianhua Road, Jinjiang Amusement Park, New Longhua Road, Caobao Road, Shanghai Stadium, Xujiahui. Hengshan Road, Changshu Road. Shaanxi Road, South, Huangpi Road, South, People's Square,

Xinzai Road, Hanzhong Road, and Shanghai Railway Station. All the stops have a clean, bright, quiet and tasteful environment, rich in the flavor of the times. The architectural style finds expression in individuality amidst generality, changing characteristics in unification. Each stop has a distinct theme in design, for instance, at the People's Square stop the mosaic murals and artistic bas-relief tally with the cultural atmosphere aboveground; the Caobao Road stop has pendant lamps with three-dimensional frames in harmony with the hi-tech micro electronics industrial zone aboveground; the Shanghai Stadium stop has pendant roofs encircled by lights, expressing the characteristic of sports; the Shanghai Railway Station stop has beams and pillars in the form of doors to express that the railway station is the gate to Shanghai. These unique designs not only express the characteristic of each stop but also create different artistic atmosphere.

No 2 Subway is an important project of municipal works planned by the city government following No 1 Subway. It runs from east to west with a total length of 27.3 km, starting from Hongqiao International Airport, passing through Beixinjing industrial and residential area, by Zhongshan Park, turning to Nanjing Road, West, near Jingan Temple, crossing with No 1 Subway at People's Square, then along Nanjing Road to the Bund and through the Huangpu River to Pudong Lujiazui, along Dongchang Road and ends at Pudong International Airport. The first phase of the project from Zhongshan Park to Longdong Road stop will be completed by the end of 1999. There are altogether 12 stops along the line. The completion of the two subways will greatly improve the traffic conditions in the city center.

ELEVATED LIGHT-RAIL PEARL LINE

The elevated light-rail Pearl Line is planned to run from Minhang in the south to Baoshan in the north with a total length of 62 km. The first phase of the project starts at Caohejing in the south and end at Jiangwan Town with a total length of 24.97 km, passing the 6 districts of Xuhui, Changning, Putuo, Zhabei, Hongkou and Baoshan. Along the line are 19 stops. Except the stops of Caohejing, Shilong Road and Shanghai Railway Station on the ground, the other 16 stops are all elevated from the ground. In consideration of the needs of passengers in transfer to other public buses, there will be additional 25 ground surface bus lines, apart from the existing bus lines, 9 of which will be extended and 5, rearranged. In the meantime, 8 stops along the light-rail line will enable passengers to transfer to subway and railway, thus linking up the passenger transport in the city with the southern and northern areas.

THE CENTURY AVENUE

The Century Avenue is located in Lujiazui Area in Pudong with a total length of 5 km and a width of 100 m. It runs from the Oriental Pearl TV Tower in the west to the Administrative and Cultural Center of Pudong New Area in the east. It is an important thoroughfare and a tourist attraction. It is featured by its unsymmetrical layout. The driving passage is 31-m wide with a sidewalk on the north side 44.5-m wide and that on the south side 24.5-m wide. It is a magnificent boulevard with 6 rows of trees and 8 botanical gardens, unifying the road with the landscaping. This highway in Pudong as a tourist attraction can be called the "the Avenue des Champs Elysees in the East."

SIGHTSEEING TUNNEL AT THE BUND

The sightseeing tunnel at the Bund will be built between the Bund at Nanjing Road, East, and the Oriental Pearl TV Tower in Pudong, with a total length of 646.70 m. It is the first passenger tunnel in China. Tourists may take the escalators at the entrance and the exit, while the handicapped may use the hydraulic pressure elevator. In the tunnel, passengers will take a '90s-internationally up-to-date, automatic, no-driver, cable-drawn, closed car to cover the distance in 2.5-5 minutes. The transport capacity will reach 5280 persons/hour. The passenger tunnel once completed will be one of the traffic facilities for tourists in Shanghai.

RIVERSIDE PROMENADE

The Riverside Promenade runs from Dongchang Road Ferry Crossing along the Huangpu River, passing by the Oriental Pearl TV Tower to Taitongzhan Wharf, with a total length of 2,500 m. The first phase of the project 1,500-m long is now completed.

Standing on the west bank of the river one can see the beautiful Riverside Promenade, called the "New Bund" of Pudong, which combines a flood-control embankment, a riverside thoroughfare, a waterside terrace, a music fountain and a yacht wharf into an attractive scenic sight. The promenade has adopted a three-dimensional design in layers. Standing on the broad terrace on top of the landscaped slope one can have a full view of the magnificent scene of the Bund on the west bank. At the foot of the terrace are fountain-heads spurting water into a bubbling waterfall, attracting tourists to the terrace — the pride of the Riverside Promenade. When the tide ebbs in the river tourists can recline on the cast-iron railings to watch the scenes on both banks of the river. When tide rises, one can go down the steps on the embankment to tread water. The yacht wharf rebuilt from an old wharf is specially attractive with a giant iron anchor erected high and several mooring columns. The huge fountain spraying water from a hundred fountain-heads is fitted with color lights that glitter with brilliance at night.

Visiting hours: 8:30–16:30

Entrance ticket: 5 yuan

Add: 700 Lujiazui Road, Pudong

Tel.: 58875487

Means of communications : Public buses 81, 82, 870, 871, 872, Tunnel lines 3, 4, 5 and 6

LUJIAZUI LANDSCAPED CENTRE

Occupying an area of 10 hectare. the Lujiazu Landscaped Center is located at the exit of Yanan Road, East, Tunnel. It is in the center of the Lujiazui Financial Zone and is the largest public landscaped area in Shanghai. The area is covered with lawns neatly and naturally laid out on an undulating ground. Through beautiful design it has formed a magnificent view in the midst of a modern financial area . The lawn in the landscaped center covers an area of 6.5 hectare. with the cold-season grass imported from Europe; it is green all year round. In the middle and on the northern side of the area are planted with flowery trees, bushes and arbors, like the willow, magnolia, gingko, pine, camphor, boxwood, metasequoia, and maple, creating an atmosphere full of freshness and vitality. The winding paths in the area are drawing up a pattern of Shanghai's city flower, the magnolia. In the midst of the magnolia pattern is a 8,600-sq.m. lake designed in the pattern of a map of Pudong. In the middle of the lake is a fountain supported by a circular accessory fountain like a dragon soaring into the air. Around the lake is set up a large awning for people to sit and watch the scenery. The awning is white, in the shape of a sea snail, and looks like a boat with the main mast 28-m high, giving people much room for imagination.

Visiting hours: 8:00–22:00

Entrance ticket: 5 yuan

Add: 160 Lujiazui Road, Pudong

Tel.: 58875487

Means of communications: Public buses 81, 82 870, 871, 872, Tunnel lines 3, 4, 5 and 6

PUDONG CENTURY PARK

Pudong Century Park is located in the horticultural area in Pudong at the end of the axial highway and north of the administrative and cultural center, Shanghai Science and Technology Capital and New Area Administration Hall. The park is designed to cover an area of 140.3 hectares with an investment of RMB 84.4 million yuan. The project consists of two phases. 100 hectares of land have been appropriated for the first phase of the project. The overall planning of the park embodies the combination of Eastern and Western cultures, of man and nature; it will be a typical Chinese garden with modern feature. The park mainly consists of large plots of lawns, woods and lakes. There is a mid-lake isle, a meeting square, a pastoral garden, an international garden and a tree-spaced lawn, plus a birds reserve, and facilities for scientific experience and open-air performance, and a children's playground.

Visiting hours: 7:00–18:00

Entrance ticket: 5 yuan
Add: 1001 Jinxiu Road, Pudong
Tel.: 58337243
Means of communications : Public buses 788, 794, Shen-Bao Line, Nan-Yang Line and Shen-San Line

SHANGHAI MUSEUM

Shanghai Museum is located in downtown Shanghai at the southern end of the People's Square. It is a treasure-house of the essence of Chinese culture and also a symbol and window on Shanghai's social civilization and culture. In visiting a place tourists of a civilized society usually wish to visit a museum to get a picture of the history and humanistic society of that place.

Before liberation, with the efforts of Chinese patriotic scholars, a municipal museum was set up in Jiangwan. In 1952, under the support of the first mayor of Shanghai Chen Yi, several museums were amalgamated into Shanghai Museum. It was then built at No 16 Henan Road (the original Zhonghui Bank building) with a collection of 130,000 cultural relics known in the country and abroad as a large-scale art museum, ranking as one of the 4 major museums in the country besides those in Beijing, Nanjing and Xian. At the end of 1995, Shanghai Museum was moved to the present new site in the People's Square. It has improved much in the area of display halls, facilities, and arrangement of exhibits and can better display the functions of a museum.

The building of the museum is designed in the shape of a dome at the upper part and a square at the lower part, implying the Chinese traditional expression of "a round heaven and a square earth". Viewed from a distance the structure with an arch above the dome-roof looks like a Chinese ancient bronze incense burner. It has a total floor space of 40,000 sq.m. with 4-1/2 floors aboveground and 1-1/2 underground and a total height of 29.5 m. The plane layout is divided into 6 areas of the public, the storage, the academic, the research, the administrative and the facilities, with 13 special exhibition halls. There are also exhibition halls for coins, jade ware, sculpture, seals and minority nationalities, handicrafts. There is altogether an exhibition space of 12,000 sq.m. On the first floor are halls for Chinese ancient bronze ware and Chinese ancient sculpture; on the second floor are halls for Chinese ancient pottery and porcelain, Zhandelou pottery and porcelain; on the third floor are halls for Chinese calligraphy, paintings and seals of different dynasties; on the fourth floor are halls for Chinese ancient jade ware, Chinese coins of different dynasties, Chinese furniture of the Ming and Qing Dynasties, Chinese minority nationalities' handicrafts. The museum has adopted up-to-date fire-prevention facilities, audio-visual educational facilities, computerized administrative system for cultural relic literature and automatic administrative system for the whole building. The exhibition halls and storerooms are equipped with automatic temperature and humidity control devices. The guiding work in all the exhibition halls is conducted by handy programmed walkie-talkies. Visitors may press the key for any commentary of the cultural relics they like. The commentary is in Chinese and many foreign languages. The exhibition halls are equipped with computer-controlled video projectors for providing visitors with pictures and professional knowledge of different cultural relics. The museum has a special room for research workers and a lecture hall equipped with simultaneous interpretation and audio-visual system for academic and instructive activities. The up-to-date facilities are providing a good environment for visiting domestic and foreign tourists and are an indication of the cultural standard of Shanghai as an international metropolis.

Visiting hours: 9:00–17:00 (to 20:00 on Saturdays)

Entrance ticket: 20 yuan

Add: 201 People's Avenue

Tel.: 63723500

Means of communications: No 1 Subway Peoples' Square stop, public buses 18, 46, 49, 71, 127, 145 and Tunnel line 6

SHANGHAI LIBRARY

Shanghai Library was first built in 1952 and located at the crossroad of Nanjing and Huangpi Road next to the People's Park. With the change of times the old library could no long satisfy the increasing needs of the time. Through three years' construction the new library was completed and opened in December 1996. The newly built library is located at 1555 Huaihai Road, Middle, occupying an area of 3.1 hectare and a floor space of 83,000 sq.m., three times of the original library. It is one of the largest libraries in China. The new library consists of two main buildings, each 55.6-m and 105.8-m tall, in the shape of towers and a 5-stories apron building. The towers are built in the shape of 3-dimensional terraced blocks, symbolizing the solid foundation of its accumulation of knowledge and people's continual aspiring for the heights of knowledge. Around the two towers is a large landscaped ground with two squares, each named respectively the "Knowledge" and the "Wisdom". The new library emphasizes on "people as the main body" and is entirely open to the public. There are 24 different reading rooms for Chinese and foreign books, journals and newspapers, open-shelf lending Chinese books and journals, ancient, contemporary and modern literature, special journals and indexes, acoustic material and electronic reading material, with one million books and journals on the open-shelves and 3,000 seats, equipped with electronic guide-reading, electronic reading, electronic indexing, information transmission and automatic book delivery trolleys. Besides, there is a multi-functional lecture hall, an academic lecture hall, an exhibition hall, all open to the public

and fully displaying the different functions. Shanghai Library amalgamated from the former Shanghai Library and Shanghai Institute of Scientific and Technological Intelligence is a large-scale center of literature, rational in structure and rich in contents, with the superiority from both institutions making up for each other. Shanghai Library with its collection of 40,000,000 copies of books and literature and its size in floor space ranks the seventh place in the world after the American Congress Library, the National Library in France, Beijing Library, National Congress Library in Japan and the National Lenin Library in Russia. At weekends and on holidays we can always see large numbers of readers absorbed in reading and seeking new knowledge. It is an attractive sight on holidays, which adds more cultural flavor to the city.

Opening hours: 8:30-20:00

Add: 1555 Huaihai Road, Middle

Tel.: 64455555

Means of communications: No 1 Subway Changshu Road stop, public buses 15, 93, 126, 526 and 911

SHANGHAI STADIUM

Shanghai Stadium, the principal sports ground for China 8th National Sports Meeting in 1997, is, at present, the most highly modernized and largest scaled in China. It is a comprehensive sports ground with international standards and able to accommodate 80,000 spectators. It occupies an area of 19 hectare. and is equipped with up-to-date facilities. The plane structure is of a dome-shape and vertically, the shape of a saddle. Over the auditorium is steel framework to shade the spectators from rain and sun and the seats are made of quake-proof and fire-proof material. Between the second and fourth spectators' stands are special boxes. Within the compound are also practice fields for track and field and football. Besides, there are accessory facilities, like a hotel, a sports club, a shopping arcade and an exhibition hall. It is not only a uniquely modeled sports ground but also a tourist attraction with multiple functions. Together with the 10,000-seat Indoor Stadium and Shanghai Natatorium form a modern sports city in Shanghai's urban areas.

Opening hours: 9:00–17:00

Entrance ticket: 20 yuan (Class A) and 10 yuan (Class B)

Add: 666 Tianyaoqiao Road

Tel.: 64266666

Means of communications: No 1 Subway Shanghai Stadium stop, public buses 15, 43, 42, 56, 73, 87, 89 and 92

SHANGHAI GRAND THEATRE

Shanghai Grand Theatre is located in the west of the City Hall on People's Square. The total investment is US$60,000,000. It has a total floor space of 70,000 sq.m. The building is 40-m high, with 2 stories underground, 6 stories aboveground and 2 stories on top, altogether 10 stories. It was designed by the French architect Salbanjie, unique in style, combining the feature of the Chinese and Western cultures.The white arched roof and the transparent lustrous glass wall ingeniously incorporated poses like a crystal palace. The stage with a space of 728 sq.m., a back stage of 360 sq.m. and side stages of 256 sq.m. is the largest in the world with the most convertible stage facilities. There are 1,800 seats in the audience hall, able to satisfy

the needs of performance by first-grade international and domestic ballet, opera and symphony orchestra troupes. In the theatre compound there is a medium-size theatre of 550 sq.m. with a seating capacity of 250 people, suitable for the performance of chamber music and song and dance shows. The Grand Theatre has become a centre of cultural life in Shanghai, providing a place for performances of world-grade operas, dances, films and music. It is an architecture of a cultural symbol in Shanghai as an international metropolis.

Opening hours: 9:00-16:00
Entrance ticket: 50 yuan
Add: 190 Huangpi Road, North
Tel.: 63875480
Means of communication: No 1 Subway People Square stop, public buses 18, 46, 49, 71, 127, 145 and No 6 Tunnel line

SHANGHAI CITY PLANNING EXHIBITION HALL

Shanghai City Planning Exhibition Hall is located in the east of the City Hall. On top of the building are 4 giant steel caps symbolizing the city flower-magnolia, glittering in the sunlight, setting off with the crystal-like Grand Theatre in the west. The main building is 43.3 m high, with 5 stories aboveground and 2 stories underground, in a total floor space of 18,393 sq.m. The exhibition hall not only enables Shanghai citizens to visit and learn about the changes and the future plans of the city development, but also plays a role in introducing to domestic and foreign visitors the planning and construction of the city, posing as an image of Shanghai as an open international metropolis.

Add: In the east of the City Hall on People's Square
Means of communication: No 1 Subway People Square stop, public buses 18, 46, 49, 71, 127, 145 and No 6 Tunnel line

SHANGHAI CIRCUS CITY

Shanghai Circus City, located on Gonghexin Road, occupying an area of 22,500 sq.m., is a cultural, sports and amusement centre in Shanghai's northern district. The Circus City is composed of 5 parts with acrobatic and circus show as the main body, a rehearsal hall, an amusement city, an animal house and a performers' reception centre. The Circus City is equipped with up-to-date facilities complete in functions, providing a place for large-scale domestic and international acrobatic competitions and performances. It can also meet the needs of the citizens' cultural lives for music, song and dance shows.

Add: 2266 Gonghexin Road

Tel.: 66527750

Means of communication: Public buses 46, 96, 114 and 222

LONGHUA TOURIST CITY

Longhua Tourist City, located in the southern part of Shanghai downtown, near the Xujiahui shopping centre, is one of the tourist areas in Shanghai with the largest scale and greatest potential for development in the century. Supported by the rich resources in indigenous culture, revolutionary traditional culture and Buddhist culture has been built into a typical tourist area with the feature of Chinese Buddhist culture and full of folk customs and life-style Chinese. The tourist city is built next to the Longhua Temple, combining the old and the new, and together with the Longhua Martyrs' Cemetery forms the Longhua Tourist City.

Add: Longhua Town

Tel.: 64696546

Means of communication: Public buses 73, 87, 41, 44 and 104

JIN MAO BUILDING

Jin Mao Building is a symbolic architecture of Shanghai in marching to the 21st century. Its height is only next to that of the Twin-Tower Building in Kuala Lumpur, Malaysia, and the Sears Tower in Chicago, U.S.A. It is the first tallest in the country and the third tallest in the world. Standing in the middle of Lujiazui

Finance and Trade Zone and by the Huangpu River, it overlooks the Oriental Pearl TV Tower in the distance, and next to the tunnel on Yanan Road, East, and will soon be reached by No 2 Subway. The main building is 420.5-m high, with 88 stories aboveground and 3 stories underground, occupying an area of 23,611 sq.m., with a total floor space of 290,000 sq.m. Jin Mao Building is an intelligence-type high-riser, combining the functions of office, business and hotel. The 3rd-50th floors are spacious, bright and pillar-less offices able to accommodate over ten thousand people at work at the same time; the 51-52 floors are electric and machinery equipment floors; the 53rd to 87th floors house are the world's tallest super 5-star Jin Mao Grand Hyatt Hotel. In the central cylinder from the 56th floor to the top of the tower is a 27 dia.-142-m high "atrium in the air" with sunlight reflecting through the glass. Around the atrium are 555 guest rooms of different sizes and styles and different Chinese and Western restaurants. On the 86th floor is the Enterprisers' Club. On the 87th floor is a restaurant in the air. The 88th floor, 341 m from the ground, is the sightseeing floor, the highest at present in the country and able to accommodate over a thousand visitors. Two elevators with a speed of 9.1 m/sec. are working to transport visitors in 45 seconds from the first basement to the sightseeing floor. Here, looking around and to the far distance, one can have a whole view of new Shanghai.

Add: 2 new century Avenue, Pudong

Tel.: 50470088

Means of communication: Public buses 81, 82, 870, 871, 872, Tunnel lines 3, 4, 5 and 6

SHANGHAI STOCK EXCHANGE BUILDING

Shanghai in the 21st century will be the most important financial centre on the west coast of the Pacific. Opened for business on Dec. 19, 1997, Shanghai Stock Exchange Building is a masterpiece of the 21st century. Located at the exit of the Yanan Road Tunnel in Pudong, it is landmark architecture in the central commercial area in Lujiazui, Pudong. The building with an exterior like the Arch of Triumph, is 109-m high, with 27 stories aboveground and 2 stories underground, and a total floor space of 100,000 sq.m. From the 2nd to the 9th floor is the business floor. The pillar-less hall is spacious and bright with an area of 3,600 sq.m., accommodating 1,810 seats. It is one of the largest and most advanced stock exchang building in Asia, even in the world, among all stock exchanges. From the 10th floor up are intelligence-type high-class offices. There is a 63-m overpass between the two parts of the building. The building has an advanced equipment control system with modern computer-control, communication and graphic display technique, which link up all the monitored areas, thus providing highly safe, protective and modernized working environment.

Add: 528 Pudong Rd, S

Tel.: 68808888

Means of communication: Public buses 81, 82, Tunnel lines 3 and 5

SHANGHAI PUDONG INTERNATIONAL AIRPORT

Located in Shanghai Pudong New Area, by the sea, Shanghai Pudong International Airport occupies an area of 32 sq.km., 30 km from the People's Square in downtown Shanghai. The first phase of the project, with an investment of RMB12 billion yuan, started on October 1997 and was completed at the end of 1999. The exterior of the main building looks like a giant sea gull, imparting a strong sense of the times and symbolic significance. Its 278,000 sq.m. floor space is three times that of the Hongqiao Airport. It is available for 36 planes to land at the same time. There are 13 luggage turn-tables, able to meet the needs of an annual 126,000 plane/times of loading and unloading. It has a yearly handling capacity of 20,000,000 person/times of passenger flow and 750,000-ton cargo transport. It can serve the taking off and landing of any types of the world's large planes. The second phase of the project is targeted to complete in the year of 2005. It will consist of a 4,000-m runway, 800,000-sq.m. passenger lobby and 4 high-class south-north runways. The new airport once completed will handle an annual passenger volume of 70,000,000 person/times and a freight volume of 5,000,000 tons. It will lay a good foundation for Shanghai's development in the near century.

Add: 100 Jiangzhenwei No 1 Road

Tel.: 38484500

Means of communication: Special bus lines (Pudong Airport – Hongqiao Airport, Pudong Airport – Shanghai Railway Station, Pudong Airport – Shanxi Road Civil Aviation Office, Pudong Airport – East Jiangwan Road, Pudong Airport – Zunyi Road)

HONGKOU FOOTBALL FIELD

Hongkou Football Field is built on the original site of the 46-year old Hongkou Stadium. It is a multi-function, multi-purpose stadium mainly for football games. It was completed in March 1999 and first hosted football fans for the national football league match in the '99 match season. The rebuilding of the football field called for international competitive tender and was contracted by the Japanese RIA Designing Institute for planning and further supplemented and undertaken in construction design by Shanghai Construction Designing Research Institute. The whole of the football field is a huge structure, without any expansion or settlement joints. The whole design took into consideration the temperature stress and body deformity. Advanced technique and equipment for ground heating and strengthened drainage cycle for the conservation of the natural lawns are introduced from abroad. The huge oblong opening above the football field gives the maximum sunlight to the field and keeps good air circulation. The rational architectural structure and flexible arrangement of space offer all spectators a good view. It nestles amidst green woods, integrating with the surrounding quiet and humanistic environment into a harmonious entirety. The football field occupies an area of 56,000 sq.m., with a total floor space of 72,557 sq.m., 35,000 spectators' seats and 47 boxes. Hongkou Football Field is not only equipped with the functions for holding high-standard international and domestic football matches, but also complete with such sports and recreational facilities as an indoor swimming pool, a ping-pong room, a billiard room, and a goal-shooting practice court. In addition, there are up-to-date accessory facilities, like a restaurant, a beauty parlour, a sauna bath and shops. Here, football fans will enjoy themselves with greatest satisfaction and the general public can have a place for their setting-up exercises, leisurely rest and amusement.

Add: 444 East Jiangwan Road

Tel. : 65400009

Means of communication: Public buses 21, 70, 18, 97, 51 and 52

ORIANA CRUISER

The Oriana is a huge British imperial cruiser and is the only large-scale ship museum. It was built 40 years ago in England with a sum of £14,000,000 . In 1999, having sailed for 40 years, at last settled down in Huangpu River and anchored at Shanghai Harbour to host Chinese and foreign visitors. On the 20,000-sq.m. exhibition floor in the cruiser one can experience the extraordinarily imperial style and the scientific mystery of an ocean-going ship, the pleasure of sea-going, the historical feature of the cabins and the delicacies of world cuisines.

Add: 2 DongChang Road

Tel.: 68875483

Means of communication: Public buses 82, 85, Tunnel lines 3 and 4

PROPOSED TOURS OF NEW METROPOLITAN SCENIC SIGHTS

A. One-day tour of new metropolitan sights

Morning: Tour People's Square, visit Shanghai Museum, the Grand Theatre - take the subway to Shanghai Stadium

Afternoon: Tour Yuyuan Garden, Nanpu Bridge and Oriental Pearl TV Tower

Evening: Take the ferry and tour the Bund

B.Two-day tour of new metropolitan sights

lst day:

Morning: Tour People's Square, visit Shanghai Museum, the Grand Theatre - take the subway to Shanghai Stadium

Afternoon: Tour Hongqiao Development Area, Gubei New Residential Area and visit Shanghai Library

Evening: Tour the Bund

2nd day:

Morning: Tour Yuyuan Garden and Nanpu Bridge

Afternoon: Tour Oriental Pearl TV Tower and Riverside Avenue

RECOMMENDED TRAVEL SERVICES

SHANGHAI HUATING OVERSEAS TOURIST CO.

Add: F/4, 503 Wulumuqi Rd, N

Tel.: 62491234

Fax: 62485470,62482781

Post Code: 200040

SHANGHAI JINJIANG TOURS LTD.

Add: 191 Changle Road

Tel.: 64662828

Fax: 64662297

Post Code: 200020

SHANGHAI CYTS TOURS CORPORATION

Add: 2 Hengshan Road

Tel.: 64331826, 64331907

Fax: 64330507

Post Code: 200031

SHANGHAI CHINA INTERNATIONAL TRAVEL SERVICE CO., LTD

Add: CITS Building, 1277 Beijing Rd, W

Tel.: 62898899

Fax: 62894928

Post Code: 200040

SHANGHAI CHINA TRAVEL SERVICE

Add: 881 Yanan Rd, M

Tel.: 62478888, 62475770

Fax: 62475521

Post Code: 200040

(II) TRADITIONAL EXQUISITE SCENES

NANJING ROAD-CHINA'S NO 1 SHOPPING STREET

The 5.5-km long Nanjing Road is the most bustling and prosperous street in Shanghai and famed as "China's No 1 Shopping Street". It was first built in 1851. Formerly it was a country path in the fields running east-westward from the Bund to Henan Road. In 1853 the Fuli Company was opened here. In 1851, 14 firms like the Watson, Lao Deji Pharmacy and others and 9 cotton and woollen fabrics stores were set up. Along with the development of the city and the import of large quantities of foreign merchandise commerce, on Nanjing Road was rapidly developing. Hundreds of big stores and famous shops were opened one after another. With the opening of five department stores, Wing On, Sincere, Sun Sun, Dai Sun and China Chinese Goods, the colourful and brightly lit Nanjing Road became the most bustling commercial street in Shanghai and in the whole country. After liberation, it has been totally remoulded and the newly rearranged Nanjing Road has become the centre of Shanghai's busy downtown. Here, one will find hundreds of modernised malls, famous old-brand stores and special product shops. It has become the largest collecting and distributing centre for retail goods and an information centre. The every-day visitor flow here reaches over a million person/times. At night, lights glitter in blazing colours, especially at weekends, it becomes a pedestrian walkway for shopping and sightseeing. Nanjing Road, with its magnificent buildings, shops standing in rows upon rows , bustling street scene and brilliant night view, is worth of its reputation as "China's No 1 Shopping Street".

On Oct. 1, 1999, "China's No 1 Shopping Street" will be opened as a 24-hour pedestrian walkway. The 1,033-m long walkway extending from Henan Road to Xizang Road has adopted an unsymmetrical design. On the northern side of the straight road there is a continuous "golden belt", collecting artistic sketches, flower-beds and bus-waiting stands, forming a number of movie-like picturesque scenes under the sun light. The commercial layout on Nanjing Road will be rearranged. There will no longer be a thousand shops with the same face. Shanghai No 1 Department Store, Hualian Commercial Building, and New World Department Store will keep their characteristics of department stores, while the other shops will be turned into "one shop, one commodity". At the same time, facilities for catering, leisure and recreation will be increased to make Nanjing Road a pedestrians walkway "graceful in the eastern section, special in the middle section and prosperous in the western section".

Means of communication: No 1 Subway People's Square stop, public buses 20, 22, 37, 42, 49 145, and 135

Proposed tour: 120 minutes

HUANGPU RIVER CRUISE

Huangpu River cruise is a traditional tourist item in Shanghai's tours. It is significant not only because of Huangpu River being Shanghai's mother river but also of the collection of the quintessences of Shanghai scenes. Here, one can find the expression of Shanghai's past, present and prospects for a brilliant future. The cruise begins at the Bund towards south against the current up to the Nanpu Bridge and turns back towards the north, passing the

Yangpu Bridge to reach Wusong Mouth and then back to the Bund. During the cruise, one can see both

the Nanpu Bridge and the Yangpu Bridge and the 468-m tall Oriental Pearl TV Tower, the first in Asia and the third in the world. The two bridges are like two dragons sprawling on the Huangpu River while the Oriental Pearl TV Tower between is like "two dragons playing with a pearl". On the west bank of the river, rows of magnificent tall buildings of different foreign architectural styles are in contrast with the modern high-risers on the east bank, presenting an attractive view to visitors. The Huangpu River and the Changjiang River meet at Wusong Mouth, where the Changjiang River empties into the sea. Here, three streams of water from the Huangpu, the Changjiang and the East Sea converge. At rising tide, one can see the famous strange sight of the "three-layer water", water from the Huangpu passing through the city is bluish grey, water from the Changjiang washing down mud and sand is yellow and that in the East Sea is green. Three streams with different colours are very distinct, forming the "three layer water". It is really a strange sight.

Service hours: 9:00-22:00
Ticket price: 45-100 yuan
Business Add: 153, 219-239 Zhongshan R, E 2
Tel.: 63744461
Means of communication: Buses 20, 22, 42, 55, 65, 71 and 135
Proposed cruise: 180 minutes

YUYUAN GARDEN

Located on Anren Street, Yuyuan Garden was built during the reign of Jiajing of the Ming Dynasty (1577), 400 hundred years from now. It is a residential garden built by Pan Yunduan, minister of finance in Sichuan Prooince in

the Ming Dynasty. Pan built the garden to "please his parents and let them enjoy themselves in their late years". In ancient Chinese "yu" means "pleasing", hence the name of the garden. The garden is typical of the gardening art south of the Changjiang River and is famed as "a wonder of beauty in south-east China". It is still a famous classical garden in south China. At the end of the Ming Dynasty the garden was deserted. It was rebuilt in the 25th year of Emperor Qianlong of the Qing Dynasty (1760). In the 19th century, during the Opium War, the beautiful garden was badly damaged. During the Small Sword Society Uprising, the Spring Hall in the Yuyuan Garden was made as the northern headquarters of the uprising army. Now, there is a number of historical relics left by the uprising, like weapons, coins and literature. After liberation, the municipal government renovated the garden several times. It was opened to the public in 1961.

On entering the gate, you will come face to face with the Three Corn-ear Hall. Standing in the hall and looking up, you will see a horizontal plaque with the characters "Mountains and Forests in the City", describing the environment of the garden being located in the midst of a bustling town yet full of the natural pleasantness of mountains and forests. Going through the "Hall of Viewing the Mountain" you can see a large rockery on the other side of a pond. It is 12-m high, piled up with 2,000 tons of yellow stones from Wukang, full of twists and turns, , looking magnificent and enchanting. The Inner Garden was built in the 48th year of the reign of Emperor Kangxi of the Qing Dynasty (1708), occupying only an area of 0.13 hectare but complete with all the rockeries, ponds, halls, chambers, pavilions and terraces, crenelated walls and corridors, cleverly arranged and proportionately laid out.

In front of the Hall of Jade Magnificence in the Outer Garden are 3 stone peaks; in the middle of these is the Exquisite Jade Stone. It is one of the famous exquisite stones south of the Changjiang River, the other two being the Duanyun Peak in Suzhou and the Wrinkled Peak in Hangzhou. It is 3.2-m tall. In the stone are 72 holes. If you burn an incense at the bottom, smoke will come out from all the holes; if you pour water from the top, there will be water dripping from all the holes. It is said that it was a piece of curio stone of the Imperial Marble Convoy in the Song Dynasty. It somehow got lost on the way and then reclaimed. The stone also has a history of more than 400 years here. In the garden there are such famous tourist attractions, like the Happy Fish Waterside Pavilion, a Thousand Flower Hall, the Hall of Mildness, the Hall of Elegance, the Nine-zig Bridge, the lotus pond, and the Mid-lake Pavilion. This classical garden, integrating the gardening art of the Ming and Qing Dynasties with chambers and halls, beautiful rockeries, luxuriant trees and plants, is featured by its gracefulness and peacefulness, delicateness and exquisiteness, small but striking you as large, presenting the artistic styles of gardens south of the Changjiang River. It deserves the fame of a masterpiece of classical gardens. It is listed as a key cultural relic protected by the state and a popular tourist attraction for both domestic and overseas tourists.

Visiting hours: 9:00–17:00

Entrance ticket: 20 yuan

Add: 132 Anren Street

Tel.: 63260830

Means of communication: Public buses 64, 24, 11 and 926

Proposed tour: 60 minutes

SHANGHAI ZOO

Shanghai Zoo, located in the western suburb of Shanghai, is a large park mainly for keeping and displaying animals. It occupies an area of 70 hectares. It was formerly a golf course. The park was built in 1954 and named West Suburban Park. On New Year's day of 1981, it was converted into Shanghai Zoo. Amidst the luxuriant trees and plants, large plots of lawns, zigzag streams and a large lake, live more than 380 kinds of precious and rare animals, like the elephant, the golden-haired monkey, the giant panda, the Yangtse alligator, the red-crowned crane, the Siberian tiger, the giraffe, the hippopotamus, etc. In the last 30 years, the zoo has successfully bred many kinds of precious animals, contributing to the scientific study of wildlife. The park is divided into several major exhibition areas: the gold fish, the reptiles, the birds, the mammals, and the primate, arranged from the low to the high-ranking species in a counter-clockwise manner. Shanghai Zoo is a favourite place for visit for the Shanghai public, especially the children. Here, visitors can admire the animals and watch

performances of animal training.
Visiting hours: 7:00–17:00
Entrance ticket: 10 yuan
Add: 2381 Hongqiao Road
Tel.: 62687775
Means of communication: Public buses 48, 57, 833, 911, 925 and 806
Proposed toru: 60 minutes

SHANGHAI BOTANICAL GARDEN

Located on Longwu Road and founded in 1974, Shanghai Botanical Garden is the largest municipal botanical garden in the country. It occupies an area of 81 hectares. It grows more than 3,000 kinds of plants. It is divided into areas of plant evolution,

environment protection, potted landscape, herbs, greenhouse for exhibition, orchid, model landscaping and plant hall. It is a comprehensive garden in the training of introduced species, scientific research, scientific knowledge popularisation, education, sightseeing and production. In the past years, the garden has introduced and collected from abroad many kinds of ornamental plants, especially the rare and almost extinct species. It has several times won prizes in the international flower shows in Canada and Holland. Shanghai Botanical Garden, with its colourful plant display, appeals to visitors with its natural charm and attracts people for a long-time admiration.

Visiting hours: 8:00-17:00
Entrance ticket: 6 yuan
Add: 1111 Longwu Road
Tel.: 64513369
Means of communication: Public buses 56, 824 and 820

Proposed tour: 60 minutes

SHANGHAI MUNICIPAL CHILDREN'S PALACE

The building of the Municipal Children's Palace was the former villa of an English businessman named Alley Kadoorie. It is wholly built of marble; it is also called the "Marble Hall". Its construction started in 1918 and was completed in 1924. In 1953, Madame Soong Ching Ling founded the China Welfare Society Children's Palace here. The main building is of a palace style. There are other halls, like the Science Hall, the Art and Recreation Hall, a small stage, and an observatory. Every year, over a million children come to take part in different kinds of activities here. There are over a hundred hobby groups, like the chorus, folk music, orchestral music, painting, calligraphy, biology, astronomy, etc. It has trained a large number of scientific and artistic personnel for our country.

Add: 64 Yanan Road, West

Tel.: 62481850

Means of communication: Public buses 37, 20, 71, 127 and 48

Proposed tour: 80 minutes

GREAT WORLD AMUSEMENT CENTRE

The Great World Amusement Centre has a history of over 80 years. It was first founded in 1917 by Huang Chujiu. The Great World used to be the most attractive amusement place for the general public in old Shanghai. There are many small stages showing in turn all kinds of operas, folk art forms, song and dance and vaudeville. In the middle of the building is an open-air show of circling flying ship. Here are also a movie house, a shopping arcade, snack bars and Chinese and Western restaurants. Visitors can spend a whole day there. Later on, it was seized by power by an

underworld gang leader Huang Jinrong and turned it into a place of evil, thus ruining its reputation as an amusement centre. After liberation, the Great World was reformed and turned into a popular place of recreation and leisure for the people. It is featured for its vaudeville and local operas of southern and northern China. It entertains Shanghai citizens and visitors from all places in China with show items suitable for both the refined and popular tastes and are much appreciated by the people. The architecture of the Great World is quite unique; it is a creamy-coloured, multiple-story hexagonal building, supported by 12 cylindrical columns, with a pointed tower on top. The main building consists of 3 inter-linking sections of 4 stories. There are 2 affiliated buildings. The whole layout is something unique and novel. The Great World Amusement Centre consists of 4 parts: the Amusement World, the Exposition World, the Stunt World and the Gourmets' World, offering 8 major series of amusement items. Especially in the '90s, the Great World Open Challenge and the Guinness Record Challenge Competition have attracted masters of skill from different places, creating many "onlys" and "firsts" in the country and in the world. Its strong Shanghai style culture and recreational facilities in pursuit of the times are attracting thousands of visitors everyday from home and abroad.

Visiting hours: 9:00–21:30
Entrance ticket: 25 yuan
Add: 1 Xizang Road, South
Tel.: 63263760
Means of communication: No 1 Subway People Square stop, public buses 71, 135, 17, 18, and 23
Proposed tour: 120 minutes

SHANGHAI MUNICIPAL ARTS AND CRAFTS RESEARCH INSTITUTE

Shanghai Municipal Arts and Crafts Research Institute is the first of its kind in the research of the traditional folk arts in our country. It was founded in 1956. Its main task is to create high-class arts and crafts works and produce a limited number of small-size arts and crafts pieces. It offers guidance in design, inspection and skill to the arts and crafts circles in Shanghai. It consists of research departments of embroidery, sculpture, folk art and fine bas-relief carving on porcelain, bamboo, ink-stone and ivory, woollen needlepoint, embroidery, knitting, box wood carving, jade carving, paper cutting, dough figurine, fancy lanterns and fine ivory carving.

Add: 79 Fenyang Road

Tel.: 64373454

Means of communication: No 1 Subway Changshu Road stop, public buses 96, 42 and 45

Proposed tour: 60 minutes

SHANGHAI GENERAL CARPET FACTORY

China's hand-made carpet and artistic tapestry has a long history. It is a traditional arts and crafts in our country. Shanghai General Carpet Factory, apart from producing hand-made high-grade woollen carpets and hand-made high-grade silk carpets, produces artistic tapestry masterpieces, which is the ultimum expression of carpet-making art and an exquisite artistic product of high artistic and national style. It describes China's famous mountains and rivers, historical relic sites, tourist attractions, such as the of Heaven Temple and the Great Wall in Beijing, the scenery on Huangshan Mountain and landscape in Guilin, and reproduces famous Chinese and foreign painting masters' works, like the "Galloping Horse" by Xu Beihong, "Mona Lisa", masterpiece by Italian great painter da Vinci, and "Holy Mother on the Chair", the famous work by Rafeillo. The artistic tapestry is exquisite in workmanship, novel in material selection, rich and varied in colours and impressive in three-dimensional expression, especially those reproductions of world famous painting works. There is only one of a kind and is valuable for collection and much appreciated by customers.

Add: 25 Caobao Road

Tel.: 64361713

Means of communication: No 1 Subway Caobao Road stop, public buses 43, 89, 93 and 830

Proposed tour: 60 minutes

SHANGHAI JADE CARVING FACTORY

Located on Caobao Road in the south-western part of Shanghai, it is specialised in producing jade and ivory artistic carvings. Jade and ivory carving is a traditional arts and crafts in our country with a history of 6,000 to 7,000 years. Here, one can see the processes of jade and ivory carving and appreciate the artistic works by skilful masters.

Add: 33 Caobao Road

Tel.: 64362660

Means of communication: No 1 Subway Caobao Road stop, public buses 43, 89, 93 and 830

Proposed tour: 60 minutes

PROPOSED ITINERARY FOR QUINTESSENCE TOURS

Morning: Tour Shanghai Zoo (or Shanghai Botanical Garden) - visit Shanghai Municipal Children Palace

Afternoon: Tour Yuyuan Garden - Great World Amusement Centre - Nanjing Road

Evening: Boat-ride on the Huangpu - tour the Bund

RECOMMENDED TRAVEL SERVICE

SHANGHAI HUATING OVERSEAS TOURIST CO.

Add: F/4, 503 Wulumuqi Rd, N

Tel.: 62491234

Fax: 62485470,62482781

Post Code: 200040

SHANGHAI JINJIANG TOURS LTD.

Add: 191 Changle Road

Tel.: 64662828

Fax: 64662297

Post Code: 200020

SHANGHAI CYTS TOURS CORPORATION

Add: 2 Hengshan Road

Tel.: 64331826, 64331907

Fax: 64330507

Post Code: 200031

SHANGHAI CHINA INTERNATIONAL TRAVEL SERVICE CO., LTD

Add: CITS Building, 1277 Beijing Rd, W
Tel.: 62898899
Fax: 62894928
Post Code: 200040

SHANGHAI CHINA TRAVEL SERVICE

Add: 881 Yanan Rd, M
Tel.: 62478888, 62475770
Fax: 62475521
Post Code: 200040

(III) HISTORICAL RELIC SITES AND FORMER RESIDENCES OF HISTORICAL CELEBRITIES

Shanghai is one of 62 famous historical cities in China. It has 130 relic sites under the state or the municipal protection. Many important historical events took place in Shanghai, therefore, it is known as "a window on China's modern history".

1. HISTORICAL RELIC SITES

SITE OF THE FIRST NATIONAL CONGRESS OF THE COMMUNIST PARTY OF CHINA

The site of the First National Congress of the Communist Party of China is located on Xingye Road. It is a typical residential

building of the '20s in urban Shanghai, a stone-framed door type built of wood and bricks. It has been listed as a key relic under state protection. On July 23, 1921, the First National Congress of the Communist Party of China was held here. Delegates from the different Communist groups: Mao Zedong, Dong Biwu, Li Da, He Shuheng, Chen Tanqiu and Wang Jinmei, altogether 13 members, came to attend the meeting to discuss the Party program and the founding of the Communist Party of China. During the meeting, owing to the interruption by spies from the French police, the meeting had to be resumed on a boat on the Nanhu Lake in Jiaxing County, Zhejiang Province.

In 1999 the city government conducted reconstruction of the memorial hall at the site. The new memorial hall is 12-m high with 2 stories at the front and 3 stories at the back. The front lobby is 300 sq.m. in area. On the 200-sq.m. ground floor, is a lecture hall equipped with TV recorder. On the second floor is the newly built exhibition hall of the "Display of Historical Relics of the History of the Founding of the Communist Party of China". The exhibition hall has a space of 450 sq.m.. On display are photos of the delegates to the First National Congress, several hundreds of precious relics, documents and photographs. There is a wax statue hall, showing the 15 attendants to the congress (2 were the representatives from the Communist International) sitting round the table. Young Comrade Mao Zedong, holding a paper in his hand, is standing in the middle. It reproduces the historical scene of the day when the First National Congress of the Communist Party of China was taking place. Visitors will feel as if they are personally on the scene. Visiting hours; 8:30-11:30, 13:15-16:00 (closed on Monday and Thursday mornings)

Add: 76 Xingye Road

Tel.: 53822171-111

Entrance ticket: 3 yuan

Means of communication: Public buses 109, 24 and 17

Proposed tour: 60 minutes

FORMER SITE OF THE CENTRAL ORGAN OF THE CHINESE COMMUNIST YOUTH LEAGUE

The former site of the central organ of the Chinese Communist Youth League is at 6 Lane 567 Huaihai Road, Middle. Since February 1920, Shanghai Communist groups carried out their

activities here. On Aug. 20, 1920, the Chinese Communist Youth League was founded and its central organ was set up here. It is now a key relic site under state protection.

Add: 6 Lane 567 Huaihai Rd, M

Tel.: 63724744

Means of communication: Public buses 02, 42, 911 and 926

Proposed tour: 30 minutes

LONGHUA REVOLUTIONARY MARTYRS' CEMETERY

The Martyrs' Cemetery is located on Longhua Road, Xuhui District, next to the ancient Longhua Temple. It is the former site of the Nationalist Party's Songhu Garrison Headquarters and where the revolutionary martyrs died. Thousands of Communists and revolutionaries had been imprisoned and executed here. Since 1949, after the liberation, the place has been protected as a memorial place for the revolutionary martyrs. In 1985, the place was approved by the Party Central Committee and the State Council to be built into the Longhua Revolutionary Martyrs' Cemetery. This is a memorial place for the education of revolutionary traditions. It occupies an area of 19 hectares, divided into the paying respect area, the tomb area and a hall for storing ash urns of senior cadres and a tablet area. The execution ground of the revolutionary martyrs is a key relic site under state protection.

Visiting hours: 6:00–16:00

Add: 2887 Longhua Road
Tel.: 64685995
Entrance ticket: 1 yuan
Means of communication: Public buses 73, 41, 44, 56, 104 and 864

FORMER SITE OF THE HEADQUARTERS OF SHANGHAI WORKERS' PICKET CORPS

On Baoshan Road in Zhabei District there is a reinforced concrete building, where the Commercial Press and Editors' Office used to be and it had been the headquarters of Shanghai Workers' Picket Corps. On Mar. 27, 1928, 850,000 industrial workers in Shanghai under the leadership of Zhou Enlai, Luo Yinong, Zhao Shiyan and Wang Shounian held the Third Armed Uprising, attacking the strongholds of the allied Zhilu allied army stationed in Shanghai. The uprising won a victory and set up the Shanghai Special Provisional Government in the city. The Picket Corps' headquarters was set up here.

Add: 584 Baoshan Road
Tel.: 64805390 × 6913
Means of communication: Public buses 18 and 21
Proposed tour: 60 minutes

SANSHAN TRADE GUILD HALL

The guild hall is located on Bansongyuan Road in Nanshi District. The building is magnificent with high artistic standard. The base of the caisson ceiling the stage is octagonal shape carved with patterns of the eight city gates in old Shanghai. It was the headquarters of Nanshi Workers' Picket Corps in the Third Armed Uprising of Shanghai Workers in 1927. It is now an exhibition hall of folk collections.

Visiting hours: 9:00–17:00
Add: 1551 Zhongshan Rd, S
Tel.: 63135582
Entrance ticket: 1.5 yuan
Means of communication: Public buses 43, 89, 65, 109, 929 and No 2 Bridge line
Proposed tour: 60 minutes

SITE OF INAUGURAL MEETING OF CHINA "LEFT-WING WRITERS' FEDERATION"

The inaugural meeting of China Left-wing Writers' Federation took place in a 3-storied building of the early '20s on Duolun Road in Hongkou District. In the early '30s it had been the school building of China Arts College. On Mar. 2,1930, a revolutionary organisation — China Left-wing Writers' Federation ("Left-wing Federation" in abbreviation), under the leadership of the Communist Party of China, held its inaugural meeting here. At the meeting Lu Xun, Shen Ruixian and Qian Xingcun were elected as the presidium. Lu Xun made an important speech. A permanent organ of the federation was elected and the theories, program for action and working principles were determined. The "Left-wing Federation" played an important role in smashing the counter-revolutionary, cultural encirclement and suppression by the Nationalists.

Add: 145 Duolun Road
Tel.:63571649
Means of communication: Public buses 18, 21 and 70
Proposed tour: 30 minutes

STATUE OF THE ANTI-BRITISH NATIONAL HERO CHEN HUACHENG

The statue of the Anti-British national hero Chen Huacheng is standing in Lingjiang Park. In June 1842, British battle ships attacked Wusong Mouth. Chen Huacheng's superior, Niu Jian, governor of Jiangsu, Anhui and Jiangxi ,planned to sue for peace. Chen Huacheng was then the military commander in Jiangsu and Anhui. He strongly opposed to the suing for peace. He had bronze canons cast, forts built, gunpowder made and army drilled, and defences set up. When the British army attacked, Chen Huacheng, at the age of 67, led his troops to counter-attack bravely. The forts at Wusong Mouth damaged a number of British ships and the soldiers fought hand-to-hand with the British army and beat back the enemy. Later, Niu Jian gave up fight and fled pell-mell from Baoshan. The Brtish army landed and assailed the forts from the back. Chen Huacheng defended his position to the last. He was wounded seven times and gave up his life for his country.

Visiting hours: 9:00–16:00

Add: 1 Youyi Road
Tel.: 56163295
Entrance ticket: 10 yuan
Means of communication: Public buses 51, 116 and 549
Proposed tour: 60 minutes

MARTYRS' CEMETERY OF THE TAIPING HEAVENLY KINGDOM

The Martyrs' Cemetery of the Taiping Heavenly Kingdom is found in Tunliang Lane, northwest to Gaoqiao Town in Chuansha County. In the first year of Qing Emperor Tongzhi (1862), the uprising army of the Taiping Heavenly Kingdom attacked Shanghai for the third time. After seizing Jinshan, Nanhui, Fengxian and Chuansha, they occupied Gaoqiao, the strategic passage to Shanghai. The Qing government troops colluded with the imperialists and set up a rifle corps with the American scoundrel Wall as the captain. The rifle corps headed by Wall and the allied troops of the British and French assaulted Gaoqiao with gunboats. The Taiping army resisted indomitably. The invaders set fire to Gaoqiao Town and the Taiping army was forced to transfer. In the battle at Gaoqiao the fallen soldiers of the Taiping army were buried here. To commemorate the Taiping soldiers, who fell in action, the graveyard was rearranged in 1954 and a tombstone erected, "Tomb of Martyrs of the Taiping Heavenly Kingdom Army".
Add: Gaoqiao Town, Chuansha County
Tel.: 68769317
Means of communication: Public buses 81, 591, 592 and 593
Proposed tour: 30 minutes

SPRING HALL

The Spring Hall in YuYuan Garden was built,first year of Qing Emperor Daoguang (1821). The name of the hall was derived from poet Su Shi's verse "The green heralds spring". It is a large hall with 6 adjoining rooms. During the Small Sword Society uprising the northern headquarters was set up here, where one of the Small sword Society leaders Chen Alin issued orders and directed the battle. In the hall there is large painting "Appreciating the Sword"

by famous late Qing painter Ren Bonian and a couplet written by calligrapher Shen Yinmo, "Brave ink embraces the space and the heart keeps the talent", in praise of the heroic spirit and noble mind. Besides, there on display are relics like the weapons used, coins cast and scripts of orders issued by the uprising army.

Visiting hours: 9:00–17:00
Add: 132 Anren Road
Tel.: 63260830
Means of communication: Public buses 64, 24, 11, 926
Proposed tour: 60 minutes

SITE OF THE PROVISIONARY GOVERNMENT OF THE REPUBLIC OF KOREA

Located in an old-fashioned building with a stone-framed door, built in 1925,the provisional government of the Republic of Korea finally settled down here after the March First Movement and several times relocation. King Jiu was then the head of the state council (equivalent to president). In 1932, some members of the provisional government were persecuted and arrested by the Japanese military and police, the provisional government was forced to evacuate from Shanghai. This place is the best preserved "former site" where the provisional government of the Republic of Korea spent the longest time for work. It was opened to the public in 1993. It has since then received 3 Korean presidents and 3 congressmen. It is called the "Shrine of the Korean National Independence Movement."

Visiting hours: 9:00–17:00
Add: 4 Lane 306 Madang Road
Tel.: 53824554
Means of communication: No 1 Subway Huangpi Road stop, public buses 17, 24, 26 and 42
Proposed tour: 30 minutes

SHANGHAI OLD CITY WALL AND DAJING PAVILION

Zhonghua Road and Remin Road in downtown Shanghai forms a circular road. This road was built in the place of the dismantled old city wall. It is a landmark of the boundary of old Shanghai downtown. It was built by Shanghai County during the Jiajing year of the Ming Dynasty (1523-1566) to guard against the pirates. After the Chinese bourgeois democratic revolution in 1911, the old city wall became an obstacle in the city's economic development and

communications; the city government decided to dismantle the wall, filled up the city moat and built a road. The project was completed on July 1912 to 1914, forming the present circular road. In the course of dismantling, a section of the wall was preserved, where the Dajing Pavilion — the Dajing Guangong Temple is. Formerly it was an arrow tower and later the Guanggong Temple was built on it. During the Qing Dynasty the Yichun Terrace was added to it. It has now become a tourist attraction.

Add: 269 Dajing Road, Xiao Beimen

Tel.: 63852443

Means of communication: Public buses 11 and 911

Proposed tour: 60 minutes

2. FORMER RESIDENCES OF HISTORICAL CELEBRITIES

DOCTOR SUN YATSEN'S FORMER RESIDENCE

Shanghai was the place where Dr Sun Yatsen travelled back and forth many times during the democratic revolution. On Xiangshan Road there is a Western-style two-storied building bought with funds pooled by Canadian overseas Chinese for Dr. Sun Yatsen. In front of the building is a landscaped garden. On the first floor is the dining room, the sitting room and on the second floor is the bed room and the study room. Dr. Sun Yatsen and his wife Madame Soong Ching Ling lived here for 6 years from 1918 to 1924. He conducted many of his important revolutionary activities here and wrote the "Program for Founding the Republic", "Theories of Sun Wen" and "Industrial Program". On August 1922, he met here with representatives from the Central Committee of the Communist Party of China Li Dazhao and Lin Boqu. In the same year, he consulted with Yue Fei, the special envoy from the Soviet Union. On January 6 of the following year, he published the "Manifesto by Sun Wen and Yue Fei". On September 1922, he called a meeting on the lawn in front of the building and invited Communist members to attend the meeting to study and formulate the reorganisation scheme of the Nationalist Party . It was the first Nationalist and Communist coalition. Dr Sun Yatsen's former residence is listed as a key cultural relic site under state protection.

Visiting hours: 9:30-11:00, 14:00-16:30

Add: 7 Xiangshan Road

Tel.: 64372954

Entrance ticket: 8 yuan

Means of communication: Public buses 17, 24, 42, 916 and 911

Proposed tour: 90 minutes

SOONG CHING LING'S FORMER RESIDENCE AND MAUSOLEUM

Soong Ching Ling was Dr. Sun Yatsen's wife. She was the honorary chairwoman of the People's Republic of China. Her former residence, a Western-style garden villa, is located at 1843 Huaihai Road, Middle. Since 1948, Soong Ching Ling had been living and working in her Shanghai residence here. She passed away in Beijing on May 29, 1981 at the age of 90. She was first buried in the International

Cemetery in the Soong Family graveyard on Hongqiao Road, Shanghai. Later the graveyard was extended and built into a mausoleum. In front of her tomb is the memorial square, in which a marble statue of Soong Ching Ling was erected. On a granite memorial tablet is carved the inscription by Deng Xiaoping: "Eternal glory to Comrade Soong Ching Ling, a patriot, a democrat, an internationalist and a communist fighter".

Visiting hours: 9:00–11:00. 13:00–16:30

Add: 1843 Huaihai Road, Middle

Tel.: 64376268

Entrance ticket: 8 yuan

Means of communication: Public buses 126, 44, 48, 926 and 911

Proposed tour: 90 minutes

FORMER RESIDENCE OF ZHOU ENLAI

Zhou Enlai's former residence, a 3-storied garden villa, located on Sinan Road, Luwan District, was the office of the Chinese Communist Party's delegation in Shanghai. On May 1946, in accordance with the "Double-Tenth Agreement" between the Nationalist Party and the Communist Party, Zhou Enlai led the Communist delegation to Nanjing to have a conference with the Nationalist Party. On June, the delegation set up its office in Shanghai. It was made known to the public as Zhou Enlai's residence; hence it is called "Zhou Enlai's Apartment". Premier Zhou Enlai came to Shanghai four times. Here he held press conferences and met with patriotic personages.

Visiting hours: 8:30–11:00, 13:00–16:30

Add: 73 Sinan Road

Tel. for information: 64730420

Entrance ticket: 2 yuan

Means of communication: Public buses 24, 17 and 96

Proposed tour: 40 minutes

LU XUN'S FORMER RESIDENCE, MEMORIAL HALL AND TOMB

At No 9 Dalu Xincun on Shanyin Road, Lu Xun lived from April 1933 to Oct. 19, 1936, when he passed away. Here, Lu Xun wrote many militant essays and translated works like the "Dead Soul", edited Ju Qiubai"s posthumous works, "Collection of Works on the Sea". In 1935, when the Chinese Worker-Peasant Red Army victoriously reached Shaanxi, Lu Xun sent them a telegram of congratulation.

Qu Qiubai stayed for some time on the third floor of Lu Xun's apartment. In 1956, Lu Xun's Memorial Hall was built inside Hongkou Park. The name of the memorial hall was inscribed by Zhou Enlai. The relics displayed there describe the ideological development and militant cause of Lu Xun, emphasizing on the ten years of his social and cultural life in Shanghai. Lu Xun's tomb was formerly located in the International Cemetery in Shanghai's western suburbs. It was moved to Hongkou Park in 1956. On the tombstone are inscribed by Mao Zedong, "Tomb of Mr Lu Xun". In front of the tomb on the lawn is a bronze statue of Lu Xun. Around the tomb are planted pines and cypresses, giving the graveyard a solemn and respectful atmosphere. It is now a key relic site under state protection.

Visiting hours: 9:00–16:00
Add: 146 East Jiangwang Road
Tel.: 56669711
Entrance ticket: 4 yuan
Means of communication: Public buses 18, 21, 70 and 97
Proposed tour: 120 minutes

ZHOU TAOFEN'S MEMORIAL HALL

The great patriot Mr. Zhou Taofen was an outstanding journalist, statesman and publisher in China's modern history. This was Mr. Zhou Taofen's former residence in Shanghai from 1930 to 1936. Mao Zedong, Zhou Enlai, Zhu De and Soong Ching Ling had inscribed to commemorate him. The horizontal tablet on the memorial hall was written by Shen Junru. In the hall are displayed many precious relics of Mr Zhou Taofen's manuscripts, works and inscriptions by state leaders.

Add: 54 lane 205 Chongqing Rd, S

Tel.: 63842811

Means of communication: Public buses 17, 43, No 1 Bridge line and No 8 Tunnel line

Proposed tour: 40 minutes

XU GUANGQI'S TOMB

Xu Guangqi's tomb is located in Guangqi Park on Nandan Road. Xu Guangqi was the pioneer in China in the study and introduction of Western sciences. He was specially outstanding in his achievements in agriculture and astronomy. In 1633, when he died, he was buried at the junction of Fahua Creek and Zhaojia Creek, where his descendants lived. The district Xujiahui was named after the Xu family ("jia" in Chinese means "family"). In 1957, the tomb was remoulded. In the graveyard there is Xu Guangxi's granite statue, 12 carved tablets of his portrait, original hand-writing and biography.

Add: 17 Nandan Road

Tel.: 64381780

Means of communication: Public buses 93, 43 and 02

Proposed tour: 30 minutes

FORMER RESIDENCES, LIVING QUARTERS AND MEMORIAL PLACES OF OTHER HISTORICAL CELEBRITIES

There are also in Shanghai many other memorial places related with the Old Democratic Revolution and the New Democratic Revolution and many residences or places of activity of celebrities with high prestige. These are tourist resources of great value and historical significance.

NAME OF RESIDENCE	ADDRESS	TIME LIVING
Mao Zedong's former residence	63 Anyi Road	1920
Zhang Xueliang's apartment	1 Langao Road	1934-1935
Liu Haisu's apartment	512 Fuxing Road, Middle	1935
Chiang Kai Shek's residence	9 Dongping Road	1927
Cai Yuanpei's former residence	16 Lane 303 Huashan Road	1937
Wu Changshuo's former residence	Lane 457 Shanxi Road, N.	1910-1927

PROPOSED TOUR OF HISTORICAL SITES AND FORMER RESIDENCES OF HISTORICAL CELEBRITIES

First day: Morning: Site of First National Congress of the Communist Party of China-former site of Central Organ of Communist Youth League-Zhou Taofen's Memorial Hall

Afternoon: Dr Sun Yatsen's former residence-Zhou Enlai's apartment-Soong Ching Ling's former residence

Second day: Morning: Xu Guangqi's tomb-Longhua Revolutionary Martyrs' Memorial Place

Afternoon: Lu Xun's tomb-Lu Xun's Memorial Hall

RECOMMENDED TRAVEL SERVICE

SHANGHAI HUATING OVERSEAS TOURIST CO.

Add: F/4, 503 Wulumuqi Rd, N

Tel.: 62491234

Fax: 62485470,62482781
Post Code: 200040

SHANGHAI JINJIANG TOURS LTD.
Add: 191 Changle Road
Tel.: 64662828
Fax: 64662297
Post Code: 200020

SHANGHAI CYTS TOURS CORPORATION
Add: 2 Hengshan Road
Tel.: 64331826, 64331907
Fax: 64330507
Post Code: 200031

SHANGHAI CHINA INTERNATIONAL TRAVEL SERVICE CO., LTD
Add: CITS Building, 1277 Beijing Rd, W
Tel.: 62898899
Fax: 62894928
Post Code: 200040

SHANGHAI CHINA TRAVEL SERVICE
Add: 881 Yanan Rd, M
Tel.: 62478888, 62475770
Fax: 62475521
Post Code: 200040

(IV) CULTURE, ART AND RELIGION

1. METROPOLITAN CULTURAL SIGHTS

SHANGHAI MUSEUM
Shanghai Museum has a collection of over 120,000 items of cultural relics displayed on a floor space of 12,000 sq.m. On the first floor are the Hall of Ancient Bronze Ware, Hall of Chinese Ancient Sculpture and a large exhibition hall; on the second floor are the Hall of Chinese Ancient Pottery and Porcelain and a large

exhibition hall; on the third floor are the Hall of Chinese Calligraphy of Different Dynasties, Hall of Chinese Painting of different dynasties and Hall of Chinese Seals of different dynasties; on the fourth floor are the Hall of Chinese Ancient Jade Ware, Hall of Chinese Coins of different dynasties. Hall of Chinese Furniture of the Ming and Qing Dynasties, Hall of Arts and Crafts of Chinese Minority Nationalities and a large exhibition hall. The 12 special topic halls displaying bronze ware, pottery and porcelain, paintings, calligraphy, sculpture, coins, jade ware, furniture, seals, arts and crafts of Chinese minority nationalities and Western arts, give a full picture of the brilliant course of the 6,000 years' Chinese ancient arts. The museum adopts an advanced system of management, guiding and enquiry to render convenience to visitors.

Visiting hours: 9:00–17:00 (to 20:00 on Saturdays)
Add: 201 People's Avenue
Tel.: 63270276
Entrance ticket: 20 yuan
Means of communication: No 1 Subway People's Square stop, public buses 18, 46, 49, 71, 127, 202, 505 and No 6 Tunnel line

SHANGHAI HISTORICAL MUSEUM

Shanghai Historical Museum was originally named Exhibition Hall of Shanghai Historical Relics. It is a museum of historical records specially describing Shanghai's historical development in the past 100 years. Through the display of precious relics, literature, archives, pictures, accompanied by advanced audio visual and acoustics facilities, it presents to visitors the historical development of the city of Shanghai in modern times. The museum is divided into 6 parts, displaying different kinds of relics, several thousands literary materials, giving an overall and systematic picture of the profound changes in the city's development since its opening-door in politics, economy, culture, society and livelihood. Shanghai Historical Museum was built on the foundation of the collections of the former historical museum and supplemented with Shanghai local historical items and literary material. It has now a collection of 20,000 items. Among these are the copper lions formerly placed at the gate of the British Hong Kong and Shanghai Banking

Corporation, an iron canon "Armstrong" cast by the Jiangnan Manufacturing Bureau, the Wuhua Hundred-character Ceremonial Sedan Chair, the gold-plated character sign of the hundred-year-old Hongyun Restaurant. All these are precious relic items with strong Shanghai local feature.

It is a window for Shanghai citizens and domestic and foreign visitors to learn about the history of Shanghai.

Visiting hours: 9:00–15:30

Add: 1286 Hongqiao Road

Tel.: 62755595

Means of communication: Public buses 72, 73, 251 and 911

SHANGHAI MUSEUM OF NATURAL SCIENCES

Located on Yanan Road, East, Shanghai Museum of Natural Sciences is one of the largest museums of natural sciences in the country. It has a floor space of 4,000 sq.m. , consisting of 9 exhibition rooms of "Animal History of Ancient Museum of Natural Sciences", "History of Ancient Man", "Chinese Ancient Mummies", "Invertebrates", "Fishes", "Amphibians", "Reptiles", "Birds" and "Mammals". It has a collection of over 240,000 items. Among these are 184 items of 100 categories of specimens of high academic value, arranged according to geologic age, vividly describing the emergence and development, the long course of evolution of animals and plants, their thriving and decline, from aquatic to terrestrial life, from the simple to the complex, from the lower to the higher. Shanghai has planned to build a science and technology city in Pudong and move the museum over there. It will change the pattern of closed display and will adopt the advanced technique of electricity, light and sound to enable visitors to participate in experimental exhibition activities with an aim to play a greater role in popularising scientific knowledge.

Visiting hours: 9:00–15:30

Add: 260 Yanan Rd, E

Tel.: 63213548

Entrance ticket: 16 yuan

Means of communication: Public buses 71, 127 and 66

SHANGHAI LIBRARY

Shanghai Library is one of the symbolic cultural buildings in Shanghai. It has a total floor space of 80,000 sq.m. with a collection of 13,200,000 volumes of books and magazines. It is one of largest libraries in the country and ranks among the 10 large libraries in the world. There are 24 reading rooms for Chinese and foreign books and magazines, Chinese books on open-shelf for loan, ancient and modern literary material, special journals and standards, audio-visual material and electronic reading material. The total number of open-shelf copies is 1 million. There are 3,000 seats in the reading rooms. The library is equipped with electronic reading guide, electronic reading, electronic indexing and information transmission and delivery of books by trolleys. Besides, the library adopts the most advanced internationally information storage indexing technique and links with major information internet in the country and abroad. The multi-functional hall, lecture hall and exhibition hall are open to the public and fully display its different functions.

Time open: 8:30–20:00
Add: 1555 Huaihai Rd, M
Tel.: 64455555
Means of communication: No 1 Subway Hengshan Road stop, public buses 15, 93 and 126

SHANGHAI ART GALLERY

Shanghai Art Gallery, located on Nanjing Road, West, was founded in 1956. It was formerly named Shanghai Fine Arts Exhibition Hall. It is a museum of plastic arts with the function of collecting and displaying fine arts masterpieces, for holding art exhibitions, conducting academic study and organising domestic and oversea fine art exchanges. It is complete in facilities and services. Along with the development of Shanghai's culture and its position in the country and abroad, the gallery shows increasingly its importance. It has become a centre for the art circle and art lovers to appreciate art works and for art exchanges.

Add: 456 Nanjing Rd, W
Tel.: 63270827
Means of communication: Public buses 20, 37, and 23

SHANGHAI GRAND THEATRE

Shanghai Grand Theatre owns the largest and most convertible stage in the world. The auditorium has a seating capacity of 1,800, able to accommodate first-class ballet, opera and orchestra performances from the country and the world. There is also a medium-size theatre with 600 seats and a small-size theatre with 250 seats, suitable for the performance of chamber music and song and dance shows. The Grand Theatre has become a centre of cultural life in Shanghai, a place for world-grade performances of opera, dance, movie and music. It is a symbolic building of culture of Shanghai as an international metropolis.

Add: 190 Huangpi Rd, N

Tel.: 63875480

Means of communication: No 1 Subway People Square stop, public buses 18, 46, 49, 71, 127, 145 and No 6 Tunnel line

SHANGHAI BOOK CITY

Shanghai Book City, opened in December 1998, is one of the 10 symbolic buildings of culture determined by Shanghai Municipal Government. It is located on Fuzhou Road, a cultural street with a hundred-year history. It co-ordinates with Shanghai Museum and Shanghai Grand Theater on People's Square in the distance. Together they form a scenic sight of culture. It occupies an area of 3,713 sq.m. with a total floor space of 40,000 sq.m., 27 stories aboveground and 2 stories underground for parking. From the first to the sixth floor is the business floor for retail of books; the seventh floor is the exhibition centre. From the eighth floor up are intelligence-type offices.

The building is magnificent and graceful, giving an atmosphere of learning. The 10,000-sq.m. business floor is a first super large-scale retail bookshop in the history of Shanghai, dealing in all kinds of books, video products and electronic publications in a variety of 120,000 kinds, covering practical life, Chinese and foreign literature, social sciences, culture and education, children's reading material, science and technology and arts. There is a large quantity of Hong Kong and Taiwan editions and foreign masterpiece originals, providing a special window for readers to explore the world.

Add: 465 Fuzhou Road

Tel.: 63522222

Means of communication: Public buses 17, 49 and 123

FUZHOU ROAD CULTURAL STREET

A century ago, on Fuzhou Road many bookstores and stationery shops were set up and has hence enjoyed the reputation of a cultural street. Now, there are more than 30 different kinds of bookstores and stationery shops, like China Science and Technology Bookstore, Shanghai Bookstore, Bookstore of Foreign Languages, Store of Ancient Books. At the end of 1998, the 27-storied Shanghai Book City, a symbolic building in Shanghai, opened for business. Here many stationery shops and sales departments of publishing houses are found. The street is a well-known in the whole country as a cultural street.

Add: Fuzhou Road

Means of communication: No 1 Subway People's Square stop, public buses 17, 49 and 123

JINGDEZHEN CERAMICS SHANGHAI ART CENTRE

Jingdezhen Ceramics Shanghai Art Centre occupies an area of 10,000 sq.m., exhibiting more than 60,000 items, including many masterpieces of famous art masters. Walking into the exhibition hall is like entering a contemporary ceramic art museum. The centre consists of exhibition, training, creation, auction and ceramic cultural sightseeing, playing the role of ceramic creation, education, sightseeing and trade. The centre has a room for ceramic art activities, able to accommodate 200 visitors in ceramic activities. Visitors can, under the guidance and with the help of masters, turn a pile of lifeless clay into jars, pots, vases, human figures or abstract objects from conception.

Add: 1253 Daduhe Road

Tel.: 62453834

Communications: Public buses 143, 567 and 754

SHANGHAI SCIENCE AND TECHNOLOGY CAPITAL

Shanghai Science and Technology Capital, jointly founded by

Shanghai New Huangpu Real Estate Co.,Ltd. and Singapore Changli International Investment Co.,Ltd., occupies an area of 23,850 sq.m. with a floor space of 200,800 sq.m. The building is magnificent, accomplished in planning, and new in facilities. The Science and Technology Capital is jointly managed by Shanghai Municipal Science Commission and Huangpu District People's Government and named by the municipal government. It will become an exhibition centre for scientific achievements and a place of gathering for large-scale Chinese and foreign hi-tech enterprises.

Add: 668 Beijing Rd, E

Tel.: 53090525, 53094781

Means of communication: No 1 Subway Xinzha Road stop, public buses 21, 19, 64, 18 and 217

2. GALLERY OF INTERNATIONAL ARCHITECTURES ON THE BUND

The Bund is a symbol of Shanghai. The best attraction of the Bund lies in its blocks of antique and graceful buildings. They were not designed by the same architect nor built at the same time, yet they harmonise in architectural tone and the outlines were treated so co-ordinately that no matter you walk in front of them or look at them in a distance, they all present you an air of dignity, elegance, magnificence and strength. The majority of the buildings belong to the style of "restoration to the ancients" and eclecticism, except the Sassoon House (now Peace Hotel) and the Broadway Mansions (now Shanghai Mansions), which belong to the early modernist school. When you take a walk along the embankment,

you will see pointed Gothic roofs, arches of ancient Greece, Baroque columns, Spanish balconies, displaying before you the rich flavour of foreign lands, so unique and attractive. When night falls and lights are on, the buildings are immersed in a sea of brilliance, each glittering like a crystal palace. Watching from the other side of the river, you will see a dazzling picture like a scene in a magnificent epic.

The Bund is worthy of its name as "a gallery of international architectures".

Add: Zhongshan Rd, E I

Means of communication: Public buses 20, 22, 37, 55, 65, 42, 126, 135 and 145

SHANGHAI MUNICIPAL GOVERNMENT NO 2 OFFICE (FORMER BRITISH CONSULATE)

No 33 on Zhongshan Road, East 1, was the British Consulate before the '60s. It was first built in 1849 and rebuilt in 1852. In 1870, it was destroyed by fire. The present building was built in 1873. It has an architectural style of the English Renaissance period. The main building is two-storied in a square shape, roofed with Chinese butterfly-tiles. The first floor is built on a high terrace for better ventilation. There are a number of windows on the front with arched or levelled tops. It is surrounded by luxuriant trees and large tracts of lawns, giving a more graceful and magnificent air.

CHINA GUANGDA BANK (FORMER FRENCH ORIENTAL HUILI BANK)

No 29 Zhongshan Road, East 1, built in 1914, was the French Oriental Huili Bank, a typical French classical architecture. At the entrance, above the arched gate is a whirly begonia, a Baroque design with French feature. In the front of the building are giant Ionian columns, separating the building into three sections.

SHANGHAI FOREIGN TRADE BUILDING (FORMER JARDIN, MATHESON & CO., LTD.

No 27 on Zhongsha Road, East 1, was originally a two-storied building and rebuilt in 1920 into a 5-storied steel-framed reinforced concrete building, imitating the architectural style of the English Renaissance. The front is decorated with Corinthian columns, connecting the first and second stories into one section and the third, fourth and fifth stories into another section, paved with roughly chiselled rectagular blocks. The windows are large and the rooms are bright.

SHANGHAI TEXTILE BUILDING (FORMER ZHENGJIN BANK)

No 24 on Zhongshan Road, East 1, built in 1924, is a 7-storied building of reinforced concrete of modern Japanese Western-styled architecture. It was originally the Japanese Yokohama Zhengjin Bank. The first floor is paved with stone blocks with distinct horizontal lines, giving a bright and lively expression. The huge columns from the second story to the fifth story, imitating classicism, add more grace and dignity to the building.

BANK OF CHINA, SHANGHAI BRANCH (FORMER BANK OF CHINA HEAD OFFICE)

No 23 Zhongshan Road, East 1, built in 1937, was one of the most successful high-risers. It consists of two parts; the western building is a 4-storied reinforced concrete structure. The eastern section is the main building of steel framed structure, and 15 stories aboveground and 2 stories underground. It has a Chinese national-styled square and tapered roof. All the balustrades and window frames are designed with Chinese national characteristics. Both sides of each story are decorated with hollowed-out patterns, expressing an air of auspiciousness.

PEACE HOTEL - SOUTHERN BUILDING (FORMER PALACE HOTEL)

No 19, built in 1906, is a 6-storied, brick and stone English-styled building and a flat roof. The front outer walls are paved with white bricks with red bricks in the waist lines in every story.

Doors and windows have different designs, mainly of Baroque style. In 1911, celebrated personages from different circles in Shanghai gathered here to give Dr Sun Yatsen a reception to celebrate his assuming the provisional presidency.

PEACE HOTEL - NORTHERN BUILDING (FORMER SASSOON HOUSE)

No 20 Nanjing Road, East, built in 1928, is an outstanding modern high-riser in Shanghai of steel frame structure in 10 stories and partly in 13 stories in the middle. The outer walls of the different stories are built of granite, except the ninth and the top floors of Taishan stone-paved bricks. The vertical lines, waist lines and eaves are all carved. The eastern side of the building is the front. Part of the roof on the eastern side is in a cone shape and covered with red copper. In the hotel there are British, French, Italian, German, Indian, Spanish, American and Chinese styled suites. The Old Men Jazz Band is well-known the world over. They play the music of tunes calling memories of the past.

SHANGHAI HOUSEHOLD TEXTILES IMPORT AND EXPORT CORPORATION (FORMER CHARTERED BANK)

No 18 Zhongshan Road, East 1, built in 1923, is an architecture of ecleticism of the Renaissance. The outer wall of the first floor is paved with granite, well balanced and co-ordinated, giving an expression ot abundant capital. The second story is supported by huge Baroque stone pillars. The design of the building differs with every story, one of the typical features of the Renaissance art.

GUILIN BUILDING (FORMER BUILDING OF NORTH CHINA DAILY NEWS) PRESENT AMERICAN ASSURANCE UNDERWRITING COMPANY, SHANGHAI BRANCH

No 17 Zhongshan Road, East 1, built in 1921, is a modern

architecture of the Renaissance. The front of the building consists of three parts; the first part is paved with crude rocks; the second part, washed with cement, expressing the balance and harmony of the Renaissance art; the third part are balconies supported by double columns with arched windows on both sides. The top story is a tower.

SHANGHAI MUNICIPAL INDUSTRIAL PRODUCTS IMPORT AND EXPORT CORPORATION (FORMER TAIWAN BANK)

No 16 Zhongshan Road, East 1, built in 1924, of reinforced concrete structure, is a modern Japanese Western-styled building, absorbing the good points of architecture in different countries to form a mixture of different architectural styles.

SHAGHAI SPACE BUREAU (FORMER SINO-RUSSIAN DAOSHENG BANK)

No 15 Zhongshan Road, East 1, built in 1910, is a 3-storied mixed structure of brick and stone and reinforced concrete, regular in plane, with the front decorated with classical pillars and sculptured figures. The outer walls are paved with white ceramic tiles. This was quite unique at that time. The rooms have high ceilings. The floors are paved with coloured floor tiles.

SHANGHAI CUSTOMS HOUSE (FORMER RIVER AND SEA CUSTOMS)

No 13 Zhongshan Road, East 1, built in 1927, is a 3-storied, eclectic building combining European classical and modern architecture. It consists of two parts; the eastern part on the Bund is 7-storied, built of Jinshan stones; the western part extends to Sichuan Road, Middle, 5 storied high built of machine-made red bricks from the second story up. There are Greek Doric pillars at the front gate on the Bund. On entering the gate, you will find the lobby decorated with elaborate plaster patterns and floor lining. The flat roof is gold gilded and inlaid with coloured mosaic. On top is a clock tower.

PUDONG DEVELOPMENT BANK (FORMER HONG KONG AND SHANGHAI BANKING CORPORATION

AND SHANGHAI MUNICIPAL PEOPLE'S GOVERNMENT)

No 12 Zhongshan Road, East 1, built in 1925, with 5 stories and 7 stories in the middle part, and an exterior of square shape and a semi-domed roof is a steel frame structure, and an imitation classic brick and stone exterior and interior of a style of classicism, such as Ionian pillared corridors and caisson ceilings. The interior was beautifully decorated; the pillars, wall planks and floor in the lobby were all paved with marble. It was equipped with central heating and the most advanced air conditioning equipment of that time.

SHANGHAI HARBOUR SUPERVISORY BUREAU (FORMER MERCANTILE SHIPPING CO.)

No 9 Zhongshan Road, East 1, the former Mercantile Shipping Co., was founded on trial basis by Li Hongzhang in 1872 and officially opened in 1873. In 1879, its fleet sailed as far as to the United States. In 1916, it was turned into merchant-run and a brick and stone 3-storied office building was built on the Bund. The waist line between every two stories was laid with stone slabs. The front of the second and third stories was built with classical pillars; the second story, of Doric structure and the third story, of a mixed structure. The stone material is all red granite. Above the gate is a protruding balcony.

DONGFENG RESTAURANT (FORMER SHANGHAI CLUB)

No 2 Zhongshan Road, East 1, built in 1910, the former Shanghai Club, was a place for social gathering. The exterior was built in well-balanced three sections. Between the second and third stories are 6 Ionian pillars, increasing the three-dimensional appearance of the building. The two sides of the building are symmetrically positioned, each with a Baroque pavilion on top. The windows have various shapes and beautifully carved frames. The whole building looks graceful with artistic appeal. The interior decoration is even more magnificent. There is a 34-m long bar counter built of black and white marble. It was then known as the longest bar in the Orient.

TAIPING INSURANCE COMPANY (FORMER ASIA PETROL COMPANY)

No 1 Zhongshan Road, East 1, built in 1913, was originally a 7-storied building and later another story was added to it. The exterior is of Baroque structure with most of the pillars in Ironic style. The arches on the first floor are built with rocks. The outer walls are built of stone-paved bricks. The whole structure is of steel-framed reinforced concrete.

SHANGHAI CIVIL CONSTRUCTION DESIGNING INSTITUTE (FORMER YOULI BANK)

No 17 Guangdong Road at the corner of the Bund was formerly the site of the Tianxiang Firm. In 1916, the building was dismantled and replaced with a 5-storied building with a tower on top. The rooms are spacious and ceilings are high. It was the first steel-framed structure in Shanghai.

FORMER STOCK EXCHANGE (FORMER RICHARD HOTEL)

At the northern end of the Waibaidu Bridge, built in 1910, a 5-storied steel-framed concrete, brick and wood mixed structure with an English new classic exterior. On the windows of the fifth story are large arches. The third and fourth stories are partly decorated with Ionic columns. Some of the window frames are domed-arches, others are flat ones. There are convexes and concaves in the whole building. The rooms are long, therefore, a little dark.

SHANGHAI POST OFFICE

At the end of the Sichuan Road Bridge, built in 1924, it is a large English classic building of steel frame and concrete structure. The main building is 4-storied. The tower on the corner is 8-storied. There is a basement. The front is of classic style. Several fronts are connected by new-styled Corinthian columns extending in 3 stories. The tower is of Baroque style. The outer walls are washed with fine granular stone powder. The wall on Tiantong Road is built of machine-made red bricks. On the top are two sculptured statues. The whole building looks magnificent and imposing.

SHANGHAI MANSIONS (FORMER BROADWAY MANSIONS)

On No 2 Suzhou Road, North, built in 1934, is a 22-storied, 88-m high apartment building of early modern style. Both the exterior and the interior are decorated in a bright and unsophisticated way with an exterior looking very dignified. It is now a 3-star hotel. It used to be the highest point on the northern Bund. There is a terrace on the eighteenth floor, good for getting a bird's eye-view of the whole Bund.

WAIBAIDU BRIDGE

Spanning the Suzhou Creek on Zhongshan Road, East 1, built in 1907, it is an iron bridge, enjoying a fame of the most magnificent and best-quality iron bridge in the history of Shanghai. It is an iron and steel bridge with a steel frame beautifully designed and appealing with charm.

3. RELIGIONS IN THE METROPOLIS

In China, the religions in Shanghai are the most pluralistic and coexistent. The majority of religions in the world are developing and propagating in Shanghai. Religious sites are found in urban areas and suburban counties. There are over a hundred temples and religious gathering places. Among these there are famous ones like the Xujiahui Catholic Cathedral, the Catholic Cathedral on Sheshan Hill, the Christian Community Church on Hengshan Road, the Moen Church on Xizang Road, Middle, the Buddhist Jade Buddha Temple, Longhua Temple and Jingan Temple; the Islam Songjiang Mosque and Taoist Baiyun Temple on West Linshi Road. The Sheshan Catholic Monastery on Sheshan Hill, the East China Christian Academy of Theology, the Buddhist College, the Taoist College have been either restored or founded to train the clergy and successors. A tour of religious sites in Shanghai will enable you to learn more about the religious history, culture and religious architecture in China.

BUDDHISM

LONGHUA TEMPLE

Located in Longhua Town, Xuhui District, it is a famous thousand-year-old ancient temple south of the Changjiang River. It has the longest history and the largest scale among Buddhist monasteries in the history of Shanghai. It occupies an area of more than 20,000 sq.m. with a floor space of 5,219 sq.m. It is said that Longhua Temple and Longhua Pagoda were built in the 5th Chiwu year of King Sun Quan of the Wu State during the Three Kingdoms Period (242 A.D.). There are four adjoining halls: the Grand Hall, the Three Sages Hall, Hall of Maitreya and the Abbot Chamber.

On the sides are the bell tower and the drum tower, arhats hall and preaching hall. Longhua Pagoda is by the side of the temple, also built during the Three Kingdoms Period. The pagoda is of brick and wood structure. It is 40-m tall with 7 stories in octagonal shape. There are eaves on every story and bells hanging on the corners and corridors around the body. The modelling is graceful and appealing. Longhua Pagoda is the largest among the 16 pagodas in Shanghai. Its architecture is magnificent and the sculpture, exquisite, with precious Buddhist musical instruments and beautiful landscaping. There are a large number of valuable inscriptions written by celebrated calligraphers. Gui Mao of the Qing Dynasty praised the bell chimes in Longhua Temple as "better than the bell chimes heard at midnight in Hanshan Temple" (The Longhua evening bell chimes on New Year's Day ring in the new and ring out the old.) It is now a tourist attraction of folk customs and introduced to the international tourist market. Every New Year Eve thousands of Japanese and Southeast Asian tourists come here to listen to the bell chimes. On the third day of every third lunar month the temple fair, which has a history of more than 400 years, has been carried on to this day as one of well-known folk custom festivities.

Visiting hours: 7:00–16:00

Add: 2853 Longhua Road

Tel.: 64566085

Means of communication: Public buses 73, 87, 41, 44 and 104

JADE BUDDHA TEMPLE

Jade Buddha Temple is a famous monastery in Shanghai of modern times. Located at the crossroad of Anyuan Road and Jiangning road, it is known for the Jade Buddha statues enshrined. In the early years of Qing Emperor Guangxu's reign, a high monk named Huigen from Puduo Mountain went on a pilgrimage to India. He passed through Tibet and exit from Burma. In Burma he was honoured with 5 statues of Sakyamuni. On his way back, he passed Shanghai and left two statues, one in sitting posture and the other, in reclining posture. A temple was built to enshrine them. The temple was built in the 8th year of Qing Emperor Guangxu's reign (1882 AD) in Jiangwan area. The temple was deserted during the 1911 Revolution and then rebuilt at the present site in 1918. The new temple was completed in 1928. The building is a Song Dynasty palace-type architecture, compact in structure, magnificent in appearance. The sitting jade statue in the Jade Buddha Chamber is 1.9 m tall, lustrous in colour and dignified in bearing, inlaid with precious stones, like agate, emerald and jadeite. It is a rare masterpiece in the world. The reclining Buddha statue is in the Reclining Buddha Hall. It is 1-m long, half reclining on a mahogany couch, in a state of nirvana, looking serene and peaceful. In the temple are kept Buddhist scripture and different kinds of Buddhist relics. The vegetarian food in the temple is quite well-

known. It is famous for its culinary skill in colour, shape, and flavour. To have a taste of the vegetarian food in Jade Buddha Temple is an enjoyment for the gourmets in Shanghai. At present, around the temple are complete facilities for catering, accommodation, amusement and shopping are being built. The temple area will soon become a tourist area in urban Shanghai.

Visiting hours: 8:00–17:00

Add: 170 Anyuan Road

Tel.: 62663668

Means of communication: Public buses 19, 63, 76, 112 and 113

JINGAN TEMPLE

Jingan Temple, located at the crossroad of Nanjing Road West, and Huashan Road in Jingan District, is a famous monastery in Shanghai and protected as a municipal key relic site. It is said that it was first built in the 10th Chiwu year of King Sun Quan of the Eastern Wu State during the Three Kingdoms Period (247 A.D.). The existing architecture was built during the reign of Qing Emperor Guangxu. It has been repaired many times after liberation. Major architecture in the temple are the Mountain Gate, the Tusita Hall, the Grand Hall, the Guanyin Hall, the Abbot's Chamber and the Prayer Hall. It is a completely furnished monastery.

Add: 1686 Nanjing Rd, W

Tel.: 62566366

Means of communication: Public buses 20 and 37

ZHENRU TEMPLE

Located in the northern part of Zhenru Town in Putuo District, it is a famous temple in Shanghai and a key cultural relic site under state protection. It was originally named Wanshou Temple, commonly known as the "Grand Temple". It was first built during the Jiading years of the Southern Song Dynasty (1208-1224), rebuilt in 7th Yanyou year of the Yuan Dynasty and renamed Zhenru Temple. After liberation, our government had the Grand Hall rebuilt. The existing main structures of beams, pillars, square columns and caissons and most of the parts in the building are the originals from the Yuan Dynasty. The Yuan Dynasty structures preserved to this day are rarely found among all the temples in the country. Therefore, the Grand Hall built in the Yuan Dynasty is even more precious.

Add: In the northern part of Zhenru Town

Means of communication: Public buses 105, 136, 62, 827, 858 and 129

YUANMING PREACHING HALL

Located on Yanan Road, West, a Jingtu Sect Buddhist temple founded in 1934 by a high monk named Yuan Ying. It consists of 3 divisions: Yuanming Lianchi Society, Yuanming Fashi Society and Yuanming Dabei Society. The main prayer hall is the memorial hall of priest Yuan Ying. On the 2nd day of every 12th lunar month, a prayer ceremony is held to commemorate priest Yuan Ming. It attracts many visitors from home and overseas.

Add: 434 Yanan Rd, W

Tel.: 62482846

Means of communication: Public buses 57, 71 and 127

SHANGHAI BUDDHIST LAYMEN SOCIETY

Founded in 1919, it is located on Changde Road. The buddha hall is downstairs and the preaching hall, upstairs. The 8th day and the 23rd day of every lunar month are buddhist festival days, when ceremonies of buddhist scripture reading and prayer saying are held. Special ceremonies are also held on birthdays of the Buddha and the Boddhisatva. It also conducts study on Buddhism and lectures on basic knowledge of Buddhism.

Add: 418 Changde Road

Tel.: 62471866

Means of communication: Public buses 20, 37, 138 and 21

CHENXIANGGE

Located on Chenxiangge Road, it is a typical Bhiksuni nunnery, a key relic site under state protection. On the front is an archway with 4 pillars and 3 gates with upturned eaves. Chenxiangge was also named "Ziyun Chan Temple" in the old days. It occupies an area of 2,378 sq.m. There are the Heavenly King Hall, the Grand Hall, Guanyin Pavilion on one axis. On two sides are the Jialan

Hall and the Memorial Hall of the MonkYingci.
Add: 29 Chenxiangge Road
Tel.: 63203431
Communications: Public buses 11 and 66

XIAHAI TEMPLE

It is located on Kunming Road, Hongkou District. According to historical records, Xiahai Temple was originally named Yiwang Temple, first built during the reign of Emperor Qianlong, 250 years from now. Fishermen used to go to the temple to pray for safety going to sea.

Add: 73 Kunming Road
Tel.: 65410761
Means of communication: Public buses 19, 22, 13, 28 and 145

CATHOLICISM

XUJIAHUI CATHOLIC CATHEDRAL

Located on Caoxi Road, North, with a full name of the Cathedral of St. Ignacio, was first built in the 22nd year of Qing Emperor Guangxu's reign (1896). It is a medieval Gothic architecture. There are two bell towers, one on each side, 60 m high. The whole cathedral is built of red bricks and lined with granite. On the front wall there are huge round windows fitted with stained glass. The building, standing erect and imposing, appeals to people with a solemn and sacred air. It was then the first grand architecture in Shanghai. Before liberation it was the Catholic centre south of the Changjiang River. After liberation, it has become the centre for Catholic activities. It can accommodate 2,000 worshippers at the same time.

Add: 158 Puxi Road

Tel.: 64690930

Means of communication: No 1 Subway Xujiahui Road stop, public buses 15, 42 and 93

SHESHAN CATHOLIC CHURCH

Sheshan Catholic Church (also named Church of Holy Mother in China), located on Sheshan Hill in Songjiang County is a Roman church architecture, occupying an area of 1 hectare with a height of 20 m. It was built in the 13th year of Qing Emperor Tongzhi (1857). The tower-fortress type architecture looks magnificent and imposing. It is famed as the second grandest church in East Asia. On Holy Virgin's Day every May, pilgrams swarm here from all places in the country to line up in long queues in entering the church for mass. It is really a spectacular occasion.

Add: On Sheshan Hill, Songjiang County

Tel.: 57651651

Means of communication: No 1 Tourist Bus

DONGJIADU CATHOLIC CHURCH

Located on Dongjiadu Road in Nanshi District, it is also named Catholic Church of Savorett. Built in 1853, it was then the first Catholic church in China. It is of wood and brick structure, rectagular in shape, with a front of the Baroque style of the Renaissance. There are over 200 large and small rooms, still preserved intact.

Add: 185 Dongjiadu Road

Tel.: 63787214

Means of communications Public buses 576, 868, 65 and 910

ST JOSEPH'S CATHOLIC CHURCH

St Joseph's Catholic Church, located on Sichuan Road, South, built in 1860, is a Catholic church built in the early days in Shanghai. It is a Gothic structure built of red bricks with a steeple, 50-m high. On the roof are four 3-m high small bell towers surrounding a 5-m high giant bell. Around the bell pedestal are stained-glass windows and beautiful shutters.

Add: 36 Sichuan Rd, S

Tel.: 62380293

Means of communication: Public buses 71, 127, 126, 11 and 64

CHRISTIANITY

COMMUNITY CHURCH

It is located on Hengshan Road in Xuhui District. In 1917, an oversea American Christian, living in Shanghai, organised a choir on Donghu Road. On March 1930, a church was officially founded. In 1925, the Community Church was built, mainly for the American Christians. The church was once named the American Church and later renamed the Community Church. The church occupies an area of 7,300 sq.m. with a floor space of 1,372 sq.m. The building is a wood and brick structure of modern Gothic architecture. The roof is a wooden frame of the shape of a pair of scissors, an architectural style of modern churches. There are 1,400 seats in the church. It is the largest Christian church in Shanghai. It has a high-standard choir. On every Christian festival and the third Sunday every month a music gathering is held in the church. Many overseas personages have visited the church. Among them was the expresident Carter and Bishop Tutu, the Nobel Prize winner.

Add: 53 Hengshan Road

Tel.: 64376576

Means of communication: No 1 Subway Hengshan Road stop, public buses 15, 126 and 93

HUAIEN CHURCH

Located at the crossroad of Shaanxi Road, North, and Beijing Road, it was built in 1910. In 1955, the spare-time Huaien Church School of Theology was incorporated into China Lingxiu Academy of Theology.

Add: 375 Shaanxi Rd, N

Tel.: 62539394

Means of communication: Public buses 15, 21, 24, 41, 104, 20 and 37

MOEN CHURCH

Located at the crossroad of Xizang Road, Middle, and Jiujiang Road, facing the People's Park, is a Christian church with a tall bell tower. "Moen" in Chinese means "immersed in the grace of God". It is a wood and brick structure. It can accommodate 1,000 people.

Add: 316 Xizang road, Middle

Tel. for information: 63225069

Means of communication: Public buses 18, 46, 49, 145, 123 and 37

ISLAMISM

SONGJIANG MOSQUE

The mosque is also named Zhenjiao Mosque. Located on Zhongshan Road in Chengxiang Town, Songjiang District, it is an ancient Islam architecture so far well preserved in the country. The shrine hall and the Bangke tower were built at the end of the Yuan Dynasty. In the Yongle years of the Ming Dynasty (1404-1423) the mosque was extended. It consist of a Bangke tower, a prayer hall, a bath and a shrine. The Bangke tower and shrine are Arabian "Gongbaille" architecture. The prayer hall is in the structure of a Ming Dynasty hall. In the mosque are kept tablets carved with the inscriptions from the reigns of Qing Emperors Kangxi, Jiaqing, Daoguang and Tongzhi.

Add: 21 Gangpang Alley, Songjiang town

Tel.: 57823684

Means of communication: No 1 Tourist Bus

MOSQUE ON XIAOTAOYUAN STREET

Located on Xiaotaoyuan Street the mosque was formerly named the Western Muslim Mosque or Shanghai West City Muslim Mosque. It is next to a little peach garden ("xiaotaoyuan" in Chinese means "little peach garden"). Its front gate faces Xiaotaoyuan Street, hence the name "Mosque on Xiaotaoyuan Street". Built in 1917, it is a West Asian Islamic architecture with four domed roofs. Shanghai Municipal Islam Association is found here. The main structure of the prayer hall is a reinforced concrete. Part of its roof is a terrace. In the middle of the roof is a four-cornered "Moon Viewing Pavilion", on top of which is hoisted a star and moon flag, a symbol of Islamism.

Add: 56 Xiaotaoyuan St, Fuxing Rd, E

Tel.: 63775442

Means of communication: Public buses 24, 66, and 64

TAOISM

WHITE CLOUD TAOIST TEMPLE

Located on Xilin Back Road at Laoximen, the Taoist Temple is the headquarters of the Taoist Association. In the last year of the Qing Dynasty, a Taoist monk from Jiading named Xu Zhizheng solicited for donations to build a hall for the Thunder God at Dongxinqiao. In the 8th year of Qing Emperor Guangxu (1882) it was moved here. Later, Xu collected more than 8,000 volumes of Taoist scripture and changed the name of the Thunder Good Hall into White Cloud Taoist Temple on the Sea. The scale of the temple has been extended several times and become the top of Taoist temples in Shanghai. Here preserved the Linggong Hall, Lingxiao Gold Hall, Lao Jun Hall, and Thunder God Hall. There are also 7 well preserved Ming Dynasty bronze statues, not

found in any other Taoist temples in China.
Add: 8 Lane 100 Xilin Back Rd, Laoximen
Tel.: 63855366
Means of communication: Public buses 11, 18, 23, 24 and 43

EMPEROR GRANTED REVEREND HALL

Located on Yuanshen Road, it is also named East Peak Temporary Palace. It is one of the earliest Taoist temples in Shanghai. As said by ancestors, it was built for his mother by Sun Quan, King of the Eastern Wu State, during the Three Kingdoms Period. It is famed as "a thousand-year-old Taoist temple". Qing Emperor Qianlong renamed it the "Emperor Granted Reverend Hall" to enshrine the East Peak God. There are a dozen halls, such as the Halls of the East Peak, San Qing (Three Gods), City God, and Guangong. and over 600 statues of gods. Every lunar 3rd, 4th, 7th and 9th month worshippers come in crowds. On the lst and 15th of every lunar month and other Taoist festivals, Taoists crowd the place to burn incense and worship. It is really a bustling scene!
Add: 12 Yuanshen Road, Pudong
Tel.: 58828689
Means of communication: Public buses 81, 85, 981, 870, 571 and No 6 Tunnel line

DAJING GOD GUANGONG TEMPLE

Located on Dajing Road in Nanshi District, it was originally an arrow fort on the western gate of the northern part of the old Shanghai's city wall. During the Wanli years of the Ming Dynasty a temple was erected to enshrine the statue of Guangong. It has been renovated several times and is now a key relic site under municipal protection.
Add: 259 Dajing Road
Means of communication: Public buses 11, 42, 64, 66, 126 and 926

OLD CITY GOD TEMPLE

Located inside Yuyun Commercial City, it is one of the major Taoist temples of the Zheng Yi discipline. It occupies area extending

from Fangbang Road, Middle, to Anren Street in the east, Fuyou Road in the north and Jiujiachang Road in the west. During the Yongle years of the Ming Dynasty reign (1403-1423) the county governor Zhang Shouyue rebuilt the Jinshan God Temple into the City God Temple to enshrine in the front hall Bolu Marquis, General Hoguan of the Han Dynasty and in the back hall the statue of Qin Yubo, the ordained city god. In the past years, the temple has been damaged and rebuilt several times. The existing temple was rebuilt in 1926.

Add: Inside the Yuyuan Commercial City
Tel.: 63868649
Means of communication: Public buses 11, 42, 64, 66, 126 and 926

PROPOSED TOURS OF CULTURE, ART AND RELIGIONS

2-day tour of metropolitan culture
Ist day: Shanghai Museum - Shanghai Grand Theatre - Fuzhou Road - Shanghai Book City
2nd day: Shanghai Gallery - Shanghai Library - Shanghai Historical Museum
2-day tour pf metropolitan religious sites
Ist day: Longhua Temple - Jingan Temple - Jade Buddha Temple - Moen Church - City God Temple
2nd day: Xujiahui Catholic Cathedral - Sheshan Catholic Church - Songjiang Mosque

RECOMMENDED TRAVEL SERVICE
SHANGHAI HUATING OVERSEAS TOURIST CO.

Add: F/4, 503 Wulumuqi Rd, N
Tel.: 62491234
Fax: 62485470,62482781

Post Code: 200040

SHANGHAI JINJIANG TOURS LTD.

Add: 191 Changle Road
Tel.: 64662828
Fax: 64662297
Post Code: 200020

SHANGHAI CYTS TOURS CORPORATION

Add: 2 Hengshan Road
Tel.: 64331826, 64331907
Fax: 64330507
Post Code: 200031

SHANGHAI CHINA INTERNATIONAL TRAVEL SERVICE CO., LTD

Add: CITS Building, 1277 Beijing Rd, W
Tel.: 62898899
Fax: 62894928
Post Code: 200040

SHANGHAI CHINA TRAVEL SERVICE

Add: 881 Yanan Rd, M
Tel.: 62478888, 62475770
Fax: 62475521
Post Code: 200040

(V) FOLK CUSTOMS AND LIFE STYLES

1.NEW YEAR CUSTOMS

SPRING FESTIVAL FAIR

Shanghai people visit relatives and friends during the Spring Festival. A visit to the festival fair is also a pleasure. There is an old custom in Shanghai "Go to 10 temples to burn incense". In the beginning of the New Year many Buddhists pay a round visit to about 10 temples, like the City God Temple, the Land God Temple and others.

YUANXIAO FESTIVAL

(Note: "yuanxiao" in Chinese means "glutinous rice dumpling in round shape")

On the 15th of the first lunar month, people in the city and suburban areas hang up colourful fancy lanterns in different shapes; there are lanterns of the shape of an ingot, a bat, a lotus blossom. a jade toad, and a basin for collecting treasure and a boat of plain sailing. The lanterns are meticulously made. On the night of the 15th of the lst lunar month, large numbers of fancy lanterns are hung by the nine-twist bridge in Yuyuan Commercial City and visitors come in crowds. It is a bustling scene indeed!

QINGMING

"During Qingming Festival it drizzles every day, very few people are found in the streets; Where is the wine shop? one would ask; the shepherd points to the Xinghua Village." This is a verse from the poetry written by Tang poet Du Mu, describing a sad traveller during the Qingming Festival. People from Shanghai often go outing during the Qingming Festival to tidy up the tomb site and pay respect to their deceased relatives.

BEGINNING OF SUMMER

There are 24 solar terms in the lunar calendar and the beginning of summer is the 7th solar term. When summer comes, crops begin to flourish and farmers are getting busy. It is also a peak season for eggs. There is a custom of taking eggs on that day. On that day, children often hang on their neck an egg in a little, knitted red net.

DUANWU FESTIVAL (OR DRAGON BOAT FESTIVAL)

Duanwu Festival, or the Dragon Boat Festival, is a traditioal folk festival with a long history. It falls on the 5th of the 5th day lunar month. During that festival people eat "zongzi", glutinous dumplings wrapped in reed or bamboo leaves, drink realgar wine, wear little bags with sweet-grass, and smoke the rooms with moxa leaves. Dragon boat race is held in rivers to commemorate the patriotic poet Qu Yuan of the Chu State during the Warring States Period. "Zongzi" has a variety of fillings, such as bean paste, date puree, red bean, pork meat, or ham in the shape of "little feet", "pillow cases" and "triangles".

MID-AUTUMN FESTIVAL

The Mid-Autumn Festival falls on the 15th of the 8th lunar month. It is the middle of autumn, so it is called mid-autumn festival. It is also called the Reunion Festival or August Festival. During the festival people eat moon cakes and drink sweet osmanthus wine. When the moon rises, people set up altars in open air and place moon cakes, fruit, soya beans, taros and lotus roots to offer to the moon. Later, the whole family gather together to have a reunion dinner.

CHONGYANG FESTIVAL

It falls on the 9th day of the 9th lunar month. It is one of our folk customs. On that day people climb the heights and eat "chongyang" cake. Cake in Chinese is pronounced as "gao", which is homophonic "height" and implies the meaning of good wishes. Chongyang Festival is also the Festival of the Aged. In Shanghai, the aged people are treated with noodles and "Chongyang" cake with wishes for longevity.

WINTER SOLSTICE

It is also called the Ghost Festival. It is the 22nd solar term of the 24 solar terms in the year. In ancient times, it was an important day for officials to pay respects to the emperor and offer sacrifices to ancestors. It was a grand occasion for entertaining guests. Nowadays, young people go to visit their parents and present them with tonic drinks to show their care for their parents. If one member of the family is away from home on a trip, the other members at home will miss him or her all the more.

NEW YEAR EVE DINNER

On Chinese New Year Eve the dinner is specially sumptuous. After a year's hard work, it is the time to see off the old year and wish for a prosperous new year. At such dinner people give good omens to some of the dishes, such as "fish", which Chinese is homophonic with "surplus", "facai", a kind of sea weed, is homophonic with "getting rich". After dinner, people will stay up for the night, waiting for the coming of the New Year.

2. THEME FESTIVITIES

SHANGHAI TOURISM FESTIVAL

Shanghai Tourism Festival has been listed by the China National Tourism Administration as one of the 41 important festivals in the country. The festival demonstrates to domestic and overseas tourists Shanghai's metropolitan life style and culture and for them to appreciate the prosperous atmosphere of the metropolis. Every year from mid-October to November different tourist festivities are held in Shanghai. During the festival, the Bund, shopping streets like Nanjing Road and Huaihai Road, the Nanpu Bridge, the Yangpu Bridge and the Oriental Pearl TV Tower glisten under the sunlight during the day and glitter under colourful lights at night. In Yuyuan Garden, Railway Station, Xujiahui and on Yanggao Road large-scale sales promotion is underway. Art Festival, Folk Custom Festival, Fashion Festival and Gourmet Food Festival are held in different districts and counties. It is a grand occasion of integrating and combining the Chinese and Western cultures.

TEA CULTURE FESTIVAL

Shanghai International Tea Culture Festival is held once a year. It is a grand occasion with tea as the medium for meeting with friends, cherishing benevolence, passing good feelings and carrying forth the Chinese national culture. The Tea Culture Festival is held on the last Saturday of every April and lasts for a week. The tea cultural activities are held in Zhabei District in northern Shanghai. Since 1994, the festival has been held three times. People from the tea circles and tea ceremony delegations, and tour groups from the United States, Japan, Korea, Singapore, Canada, Hong Kong and Taiwan and many Shanghai citizens join in the different festivities. The opening and closing ceremonies are conducted with unique feature, combining performance, tea serving and tea tasting, expressing the characteristics of tea culture in its artistic, national, appreciative and participatory nature. During the festival a trade fair of famous teas, porcelain, tea pots and arts and crafts from different places is held. Tea experts from overseas are invited to attend academic seminars of tea culture and exchange of tea ceremonies. Visitors can enjoy the refined art performances with the warm feelings of a tea country.

SHANGHAI SWEET OSMANTHUS FESTIVAL

Shanghai Sweet Osmanthus Festival is held every year in the 8th lunar month, in Guilin Park at a time when the sweet osmanthus blossoms are in full bloom. The sweet osmanthus is one of the 10 famous flowers in China. Its refreshing fragrance floats in the air, far and wide, and is much beloved by people. In Guilin Park, different species of sweet osmanthus are grown, like the golden and the silvery osmanthus. Under a sunny autumn sky the blossoms attract crowds of visitors. While appreciating the flowers they can also enjoy the open air movie, art performances, karaoke, mask ball and fashion show. On Guilin Road there is a Sweet Osmanthus Village with bamboo fences and thatched cottages, entertaining guests with the fragrance of wine in an antique and unsophisticated environment.

NANHUI PEACH BLOSSOM FESTIVAL

Nanhui County Peach Blossom Festival is held every April, attracting visitors with pastoral landscape and simple country life-style. When you put on the farmers' clothes, work in ploughing the fields, weaving cloth, pushing the grindstone; when you sit under the fully bloomed peach trees and have a chat with farmers; when you taste a bowl of cooked rice and fresh vegetable, you will enjoy the pastoral pleasure and the simple life-style of the country folk

ORANGE FESTIVAL

The Orange Festival is held once a year on Changxing Island. The island occupies an area of 76.32 sq.km. With "pure soil, pure water and pure air" It is famed as a jadeite inlaid at the mouth of the Changjiang River entering the sea. The orange orchard is in the middle of the island, occupying an area of 451.67 hectares. It is the largest production site of "green unpolluted food". In autumn, when you take a walk among the ripe oranges, you will feel the pleasure of a bumper harvest.

SHANGHAI BEER FESTIVAL

The Beer Festival held every summer in Shanghai is a refreshing scenic sight in hot summer. Here you can have a taste of different brands and varieties of beer, while taking part in gala parties. Having a sip of the bitter and refreshing beer and enjoying the coolness of summer, you will feel gratifying and satisfied.

LONGHUA TEMPLE FAIR

Around the 3rd of every 3rd lunar month, a temple fair is held in Longhua area. During the fair, Buddhist ceremonies are held in the temple while a bazaar is going on outside. Peaches are blooming. All kinds of special articles are found in the bazaar; while delicious snacks, folk art performances and local operas are attracting crowds of visitors. You can have a taste of the vegetarian food in Longhua Temple while listening to Buddhist music. Amidst the hustle and bustle of jubilant people, you will be deeply impressed by the prosperous scene of the Chinese folk temple fair.

LONGHUA NEW YEAR BELL CHIMES

On the eve of the New Year a ceremony of "Evening Chiming of Longhua Bell" takes place in the temple. Longhua Pagoda next door standing erect in floodlight glistens in colours. On the square, amidst dragon and lion dances people celebrate the coming of the New Year. In the bell tower 108 chimes of the bell resound in the air, bringing the blessings of the New Year. In the temple, a hundred monks in kasaya (monk's robe) are conducting a ceremony to usher in the New Year and pray for luck and happiness in the midst of incense smoke and hitting of the wooden fish.

3. OLD SHANGHAI DOWNTOWN AND OLD-FASHIONED ALLEYWAY NEIGHBOURHOODS (THE HOUSES WITH STONE-FRAMED DOORS)

Old Shanghai downtown originated in today's Nanshi District.

During the Yuan, Ming and Qing Dynasties, old Shanghai downtown was the political, economic and cultural centre of the time, therefore、there are many cultural relics and tourist attractions in that area. Yuyuan Garden and the old city wall and Dajing Pavilion built during the Jiaqing years of the Ming Dynasty, the Old City God Temple, built in the Yongle years of the Ming Dynasty, are windows showing the past of old Shanghai downtown. In 1995, Shanghai city government reconstructed and restored to their original state the 50-mold city wall, the Dajing Pavilion above it and opened them to the public. On the second floor of the Dajing Pavilion is an exhibition of "History of Old Shanghai Downtown", from which visitors may learn about the history of development of old Shanghai downtown.

The construction of alleyways in Shanghai began around the '60s of the 19th century. After the Small Sword Uprising many rich people moved into the concessions. Foreign merchants began to build wooden houses for rent. Wooden houses caught fire easily; they later built wood and brick connecting houses; these were the early models of alleyway neighbourhoods. Alleyway architecture consisted of several types: old-fashioned houses with stone-framed doors, Guangdong-styled houses, new-type houses with stone-framed doors, new-type alleyway neighbourhoods, garden-type alleyway neighbourhoods and apartment-type alleyway neighbourhoods. Different strata of people lived in different types of neighbourhoods. Old-fashioned houses with stone-framed doors were generally built in bustling downtown. Shops were opened on the ground floors and the staff lived upstairs. New-type houses with stone-framed doors were generally lent to senior staff. Doctors, teachers, architects, office staff used to live in new-type alleyway neighbourhoods, while capitalists mostly lived in garden-type alleyway neighbourhoods and senior staff, in apartment-type alleyway neighbourhoods. After liberation, things totally changed. Now, along with the increasing changes in the city, many alleyway buildings have been replaced by highrisers. However, many alleyway buildings still keep their original external appearance after remoulding while the interior structure has been rearranged. The preserving of these buildings while improving the living conditions of the residents has been much appreciated.

4. FOLK COLLECTIONS

Precious folk collections are the essence of mankind's wisdom through a history of several thousand years. They are of great historical and appreciative value. The scale of Shanghai's folk collections ranks the top in the country and has been known as "half of the country's folk collections". A hundred thousand collectors have collected over 200 categories of items. There are 40 exhibition rooms. It will be a pleasure to visit some of these exhibition rooms. There are antiques, calligraphy and paintings, abacuses, ship models, tea sets, stage costumes, root carvings, clocks and watches and many, many others. Every collector has a story to tell and every item has a vast realm to describe.

SHANGHAI FOLK COLLECTION EXHIBITION HALL

Located in Sanshan Guild Hall the Folk Exhibition Hall has amassed the masterpieces of the hundred thousand collectors. The exhibition hall is not only a centre for display, appreciation and exchange of folk collections in Shanghai, but also an important key-link for the exchange of folk culture with foreign countries.

Add: 1551 Zhongshan Rd, S

Tel. n: 63135582

Means of communication: Public buses 43, 89, 65, 109, 929 and No 2 Bridge line

COLLECTION OF CLOCKS AND WATCHES

Wang Anjian, a worker, collected over some 20 years 200 clocks and watches. The oldest has a history of over 200 years. The largest is a French floor quarter-striking clock, 2.8-m tall. The smallest has only a diameter of 11 mm. The heaviest is nearly 0.5 kg and the lightest, not over 50 g. There is also a famous Swiss bronze-coloured Nading brand nautical astronomic clock, a hand-made table-plaque clock of the Qing Dynasty and a sundial, an ancient timer.

A LIST OF SHANGHAI'S PRIVATE COLLECTION HALLS

Collector	Tel.	Collection
Feng Yiyou	62816909	Old cigarette trademarks
Yang Shaorong	127-2209189	Shoes for bound feet
Tao Changpeng	62087155	Artistic stone pots
Feng Jianzhong	68738082	First issues
Ye Wenhan	63577970	School badges
Chen Baoding	64371254	Abacuses
Lan Xiang	56988415	Chopsticks
Zhao Jinzhi	57134185	Keys
Gu Azhen	58394781	Porcelain pots
Bao wanrong	50810115	Stage costumes
Xu Binjie	65615259	Ship models
Chen Baocai	56940714	Butterfly specimens
Cai Baowu.	65530088-89770	Strange rocks
Du Baojun	62970296	Coloured pebbles

(VI) PUDONG NEW AREA

Pudong New Area is situated in the east of the Huangpu River, occupying an area of 523 sq.km.and It is facing the Bund on the other side of the Huangpu River. It has a favourable geographical location and bright prospects for development. Situated on the East Sea with a topography of a triangle, it is an alluvial plain. Its land was formed since the Tang Dynasty from the gradual sediment of sand washed up by the Changjiang River. It is called Pudong because it is situated in the east of the Huangpu River. The planned development area of Pudong is 523 sq.km. with a permanent resident population of 1,480,000. On April 1990, the Chinese government decided to develop and open Pudong to make it a leading place in the economic development of the Changjiang River valley and to develop Shanghai into an economic, financial and trade centre in the country and in Asian-Pacific area. In recent years, the national economy in Pudong New Area has rapidly and stably developed, accomplished more and more infrastructure and co-ordinated development of social undertakings. It has become an area in China with the best investment environment, the best opportunity and the highest rate of success for investment. It is an important mark in China's reform and opening to the outside world. Since its opening, Shanghai has invested several tens of billion yuan (RMB) in building many key projects in Pudong New Area in energy source, communications, telecommunication and environmental protection, which have improved the environment for investment and played an important role in linking the east and west banks of the Huangpu into one entirety. These projects include the Nanpu Bridge, Yangpu Bridge, second phase of Pudong Gas Works with a daily output of 2 million cu.m., Yanggao Trunk Road, 4 wharves with 10,000-ton capacity in Waigaoqiao Harbour, 2 huge inter-linking overpasses, Pudong section of the confluent sewage project, Lingqiao Water Works. By the end of this century, the second phase of No 2 Subway, the Century Promenade and Pudong International Airport to be completed in 1999 will facilitate the thoroughgoing in communications for Pudong and create good conditions for Chinese and foreign tourists in visiting Pudong. Tourist attractions in Pudong, like the Sea World, the largest in Asia, Shanghai Science and Technology Capital, second phase of the Central Park, Huaxia Cultural Tourist Area are under construction. A number of star-rated hotels catering to foreign visitors have been completed.

LUJIAZUI FINANCE AND TRADE ZONE

Lujiazui Finance and Trade Zone is located in the golden section of Pudong New Area and is opposite to the Bund on the other side of the river. The Bund used to enjoy the fame of a financial centre in the Far East and Lujiazui is the only development area approved as a "finance and trade zone". More than 50 Chinese and foreign financial organisations have settled down here, among which there are 28 foreign-funded banks, including the world-famous Citybank, Fujiyama Bank and Hong Kong and Shanghai Banking Corp. By the 21st century, there will be in Lujiazui about 100 Chinese and foreign banks and financial organizations, 3,000 international big companies, headquarters of large financial groups and different companies once settled down in the zone will turn Lujiazui into Pudong's as well as Shanghai's most prosperous business centre. It is a common acknowledgement of the Shanghai offices of foreign-funded banks that they should be rooted in Pudong, because they believe that from here an international financial centre will arise.

Along the bank of the river a 2,500-m riverside boulevard has been built and there stands the world-famous Oriental Pearl TV Tower. Around here a number of '90s standard cultural and art buildings will be constructed, such as the Oriental Concert Hall, a museum, a cultural and art centre, a central library, and an opera house.

The planning of Lujiazui central area combines modern functions, environment, communications, scenic sights, ecology, space art in an overall and three-dimensional design. A meticulous plan has been made to landscape the riverside plots, with high-risers setting off each other, to furnish residential areas with shopping facilities to organize a complete system of underground, water, surface and air transportation in co-ordinating the subway, the tunnel, the viaducts with surface traffic and landscaped pedestrian walkway. Lujiazui will be built into "a golden delta" on the east bank of the Huangpu River.

Add: Lujiazui, Pudong

Tel.: 58882799

Means of communication: No 3 tourist bus, public buses 81, 82, 980 and No 3 Tunnel line

WAIGAOQIAO BONDED ZONE

Located at the northern end of Pudong New Area and occupying an area of 10 sq.km., it is the largest comprehensive and multi-functional foreign trade zone on the mainland. There are many import, export trade and foreign service enterprises, bonded factories and bonded shopping arcades. As the first bonded zone set up since the reform and opening to the outside world, it is a completely new free trade zone primarily formed within isolated walls at Waigaoqiao. There are now more than 300 international trade companies and enterprises operating in the zone. It is a fast growing point in Shanghai's foreign economic relations and trade.

Add: Waigaoqiao, Pudong

Tel.: 58882799

Means of communication: No 3 tourist bus

JINQIAO EXPORT PROCESSING ZONE

Located in the middle of Pudong and occupying an area of 8.9 sq.km., Jinqiao Export Processing Zone is the largest comprehensive industrial park area in Shanghai, combining export processing, trade, commercial service and residence into one. The settling down of trans-national companies has made the zone a multi-functional and export-orientated development area of the best quality in China. Of the 500 enterprises in the world 21 have settled down in Jinqiao. Their partnership in Jinqiao has increased the value of the zone. It has now established 6 hi-tech industries, like the automobiles and their accessories, micro electronics, modern communication, new-type household appliances, machinery and automatic equipment and bio-medicines.

Add: Jinqiao, Pudong

Tel.: 58882799

Means of communication: No 3 tourist bus and No 6 Tunnel line

SUNQIAO AGRICULTURAL DEVELOPMENT ZONE

Sunqiao Town, located in the north of the Outer-ring Road, occupies a planned area of 9.5 sq.km. It has been approved as the "base for education in popularizing scientific knowledge" and "a hi-tech examplinary area". The area owns world-grade agricultural automatic temperature-controlled greenhouses from Holland, area for growing edible fungus, breeding farm for special aquatic products and potted landscape area. It will be built into a metropolitan modern agricultural park area with green ecological agriculture and for export to earn foreign exchange. With its pastoral scenery, first-grade production facilities, advanced technology and fine quality agricultural and non-staple food it attracts a great number of domestic and foreign visitors.

Add: Sunqiao Town, Pudong

Tel.: 58882799

Means of communication: No 3 tourist bus

ZHANGJIANG HI-TECH PARK AREA

Located in the mid-southern part of Pudong New Area, near the Inner-ring Road downtown in the west, by the Chuanyang River in the south and extending to the Outer-ring Road underway, it has a total planned area of 17 sq.km. It consists of the 4 areas of the technical exhibition, the technical industries, scientific research and education and living quarters. Emphasis is on the development of the 3 major industries of biomedicine, micro electronics and information technique, and the combined photo-machinery and electric equipment. It will be built into China's "Silicon Valley". Many well-known companies have already settled down in that area.

Add: Jinqiao, Pudong

Tel.: 58882799

Means of communication: No 3 tourist bus

HUAXIA CULTURAL AND TOURIST AREA

Located in southeastern part of Pudong New Area, it has a planned area of 7.5 sq.km. It is divided into two parts: the western part is in the west of Chuansha Town with an area of 2.3 sq.km. It is mainly devoted to cultural, residential, recreational and business development. The Huaxia Cultural Park in the area has been completed and opened to the public. In the park there is a memorial hall for the famous painter Wu Changshi, a memorial hall of celebrated personages from Pudong and a Huaxia English corner. The eastern part is a seaside tourist area, situated at Sanjia Port in Pudong. In Sanjia Port tourist area, there is a 6-km long seaside residential area, where the sea touches the sky, the air is fresh, the climate is pleasant and natural conditions are very favourable. It will be built into a seaside tourist area aiming at offering tourism and leisure with hi-tech means and to be participated by tourists. It will be featured for its seaside scenery, modern architecture, pastoral atmosphere, and a green sky and a green earth. It will meet the needs of different strata of tourists.

Add: Jinqiao, Pudong

Tel.: 58882799

Means of communication: shen-chuan line

PROPOSED TOURS FOR PUDONG

Morning: Oriental Pearl TV Tower-Riverside Boulevard-Lujiazui Finance and Trade Zone

Afternoon: Central Park-Huaxia Tourist City-Sunqiao Agricultural Development Zone

Evening: Dongfang Road-No 1 Yaohan Department Store

RECOMMENDED TRAVEL SERVICE

SHANGHAI HUATING OVERSEAS TOURIST CO.

Add: F/4, 503 Wulumuqi Rd, N
Tel.: 62491234
Fax: 62485470,62482781
Post Code: 200040

SHANGHAI JINJIANG TOURS LTD.

Add: 191 Changle Road
Tel.: 64662828
Fax: 64662297
Post Code: 200020

SHANGHAI CYTS TOURS CORPORATION

Add: 2 Hengshan Road
Tel.: 64331826, 64331907
Fax: 64330507
Post Code: 200031

SHANGHAI CHINA INTERNATIONAL TRAVEL SERVICE CO., LTD

Add: CITS Building, 1277 Beijing Rd, W
Tel.: 62898899
Fax: 62894928
Post Code: 200040

SHANGHAI CHINA TRAVEL SERVICE

Add: 881 Yanan Rd, M
Tel.: 62478888, 62475770
Fax: 62475521
Post Code: 200040

(VII) SCENERY IN SUBURBAN COUNTIES

1. SONGJIANG

Songjiang City was originally Songjiang Town, from where the ancient history of Shanghai originated. Early in the 10th Tianbao years of the Tang Dynasty (751), Huating County was set up in Songjiang Town. By the end of the Yuan Dynasty it was promoted to Songjiang Prefecture. Songjiang has a long history and is rich in humanistic sights. A large number of cultural relics are preserved in the city, such as ancient pagodas, gardens, architectures and temples. Songjiang is the only area in Shanghai where hills are found on the northwestern alluvial plains. According to historical records there were nine peaks and twelve hills in the midst of groups of hilly mounds in the northern part of Songjiang, among which the Kugong, Phoenix, Xueshan , Sheshan, Chenshan, Tianma, Jishan, Hengyun and Lesser Kunshan Hills used to be called the "Nine Peaks of Songjiang Prefecture", and among which the Hengshan, Tianma and Sheshan Hills are well-known. The Tianma Hill is the highest of the nine peaks, with the main peak 97.8-m high. On top of the southern peak a pagoda called the Pearl Protecting Pagoda was built in the last Yuan years of the Northern Song Dynasty (1079). The pagoda is 18.82-m high, in hexagonal shape, looking antique and imposing. Now, the pagoda leans at 6°51' 5" (5°3' more than the Pisa Tower in Italy). It is rarely seen in the world. The Sheshan Hill consists of two parts, 60-m and 97.2-m high respectively. The scenery is beautiful on the hill, the best of the nine peaks. On the western part of the hill are towering ancient trees and a large tract of bamboos. On top of the hill are a Catholic cathedral and an observatory and a newly built seismology laboratory. Songjiang is rich in tourist resources. The beautiful nine peaks lie in the northwest and the Huangpu River runs by it east-westward. Amidst green hills and blue waters the ancient pagoda stands gracefully and exquisite Ming and Qing Dynasty gardens appeal with natural beauty and humanistic sights. Songjiang ranks the top in cultural relics and historic sites among all districts and counties in Shanghai, such as the Tang Dynasty Buddhist Sutra

Stela, the Song Dynasty stone bridge, the Yuan Dynasty Mosque, the Screen Wall, the Garden of the Drunken Bai Pond, etc. We can see the sights of the Tang, Song, Yuan, Ming and Qing Dynasties up to present day. Large numbers of cultural relics vividly describe the traces of the economic and cultural development of ancient Shanghai. Songjiang is well developed in communications and accomplished in tourist infrastructure, complete in the service facilities of accommodations, shopping, recreation and leisurely pleasure. It is an ideal place for developing the tourist business.

GARDEN OF THE DRUNKEN BAI POND

The Garden of the Drunken Bai Pond, first built in 1644, is a remolded Ming Dynasty garden. It consists of the Inner and Outer Gardens. The Outer Garden is newly built while the Inner Garden is the original, the cream of the whole garden. There is a square pond in the center, surrounded by pavilions, terraces, chambers, waterside pavilions and long corridors. There is also a crenelated wall separating the scenic spots of the Thatched Cottage, the Hexagonal Pavilion, the Four-sided Hall and the Yinfang Boat. In the corridor are more than 40 carved stone tablets of Zhao Mengzhao's calligraphy. There is a tablet inscribed by the painter Zheng Banqiao, one of the Eight Eccentric painters from Yangzhou, saying, "Seldom mixed up". These are all of high value of artistic appreciation.

Add: 64 Renmin Rd, S, Songjiang District
Tel.: 57814763
Means of communication: No 1 tourist bus

TANG DYNASTY TUOLONI BUDDHIST SUTRA STELA

Located in the center of Songjiang Town inside Reifeng Primary

School on Zhongshan Road, Middle, Songjiang Town, erected in 859 (the Tang Dynasty), 9.3-m tall, in octagonal shape, composed of 21 sculptured steps, is carved with the holy Tuoloni scripture accompanied by inscription record. It is tall and beautiful in shape with the characteristic of the flourishing period of the Tang Dynasty. The most precious part is the bas-relief of the cylindrical top of the scene of the governor worshipping the Buddha. It represents the artic style of the most flourishing period of the Tang Dynasty. It is a key cultural relic under state protection.

Add: On the campus of the primary school on Zhongshan Rd, M, Songjiang District

Tel.: 57822157

Means of communication: No 1 tourist bus

SQUARE PAGODA

Located in Square Pagoda Park in the southeast of Songjiang county seat and built during the Northern Dynasty (1068 to 1094), it is a wood and brick structure with 9 stories, 48.5-m tall and in square shape. It is a copy of Tang Dynasty style and structure of wood and brick pagodas. About 60% of the original Song Dynasty wooden supports are still preserved.

Add: 235 Zhongshan Rd, E, Songjiang District

Tel.: 57822157

Means of communication: No 1 tourist bus

SCREEN WALL

Located in Square Pagoda Park in the southeast of Songjiang county seat, built in the Ming Dynasty (1370), it is 47.5-m tall and

6.1-m broad, with an area of 30 sq.m. There is huge monster on the surface. It has the horns of a deer, the tail of a lion, the hoofs of an ox, and the scales of a dragon. A legend says that this monster was attempting to swallow the sun on the sea and got drowned. It is lesson for greediness.

Add: 235 Zhongshan Rd, E, Songjiang District

Tel.: 57822157

Means of communication: No 1 tourist bus

CATHOLIC CATHEDRAL ON SHESHAN HILL

Located on Sheshan Hill in Songjiang and occupying an area of about one hectare, the 20-m high cathedral (officially named China Holy Virgin Cathedral) was first built in 1863 and rebuilt in 1935. The hall has a reinforced concrete domed roof and the lower part of the body built of Jin shan stone. The outer wall is built of red bricks. The windows are pointed at the tops fitted with stained glass inlaid with pictures of saints. The architecture is of the Roman style of the Renaissance. The auditorium can accommodate 3,000 people. It is famed as the second largest cathedral in East Asia. On every Holy Mother's Festival in May catholics come from all corners of the country and line up in long queues in entering the church for mass. It is really a grand occasion!

Add: Sheshan Hill, Songjiang District

Tel.: 57651651

Means of communication: No 1 tourist bus

SHESHAN OBSERVATORY

Located on Sheshan Hill, Songjiang, and built in the 25th year of the reign of Qing Emperor Guanxu and founded by a French priest, is the earliest observatory in China. It is now Shanghai Astronomical Sheshan Station and one of our country's centers of astronomical research.

Add: Sheshan Town, Songjiang District
Tel.: 57651609
Means of communication: No I tourist bus

XILIN PAGODA

Located in Xita Lane, Zhongshan Road, West, in the west of Songjiang county seat and built during the Southern Song Dynasty. It is officially named Chongen Main Pagoda but popularly known as the Xilin Pagoda. It was rebuilt in the Ming Dynasty. It is of a wood and brick structure with 7 stories and in octagonal shape. The brick body of the pagoda is still intact, but the waist eaves and palings were removed. The people's government has it repaired and restored to its original shape.

Add: Xita Lane, Zhongshan Rd, W, Songjiang District
Tel.: 57822157
Means of communication: No 1 tourist bus

SHEHSHAN STATE FOREST PARK

Located 10.5 km in the suburbs north of Songjiang City, it was approved in 1993 by the National Ministry of Agriculture as a state-level forest park. The main rhythm of the part is returning to nature. A number of historic sites and scenic spots have been restored and 20 more new tourist attractions and amusement centers built, such as the Forest Bathing Ground, the "Happy Little Bamboo Cottage" and bamboo artistic products. With bamboo as the main theme and the top of scenic spots, together with blooming flowers, birds chirping and fragrance of flowers and ever spring all year round, it is an epitome of nature. The Hundred Birds Garden is on the

eastern slope of Eastern Sheshan Hill, occupying an area of 20,000 sq.m.. There are in the garden 5,000 birds of 50 rare species. The elegantly quiet and peaceful forest park is an ideal place as a summer resort for tourists.

Add: Sheshan Hill, Songjiang District

Tel.: 57651666

Means of communication: No 1 tourist bus

PROPOSED TOUR OF SONGJIANG TOURIST ATTRACTIONS

1st day: Sheshan State Forest Park - Sheshan Cathedral - No 1 cable in open air - Observatory - European World Amusement Park - Hundred Birds Garden

2nd day: Square Pagoda Park - County Museum - Tang Dynasty Tuoloni Buddhist Sutra Stela - Garden of the Drunken Bai Pond - Mosque

RECOMMENDED TRAVDEL SERVICE

SHANGHAI HUATING OVERSEAS TOURIST CO.

Add: F/4, 503 Wulumuqi Rd, N

Tel.: 62491234

Fax: 62485470,62482781

Post Code: 200040

SHANGHAI JINJIANG TOURS LTD.

Add: 191 Changle Road

Tel.: 64662828

Fax: 64662297

Post Code: 200020

SHANGHAI CYTS TOURS CORPORATION

Add: 2 Hengshan Road

Tel.: 64331826, 64331907

Fax: 64330507

Post Code: 200031

SHANGHAI CHINA INTERNATIONAL TRAVEL SERVICE CO., LTD

Add: CITS Building, 1277 Beijing Rd, W
Tel.: 62898899
Fax: 62894928
Post Code: 200040

SHANGHAI CHINA TRAVEL SERVICE

Add: 881 Yanan Rd, M
Tel.: 62478888, 62475770
Fax: 62475521
Post Code: 200040

2. QINGPU

Qingpu has a long history. As early as 6000 years ago,the "Songze Culture" representing the civilization of Taihu area developed from here. It was the birthplace of some ten ancient cultural sites like Songze, Fuquan, etc. It is so far discovered as the earliest inhabited area by Shanghai people and the origin of ancient Shanghai culture.

Qingpu has an area of 677.8 sq.km., of which 1/5 is covered by water. The area is crisscrossed by rivers, lakes and marshes. There are ancient towns and little alleyways, rivers winding around the villages and towns and little bridges spanning the rivers. These are typical scenes in watery regions south of the Changjiang River, especially the famous Dingshan Lake scenic area, where the water surface is 11 times that of the West Lake in Hangzhou. Here the water is clear and pure. Looking at it from a distance you will see a vast stretch of water touching the sky.

Shanghai Dingshan Lake scenic area is a key tourist area developed with the approval of the municipal government. Here a number of scenic spots are found, such as an ancient pagoda of the Tang Dynasty, an ancient bridge of the Song Dynasty, an ancient temple of the Ming Dynasty, picturesque scenes of "little bridges, bubbling streams and families" and ancient towns of the Ming and Qing Dynasties like traditional Chinese paintings. In recent years, the Grand View Garden, a water sports ground, a yacht club, a golf course, a swimming pool, a campsite and other recreational facilities have been developed. Accommodation and catering facilities have also been built for tourists, like the Sun Island Holiday Resort, the

Hongzhu Garden, Diangshan Lake Hotel, Yuanhu Garden Hotel to accomplish the building up of the scenic area.

GARDEN OF MEANDERING STREAM

Located in Chengxiang Town, Qingpu County, it is one of the five famous gardens in Shanghai. It was built in the 10th year of Qing Emperor Qianlong's reign (1745). The garden is centered by a pond. Around the pond are chambers, pavilions, waterside

pavilions and bridges and decorated with long corridors, rockeries, pines, wisteria, presenting to visitors an environment of peace and tranquility. There are a together 24 scenic spots in the garden. In the southern part are the Hall of Harmony and Temple of Flower God; in the middle is a lotus pond surrounded by Dawn Welcoming Pavilion, Little Waterfall Bridge and Happy Rain Bridge; in the northern part ranges of rockeries and grotesque peaks and stones are found.

Add: 112 Park road, Qingpu County

Tel.: 59732996

Means of communication: No 4 tourist bus

BLUE DRAGON TEMPLE PAGODA

Located in the Old Qingpu Town (the ancient Blue Dragon Town) 1 km away from the present town, built in the Tang Dynasty (743) and rebuilt in the Northern Song Dynasty (1041-1048), is a structure of wood and brick of 7 stories, in octagonal shape. Now, only the pagoda body is preserved.

Add: Old Qingpu Town

Tel.: 59716710

Means of communication: No 4 tourist bus

ZHUJIAJIAO

Zhujiajiao is known as "Shanghai's Venice". It is the best preserved ancient town in the watery regions south of the Changjiang River. As early as 1700 years ago, during the Three

Kingdoms Period, there were already villages and bazaars here. During the Ming Dynasty it became a gathering place of merchants and a bustling town with large numbers of households. Nowadays, we can still find the streets and markets of the antique Ming and Qing-Dynasty style buildings and the simple life style of the country folk. Zhujiajiao, with antique simplicity, peacefulness, tranquility and graceful taste, is known for its antique style of an ancient town. When you take a walk along the winding little paths paved with stone slabs through the zigzag narrow alleyways flanked by little stores you will find yourself before a quietly elegant traditional Chinese ink painting of little bridges over bubbling streams, homes with courtyards of the Ming and Qing Dynasties, and little boats with black awnings. The willows along the river and the stone bridge over the Dingpu River will bring you away from the hustle and bustle of town into the peace and leisure of Zhujiajiao.

Add: Zhujiajiao town, Qingpu County

Tel.: 59242771

Means of communication: No 4 tourist bus

SONGZE ANCIENT CULTURAL RELIC SITE

In 1958, the Songze ancient cultural site was discovered in Songze Village, Qingpu County. On the upper layer was found the painted pottery culture of the Western Zhou Dynasty, on the middle layer, a group grave of the Neolithic Age, typical of the culture of the Taihu Lake valley, hence called the Songze Culture, and on the lower layer, the Majiabang culture, belong to the matriarchal society. It is the earliest cultural relic side so far discovered in Shanghai, 6,000 years from now.

Add: Songze Village, Qingpu County

Tel.: 59716710

Means of communication: No 1 tourist bus

BRIDGE FOR SETTING FISH FREE

Located in Zhujiajiao and built during the Ming Dynasty (1573-1620) and rebuilt in the Qing Dynasty (1812), it is 70.8-m long and 5.8-m wide with 5

arches. It is the largest arched stone bridge in Shanghai. It was meticulously built with a graceful shape. It is known as one of the 10 scenic spots in Zhujiajiao. "Setting free" implies the act of virtue in setting free creatures. Monk Xingchao set a rule that the bridge was only for setting free fish and turtles and fishing was forbidden.

Add: Zhujiajiao Town

Tel.: 59242771

Means of communication: No 4 tourist bvus

DIANGSHAN LAKE

Located in the southwest of Qingpu County, 50 km from downtown, it covers an area of 62 sq.km,, on the boundary of Jiangsu and Zhejiang Provinces, Dianshan Lake belongs to the Taihu Lake water system. The water is clear and pure. Around the lake are found little watery towns of Jinze, Shangta and Xicen.

Add: West of Qingpu County

Tel.: 59716710

Means of communication: No 4 tourist bus

GRAND VIEW GARDEN

Located in the southwest of Qingpu County, 50 km from town, the Grand View Garden is a present-day large-scale garden of imitation of ancient buildings built in 1979 by Shanghai Forestation Department. By the east side of the Dianshan Lake, it is divided into two scenic areas: in the eastern part are found the Folk Cultural Village, Plum Flower Garden, Hundred Flower Garden and Sweet Osmanthus Garden; in the western area are the imitation ancient buildings of the Chinese classic "The Dream of the Red Mansion" with pavilions, terraces, chambers, towers, rockeries, caves, winding and zigzag paths, describing a beautiful picture of the "Dream of the Red Mansions". Here, the Garden of Spring Plums is the best place in Shanghai for admiring plum blossoms. Here, one

can enjoy the Red Mansion music, the taste of Red Mansion feast and dress up as a character in the Red Mansion. It is an enjoyment of the pleasure of the Red Mansion. The garden occupies an area of 8 hectares with a floor space of 8,000 sq.m. It took 9 years to complete. In the neighborhood of the Grand View Garden and Dianshan Lake are the newly built Qingpu Golf Course Country Club, the Yacht Club, Water Sports Ground, Zhujiajiao Swimming Pool, Adolescents Campsite, together forming the Grand View Garden scenic area.

Add: 701 Qingshang Highway, Qingpu County
Tel.: 59262831
Means of communication: No 4 tourist bus

SUN ISLAND INTERNATIONAL CLUB

Located in the midst of the beautiful Maohe River, the island covers an area of 160 hectares, 3,800 m in length from south to north and 700-m in width, and surrounded by water on all sides. The landscape is pleasant and enjoyable. On the island an 18-link golf course is built, complete with a club, a meeting hall, an international convention hall, a pastoral holiday resort, a sports and recreational center, a bowling room, a water sports ground, a cultural square, a horse-walking club, a cultural gourmets street, an angling pond and other recreational projects. Visitors can spend long hours there and feel sorry to leave. The island was originally named Mao Island. Our ancestors were found living and working there since the Western Zhou Dynasty. Scholars and literary men have left their traces there as evidence of the history of the island.

Add: Sun Island, Shenxiang Town, Qingpu County
Tel.: 59830888

Means of communication: Special bus

PROPOSED TOUR OF QINGPU SCENES AND LIFE-STYLE

Morning: Dianshan Lake – Grand View Garden – Zhujiajiao
Afternoon: Sunny Island International Club

RECOMMENDED TRAVEL SERVICE

SHANGHAI HUATING OVERSEAS TOURIST CO.

Add: F/4, 503 Wulumuqi Rd, N
Tel.: 62491234
Fax: 62485470,62482781
Post Code: 200040

SHANGHAI JINJIANG TOURS LTD.

Add: 191 Changle Road
Tel.: 64662828
Fax: 64662297
Post Code: 200020

SHANGHAI CYTS TOURS CORPORATION

Add: 2 Hengshan Road
Tel.: 64331826, 64331907
Fax: 64330507
Post Code: 200031

SHANGHAI CHINA INTERNATIONAL TRAVEL SERVICE CO., LTD

Add: CITS Building, 1277 Beijing Rd, W
Tel.: 62898899
Fax: 62894928
Post Code: 200040

SHANGHAI CHINA TRAVEL SERVICE

Add: 881 Yanan Rd, M
Tel.: 62478888, 62475770
Fax: 62475521
Post Code: 200040

3. JIADING

Jiading, belonging to the Wu and Yue States in ancient times and established as a county in the Southern Song Dynasty (1218), 800 years from now. Jiading, known since ancient days as a cultural state, has been flourishing in culture and education and famous for talented personages. The two famous historical and cultural towns of Jiading and Nanxiang are exceptionally known for their respective Garden of Autumn Clouds and Guyi Garden. Present-day Jiading has become a satellite town in the northwest of greater Shanghai, known for its science city, automobile city and tourist city.

In the formation of tourist areas around Shanghai, Jiading is the nearest to Shanghai downtown. It is the most accessible in communications and most rapidly developed recreational area with theme parks. Now, Jiading is popular for its classical gardens of Autumn Clouds and Guyi as its traditional scenic spots, for its newly developed tourist attractions of the American Dream Park representative of a modern theme, for its indigenous tourist resources on Mao Island, which is a potential hot spot for tourism. Straw weaving of Xuhang, bamboo carving of Jiading, and meat dumplings of Nanxiang are well accepted by tourists. Jiading is well developed in communications. Shanghai-Nanjing, Shanghai-Hangzhou railways, 312 state highway, 204 state highway, Shanghai-Nanjing and Shanghai-Jiading freeways all pass through the county. Accessible in all directions, it is the best choice for spending holidays and seeking leisure by citizens from Shanghai and neighboring provinces and cities.

GARDEN OF AUTUMN CLOUDS

Located on East Grand Street in Jiading and occupying an area of 3 hectares, it is one of the five major classical gardens and the oldest one in Shanghai. It was built in the Ming Dynasty (1502), 490 years from now. It is a cultural relic protected by the municipality. In the center of the garden is a pond surrounded by rockeries and the scenery is partitioned into 4 scenic areas of the

Peach Blossom Pool, the Cloud Condensing Pavilion, the Clear Mirror Pond and the Town Temple. There are pavilions, terraces, chambers and halls, beautiful ponds and winding paths, luxuriant trees and bamboos, low balustrades and stone bridges, broken slopes and dripping fountains, rockeries and caves, all ingeniously arranged, forming a garden within a garden, a scene outside a scene, with hills like peaks with deep valleys, streams with tranquil beauty, a broad vista in a small garden. Therefore, it is reputed as "mountains and forests in a city" and a masterpiece of gardening of the Ming Dynasty. In the hall of the City God Temple in theTown Temple area there is an exhibition center of Shanghai Folk culture, A True Picture of Shanghai Folk Customs and Habits, which shows Shanghai folk customs in the past hundred years.

Add: 314 East Grant Street, Jiading District
Tel.: 59531949
Means of communication: No 6 tourist bus

FAHUA PAGODA

Fahua Pagoda is located on Lao Jie Street, Zhengzhou Bridge, Jiading. Together with a winding stream, deep and quiet alleys and antique buildings make up a picturesque scene of Jiading. The pagoda was first built during the Song Dynasty. In January 1996, in excavating the underground palace of the pagoda a number of precious relics of Buddha statues, books, ancient coins and jadeware of the Song, Yuan, Ming Dynasties were discovered. At present, the pagoda is under repair to restore to its original Ming Dynasty style. Once completed, Lao Jie Street will form into a water region scenic spot with one pagoda, two rivers, three streets and four bridges.

Add: Lao Jie Street, Zhou Bridge, Jiading District
Tel.: 59525688
Means of communication: No 6 tourist bus

CONFUCIUS' TEMPLE

Confucius' Temple in Jiading is located on South Grand Street and used to be known as No 1 temple in Wu State in ancient days. It was built in the Southern Dynasty (1219). It is now listed as a cultural relic site under the protection of the municipality. In the temple are checkered wooden gates, a jade-white ancient bridge on the pond, large numbers of craved tablets and

twisted ancient cypresses. There is the Minglun Hall, a school of the ancients, and the Dacheng Hall, where the statue of Confucius is kept. The temple is now the Jiading Museum. Here, the "Exhibition of Cultural Relics of the Imperial Examination System" disclosing the mystery of the thousand-year-old imperial examination system since the Sui and Tang Dynasties appeals to visitors with great interest. There are in the temple antique and dignified-looking tablets, the Lingxing Gate where scholars used to gather, the Sanban Pool, Dacheng Hall, the Sage Arch, and the Minglun Hall. Beside the Danghu Academy is a newly built corridor with tablets displaying the carved inscriptions and calligraphy of famous scholars like Huang Tingjian of the Song dynasty, Shen Kang, Wen Chengming and Dong Qichang of the Ming Dynasty.

Add: 183 South Grand Street, Jiading District
Tel.: 59530379

Means of communication: No 6 tourist bus

PARK OF DRAGONS MEETING POOL

Located on Tacheng Road, Jiading Town, next to Confucius' Temple, the park occupies an area of 50,000 sq.m. It was dredged in the Ming Dynasty (1588), 400 years from now. It occupies an area of 4 hectares. There are relics of stone pavilions, stone pagodas and stone tablets. The Yingkui Hill and Kuixing Pavilion stand setting off with Confucius' Temple. The park looks antique, graceful and elegantly quiet. Major scenic spots are the Free Watching Hall, Ten-thousand Buddha Pagoda, Magnificent Decoration Hall, Sunset Pavilion, Banana Little Courtyard, Broken Jade Spring, Jade Lotus Pond, Wave Shadow Waterside Pavilion, Hall of Peace, Terrace of Hundred Birds Worshipping the Phoenix and Pavilion of Clouds.

Add: 299 Tacheng Road, Jiading District
Tel.: 59529604
Means of communication: No 6 tourist bus

NANXIANG BRICK PAGODA

First built during the period from the Five dynasties to early Song Dynasty the brick pagoda has a history of over 1000 years. It was standing inside the gate of the White Crane Nanxiang Temple. The temple was damaged by fire in the 31st year of Qing Emperor Qianlong's reign (1766), but the brick fagoda remained. Beginning from the end of 1985, after one year's repair, the pagoda was restored to its original state. The newly restored pagoda is 11-m high with 7 stories in octagonal shape, all built of bricks. The exterior is a copy of a wooden tower-type pagoda. The flame-like gates, simple wooden barred windows, the exquisitely made beam supports, the delicate partition boards and erect pagoda top are typical of Song dynasty architectural style.

Add: Nanxiang Town, Jiading District
Tel.: 59525688
Means of communication: No 6 tourist bus

GUYI GARDEN (GARDEN OF ANCIENT BEAUTY)

Guyi Garden is located in the east of Nanxiang Town. It was first built during the Ming Dynasty. The trees and rockeries were arranged by the famous bamboo carver Zhu Sansong in the Ming Dynasty. The name Yi Garden was derived from the verse "The green bamboos are beautifl" in the "Book of Song". Guyi Garden is featured by historic relics and covering of bamboos. The tall halls and delicate pavilions, the stone boats and waterside pavilions, bamboo lined paths leading to quiet corners, ancient trees and famous flowers, pebble paths and winding streams guide visitors to antique and interesting sites and mould people's temperament. The Hall of Interest of the Wild, the Little Pine Mount, the Little Cloudy Mound, the Geese Playing Pond, the Floating Cloud Pavilion, the Pine and Crane Garden, the Wild Ducks Lake, Nanxiang Wall, the Nine-twist Bridge, the Plum Blossom Hall and the Mid-lake Pavilion each has its own feature. There are also cultural relics like the Tang Dynasty Buddhist Sutra Stela, the Song Dynasty Stone Pagoda, etc.

Add: 218 Huyi Road, Nanxiang Town, Jiading District
Tel.: 59121535
Means of communication: No 6 tourist bus

WUXING TEMPLE

Located in Waigang Town, Jiading District and first built in the South and North Dynasty (512), it is one of the earliest temples in Shanghai. It is a historic site of the Buddhist Chan Sect. Many high monks came from it. The Heavenly King Hall, the Grand Hall, the Mercy Pavilion, the Chongfu, Yongde and Wenchang Pavilions were respectively damaged during the Anti-Japanese War. Now, the Heavenly Hall and the arches have been restored. A new Grand Hall is being built. All the other structures will be gradually restored. Now, there is an increasing number of worshippers and its name is well-known at home and abroad.

Add: Waigang Town, Jiading District

Tel.: 59525688
Means of communication: No 6 tourist bus

OSTRICH BREEDING FARM

It is located in Anting Town and occupies an area of 4 hectares. The ostrich is bred in Africa and known as typical of a fine species of the breeding business. Besides breeding ostriches the farm also processes ostrich tourist souvenirs. It will become a multiple tourist attraction for appreciation, tasting, recreation and shopping.
Add: Anting Town, Jiading District
Tel.: 59525688
Means of communication: No 6 tourist bus

SCENIC AREA ON MAOHE ISLAND

Maohe Island is in Tanghang Town, Jiading District, on Changjiang River mouth in the east, and occupies an area of 108 hectares. The climate is pleasant and the air is fresh. It is abundant in flowers and fruit. Through 10 years of development the afforested area has reached 27 hectares. 10,000 pieces of 84 kinds of flowering trees and plants have been planted in 20 gardens of the gingko, the sweet osmanthus, the yew podocarpus, the camphor, the magnolia, the wintersweet, the wisteria and the metasequoia. Flowers bloom and leaves are green all year round. There is a group of newly built villas in new-style architecture and together with the antique structure of Zhuangyuan Restaurant and Qianyan Hall form a unique picture of the antique and the modern.
Add: Tanghang Town, Jiading District
Tel.: 59525688
Means of communication: No 6 tourist bus

THOUSAND-YEAR-OLD GINGKO

Found in Lu Family Residence in Guangming Village, Fangtai Town and planted at the end of the Tang dynasty, 1000 years from now, it is a male tree. It is 24.5-m tall with a trunk of 6.5 m and a crown of 20 m x 13,5 m. Its roots stretch around an area of one hectare. It is a " god of longevity" among all the ancient trees in Shanghai. It is numbered as No. 1 famous ancient tree by the Municipal Gardening and Forestation Bureau.

Add: Fangtai Town, Jiading District
Tel.: 59525688
Means of communication: Special bus line

PROPOSED TOUR OF JIADING SCENERY AND FOLK LIFE

Morning: Guyi Garden – Park of Dragons Meeting Pool – Jiading Confucius' Temple
Afternoon: American Dream Amusement Park

RECOMMENDED TRAVEL SERVICE

SHANGHAI HUATING OVERSEAS TOURIST CO.

Add: F/4, 503 Wulumuqi Rd, N
Tel.: 62491234
Fax: 62485470,62482781
Post Code: 200040

SHANGHAI JINJIANG TOURS LTD.

Add: 191 Changle Road
Tel.: 64662828
Fax: 64662297
Post Code: 200020

SHANGHAI CYTS TOURS CORPORATION

Add: 2 Hengshan Road
Tel.: 64331826, 64331907
Fax: 64330507
Post Code: 200031

SHANGHAI CHINA INTERNATIONAL TRAVEL SERVICE CO., LTD

Add: CITS Building, 1277 Beijing Rd, W
Tel.: 62898899
Fax: 62894928
Post Code: 200040

SHANGHAI CHINA TRAVEL SERVICE

Add: 881 Yanan Rd, M
Tel.: 62478888, 62475770

Fax: 62475521
Post Code: 200040

4. BAOSHAN

Baoshan, located at the mouth of the Changjiang River, in the north of Shanghai, occupies an area of 425 sq.km. With both the Huangpu and Changjiang Rivers passing by and an island in the distance, the scenery there is beautiful.

In the Ming Dynasty (1412), an earth mound was built at the junction of Changjiang and Huangpu Rivers to guide ships in entering the Changjiang. Emperor Yongle named it "Baoshan", which in Chinese means "treasure hill". It is not only a base for the metallurgical industry but also a port and a center for storage and shipping.

Standing on the Changjiang River Mouth Commercial Building - No 1 building on the Changjiang, one can see the famous "three-layer water" at Wusong. From the River Viewing Hall in Lingjiang Park one can watch the waves of the river rolling towards east and the immense stretch of water in the river dotted with masts and ships sailing back and forth, you will feel as if you are in the midst of a magnificent painting scroll.

There are in the area 48 historic and revolutionary sites and humanistic sights, like the famous ancient Wusong Fort, Chen Huacheng Memorial Hall, Tao Xingzhi Memorial Hall and Navy's Shanghai Museum.

There are also modern tourist attractions, such as the well-known large-scale Iron and Steel Complex - Baogang, the largest container terminal in Shanghai - Baoshan, Zhanghuabang and Jungong Road container terminals, the assembly workshop of Murdock airplanes - Shanghai Airplane Manufacturing Plant, the largest commercial and trading market in East China - East China Trading Square. There you can experience the modern flavor of big industries, big businesses, big markets and great circulation.

CHANGXING ISLAND AND HENGSHA ISLAND

In the north of Chongming Island are the two islands of Changxing and Hengsha, which have very good natural environment and are regarded as pieces of "pure land" amidst the bustling metropolis. The air above the island has attained first grade of the state's standard and the temperature in summer is 2 C lower than that in downtown Shanghai. They are ideal places as holiday resorts. There is a sea beach bathing ground and water sports ground on Hengsha Island. Every summer crowds of Shanghai residents go there to spend their holidays. Changxing Island has an area of 76.32 sq.km. and is famed as a "green jadeite" inlaid at the mouth of the Changjiang River entering the sea. In the middle of the island is Qianwei Farm with an area of 451.67 hectares, the largest orange growing base in the country and model and research center for orange growing in East China and known as the largest production base of "green food" in Shanghai. The oranges produced in the farm called "Qianwei sweet oranges" have very thin rinds and no kernels, lustrous and smooth in appearance, juicy and sweet. In the orchard there are rockeries, long corridors, potted landscapes, a Mongolian village, a horse track, a sea conch hall and a hotel. In the east to the orchard gate is a potted landscape garden and in the east is a ingeniously designed exhibition corridor of orange culture. At the end of every spring and beginning of summer, the fragrance of white orange blossoms amidst green foliage permeate the air. In late autumn, golden yellow fruit hang on the branches, appealing to the palate of visitors. Since the mid '80s, an orange festival is held every autumn, attracting thousands of visitors to enjoy the beautiful scenery and the taste of sweet oranges. It is one of the the most popular tourist attractions in Shanghai.

Add: Changxing Island and Hengsha Island

Tel.: 56109850

Means of communication: Public buses 51, 116 and ferry at Wusong Road Wharf

ANCIENT TOWN - GOLDEN LUODIAN

Luodian was first built during the Yuan Dynasty, 500 years from now. It is next to Jiading in the west, by the Liuhe River in the north and Dachang in the south. A leading town in Baoshan, it is well developed in land and water communications and prosperous in economy, a leading town in Baoshan. As early as the Ming Dynasty, Luodian was already an important commercial town for commerce, abundant in produce and prosperous in trade. By the years of Qing Emperor Kangxi's reign, trade of cotton and cotton cloth was thriving, hence it was named the Golden Luodian. Developed economy brought along prosperity in the town market. On the 15th of the 5th lunar month, the Lantern Festival, two lighted pagodas are erected before the temple, where vegetarian banquets are held, attracting great numbers of visitors. On the 5th day of the 5th lunar month there is usually a dragon boat competition going on in the river. It is a very interesting sight! Luodian is not only developed in economy but also noted for its humanistic sights. There are historic cultural sites, like such ancient architecture of the Fanwang Palace, the Datong Bridge, the Fengde Bridge and the Lailong Bridge. The old Town of Luodian is known for its "three turns, nine lanes and eighteen streets", typical of the feature of a watery region. There is also a hi-tech vegetable and horticultural garden and special species breeding farm. These are also sights worth visiting.

Add: Luodian Town, Baoshan District

Tel.: 56109850

Means of communication: Public bus Song-Luo line

ANCIENT FORT AT WUSONG

The ancient fort at Wusong was the front of our national hero Chen Huacheng in resisting the British invaders. In June 1862, the British fleet attacked Wusong Mouth. Chen Huacheng led his army at Wusong Fort to resist the enemies and damaged several of the British ships. However, outnumbered by the enemies he gave up his life. At the Wusong Fort there is still kept the big canon of "General Wuyi". When you stand on the fort and watch the vast river before you, you can imagine the moving and heroic scene of the heroes in resisting the invaders.

Add: 1 Youyi Road, Baoshan District (inside Lingjiang

Park)
Tel.: 56165854
Means of communication: Public buses 51 and 116

CHEN HUACHENG'S MEMORIAL HALL

Anti-British hero Chen Huacheng's memorial hall is located in the Lingjiang Park in Wusong. During the Opium War, the British fleet invaded Wusong Mouth. Chen Huacheng, marshal of the areas south of the Changjiang River, at the age of 67, led his men to resist the invaders bravely. His men damaged several of the British ships and fought hand-to-hand with the enemies. Later, Chen's superior Niu Jian, governor of Jiangxu, Anhui and Jiangxi Provinces, defected and fled from Baoshan. The British army landed on Baoshan and encircled the western fort from the back. Chen Huacheng defended his position with his life; he was wounded seven times and finally gave up his life. In commemorating the national hero Chen Huacheng for his heroic deeds a memorial hall was built to replace the Confucius' Dacheng Hall in Lingjiang Park. In the memorial hall are kept the armour, weapon and canon used by Chen Huacheng. These are all precious collections and serve to educate the young people. The hall is now an educational base for educating Shanghai's adolescents.

Add: 1 Youyi Road, Baoshan District (in Lingjiang Park)
Tel.: 56165854
Means of communication: Public buses 51 and 116

TAO XINGZHI'S MEMORIAL HALL

Tao Xingzhi's Memorial Hall is located at the crossroad of Hutai Road and Changnan Road. The hall was founded in 1986 to commemorate the people's educator Tao Xingzhi. The hall occupies an area of 3,820 sq.m., with a floor space of 1,910 sq.m. On display are inscriptions by Mao Zedong, Zhu De, Soong Ching Ling and Feng Yuxiang. The interior of the hall has an elegantly quiet atmosphere. There is a pond, a little bridge, a rockery, a winding path, amidst which is a marble bust and a sitting statue of Tao Xingzhi with a book in his hand.

Add: 108 Changnan Road, Baoshan District

Tel.: 56509761
Means of communication: Public bus 110

NAVY'S SHANGHAI MUSEUM

The museum, located in the navy's wharf at Wusong, occupies an area of 11,000 sq.m., with a floor space of 5,000 sq.m. The exhibits describe the history of the ancient Chinese navy, the contemporary history of the development of China's navy, and the history of development of the East Sea Fleet. On display is an exhibition of wonders of the seas in the world, the armament in the world, and different kinds of weapons. A shooting practice range loans light weapons like pistols and rifles for practice. On pre-arrangement, groups of visitors may visit the modern battle ships at the navy wharf. The museum is an educational base for educating adolescents in patriotism.
Add: 68 Tanghou Road, Baoshan District
Tel.: 56163295
Means of communication: Public busdes 51 and 116

TOUR OF BAOSHAN INDUSTRIES

BAOSHAN IRON AND STEEL (GROUP) CORP

Baoshan Iron and Steel Complex is the most modernized and largest iron and steel complex in the country. The complex occupies an area of 18.9 sq.km. The first and second phases of the project were respectively completed and put into operation in 1985 and 1991. The third phase of the project once completed will have a productive capacity of 11,000,000 tons and its technology and equipment will still be of the world's first-grade standard. The landscaping covers 35% of the complex area with an average of 240 sq.m. per person. It is a model unit in afforestation and landscaping in the whole country. In 1997, Baogang Iron and Steel Complex ranked at the top of the 500 extra large enterprises in the country and among the "strong enterprises" in Asia.
Add: 1534 Maodanjiang Road, Baoshan District
Tel.: 56124821
Means of communication: No 6 tourist bus, public buses 51, 53 and 116

SHANGHAI PORT CONTAINER TERMINAL CO.,LTD.

Invested jointly by China mainland and Hong Kong with RMB5.6 billion yuan, the terminal occupies an area of 93 sq.m. with a berth line 2,281-m long and an annual handling capacity of 1,700,000 standard containers. The newly completed office building has 18 stories with a total floor space of 250,000 sq.m., consisting of offices, meeting rooms, restaurants and recreational facilities. It is a first-grade container terminal of world standard, equipped with the most up-to-date harbor administration facilities.

Add: 4333 Yixian Road, Baoshan District

Tel.: 56442328

Means of communication: Public buses 51, 53, and 101

SHIDONGKOU POWER PLANT

Located in Shengqiao Town, Shanghai Shidongkou Power Plant and Huaneng Shanghai Shidongkou No 2 Power Plant produce an annual power volume of 15 billion KW/hr, occupying 1/2 of the city's total amount of power generation. It is an advanced unit among the power industries. The buildings in the plant are magnificent and the environment is beautiful.

Add: 270 Shengshe Road, Baoshan District

Tel.: 56152222

Means of communication: Public bus Pengsheng line

SHANGHAI AIRPLANE MANUFACTURING PLANT

The plant has a history of 50 years. It has repaired several thousands of airplanes since liberation. Since '70s it has adopted China-made materials and machinery equipment and has itself researched and produced 170 large-size passenger planes, the "Yunshi" brand.

Add: 3115 Changzhong Road, Baoshan District

Tel.: 56681122

Means of communication: Public bus 110, 845 and 852

PROPOSED TOUR OF BAOSHAN TOURIST ATTRACTIONS

Morning: Tour ancient town of Luodian – Baogang Iron and Steel Complex

Afternoon: Orange Orchard on Changxing Island

RECOMMENDED TRAVEL SERVICE

SHANGHAI HUATING OVERSEAS TOURIST CO.

Add: F/4, 503 Wulumuqi Rd, N

Tel.: 62491234

Fax: 62485470,62482781

Post Code: 200040

SHANGHAI JINJIANG TOURS LTD.

Add: 191 Changle Road

Tel.: 64662828

Fax: 64662297

Post Code: 200020

SHANGHAI CYTS TOURS CORPORATION

Add: 2 Hengshan Road

Tel.: 64331826, 64331907

Fax: 64330507

Post Code: 200031

SHANGHAI CHINA INTERNATIONAL TRAVEL SERVICE CO., LTD

Add: CITS Building, 1277 Beijing Rd, W

Tel.: 62898899

Fax: 62894928

Post Code: 200040

SHANGHAI CHINA TRAVEL SERVICE

Add: 881 Yanan Rd, M

Tel.: 62478888, 62475770

Fax: 62475521

Post Code: 200040

5. NANHUI

Nanhui County is situated on the East Sea. Land in the area took form before the Tang Dynasty. The sea is in its southeast and the

Changjiang River in entering the sea is pushed back towards the south and meets with Qiantang River; hence the name Nanhui, meaning "meeting in the south". In the 4th year of Qing Emperor Yongzheng's reign the county was established. In the past thousands of years the people in Nanhui reclaimed land from the sea and built a new world in Pudong. Nanhui is crisscrossed by rivers and laid-out with harbors, abundant in natural produce and pleasant with pastoral landscape. Peaches from Nanhui, melons, muskmelons, Shanghai honey pears and the "three yellow" chickens from Pudong are well-known in Shanghai. In spring, during the famous Nanhui Peach Blossom Festival, thousand hectares of peaches paint a sea of pink under the spring sunlight; fragrance from the white pear blossoms and the yellow rapeseed flowers float in the air. In summer and autumn, the season of bumper harvest, the sweet fragrance of fruits is intoxicating. In pastoral cottages live quite well-to-do families. The life-style of the country folk is unsophisticated, warm-hearted and honest; it is like shangri-la in real life. With 45-km sea beach, the soil is clean, the water is pure, the air is fresh; you watch sunrise, walk the beaches, play in the tides, explore the reed marshes and woods and have a taste of seafood; it is an ideal place for people to return to nature and spend their leisure time and holidays. In recent years, along the beach in Sanzhao area near the county seat from Binghai to Luchao Port are a number of newly developed tourist attractions and recreational facilities like the Wildlife Zoo, Chinese Nationalities Grand View Garden, Shanghai Pudong Shooting Amusement Center, Shanghai Magnolia Sea-beach Holiday Resort, East Sea Film and TV Amusement Park, Xiqi Children's World, Shanghai Fuzda Automobile Race Amusement Center, and Nanhui Vegetable and Horticultural Co., Ltd. .Nanhui is well developed in communications. The high-grade Shanghai-Nanhui highway links the Inner-ring Road, the Nanpu and Yangpu Bridges and reaches to the county seat and the different scenic spots. The Dazhi River traverses the county. The Pudong International Airport and the new port underway will facilitate Nanhui's traffic to different parts in the country and abroad by sea and air.

LUCHAO PORT

Luchao Port is a newly developed port city and a first-grade port of Shanghai. It has a favorable geographical location and great potential for development. It has been planned by the municipal government to be built into a city-grade tourist area. It is located in the southeast of Shanghai, on the East Sea in the east, opposite to the Buddhist shrine - Putuo Mountain and Shengsi, "a Beidaihe summer resort in the South", beyond the sea, close to Pudong New Area in the north. In the area are 6 express ways and 2 surface roads leading to the Nanpu and Yangpu Bridges. There are 7 routes for passenger, freight and vehicle transport from its wharves to Ningbo, Zhoushan, Putuo Mountain, Shengsi, the Great and Lesser Yangshan Hills in Zhejiang Province.

The climate in Luchaogang is pleasant. The location is favorable, with beautiful flowers and green waters and a number of talented people. There are rich tourist resources such as a natural fishing harbor, thousand hectares of peaches, a long sea-beach, and a dam protection forest. It is complete with up-to-date tourist facilities of catering, accommodation, travel, sightseeing and recreation. There are more than 70 restaurants serving seafood, like the Luchaogang Hotel, Hangzhou Bay Club, Jinggang Hall, and recreational facilities, like the super class Labyrinth Palace. There are resort villas built by the Xinya, Taipingyang and Jingan Huanwei Groups amidst the peaches; we call them a

"Land of Peaches Away from the Bustling World". The Golden Beach Hotel invested by Australia, containing offices and an amusement center, the 16-story Yongmao Mansion, a heated swimming pool, a golf course, a beach bathing ground and a garden on the sea are under construction. Luchaogang combines the cosmopolitan prosperity with pastoral peacefulness, freshness of the watery region and picturesque scenery on the sea-beach. It is something unique to watch the sun rise from the sea, have a taste of sea-food and fruits, experience the peacefulness of the forest, pick sea shells on the beach, and admire the landscaping. It is an ideal place for spending your holidays.

Add: Luchaogang, Nanhui County

Tel.: 58025111

Means of communication: Public buses Zhou-Nan line and Nan-Lu Line

NANHUI PEACH BLOSSOM FESTIVAL

Nanhui is a newly developed Land of Peach Blossoms. Peach is grown on 2,700 hectares of land. It ranks the top in East China in area and variety. When you sail down the river, miles of peach blossoms will catch your eye. Before you is a sea of pink, you are amidst a sea of pink clouds, a world of beauty. When you go ashore and enter the orchard, the "Peach Village", you will find yourself in a world of pink. Walking amidst the peach trees and in a sea of blossoms you will be intoxicated by the fragrance of the blossoms. The feature of Shanghai Nanhui Peach Blossom Festival is the natural landscape and the simple life-style of the country folk. Tourists can take a walk on the little paths in the fields or among the flowers, or fish angling, or plow in the fields, have a taste of wild jicai dumplings, pumpkin cakes, "three-yellow"chicken, fresh fish and shrimps and have a good time in the light of a pastoral spring.

Shanghai Nanhui Peach Blossom Festival offers a refined taste. It designs scenes and arranges activities with traditional culture, such as the performances of the dragon and lion dances, the peach blossom basket dance, traditional Chinese music, drum and brass ballad singing, and boat dance.

Add: Nanhui County

Tel.: 58025111
Means of communication: No 2 tourist bus

ANCIENT BELL GARDEN

A giant bronze bell cast in the Ming Dynasty (1571) is placed in the Ancient Bell Garden in Huinan Town, Nanhui County. It is 1.62-m tall with a 3.4-m circumference, weighing 1,600 g. The garden is arranged with pavilions, terraces, chambers, corridors, bridges, halls with upturned eaves and little paths paved with pebbles. It is featured by its buildings with white-washed walls and black tiles, a bronze bell and gingkos. It presents a typical scene of antique Ming garden. During the Peach Blossom Festival a lantern fair is held in the garden, attracting a great number of tourists.
Add: Huinan Town, Nanhui County
Tel.: 58025111
Means of communication: No 2 tourist bus

NANHUI VEGETABLE AND HORTICULTURAL CO., LTD.

Located in Changqiao Village, Xinchang town in Nanhui, it is a modern, computerized vegetable production base. It occupies an area of 7.6 hectares. 3.06 hectares of the land is devoted to green houses equipped with imported vegetable production technology and equipment from Israel. It mainly grows tomatoes, sweet peppers, cucumbers and muskmelons. It is a typical base for modern and hi-tech agricultural production.
Add: Changqiao Village, Xinchang Town, Nanhui County
Tel.: 58025111
Means of communication: No 2 tourist bus

XIQI CHILDREN'S WORLD

Located in Hangtou, Pudong, it occupies an area of 41.8 hectares and built with an investment of 250 million yuan. It is a new, trans-century tourist attraction. The main theme of the park is water. There is the Venice Holiday Resort, a water sports world, a star square, an open-air hunting ground, a children's intelligent amusement city and a stunt sports ground (including a convalescent and therapeutic center). It is a combination of science, technology, humanistic sights, gardening, landscaping, business, leisure and recreation. Many of the items are the first in the country, worth appreciating, participating, imparting knowledge and attracting great interest. In the park there is the largest swimming pool in the country with an area of 35,000 sq.m., a 8,600-sq.m. surfing pool and 200 guest rooms in the Venice Holiday Resort. There is a 10-m wide water channel connecting the different parts in the park available for visitors to take a boat and visit the different spots of interest. The children's world is a center for educating children in science and technology. It is also open to the general public as an ideal place for meetings, convalescence, rest and recreation.

Add: In the north of Hangtou Town, Pudong

Tel.: 58221987

Means of communication: No 2 tourist bus

SHANGHAI WILDLIFE ZOO

Located in Sanzao Town, Nanhui County, it occupies an area of 200 hectares. It reproduces a natural habitat for the wild animals. The zoo is divided into the free grazing area for the herbivores, the free preying area for the carnivores, the flamingo area, the scattered feeding area, the water fowl lake and precious species enclosed area, keeping altogether over 10,000 heads of 200 categories. Visitors will find themselves amidst a kingdom of wild animals.

Add: Sanzao Town, Nanhui County

Tel.: 58036000

Means of communication: No 2 tourist bus

EAST SEA FILM AND TV AMUSEMENT PARK

It is the shooting ground for filming movies and TV films. It consists of 3 areas for living, production and outdoor scene shooting. In the living area there is a hotel with 70 guest rooms, a restaurant, a chess and card room, and a karaoke room, a billiard room, and a meeting room. The rooms are equipped with satellite TV transmission channels. In the production area there is a 960-sq.m. film studio. In the outdoor shooting area there are reproductions of "a street in old Shanghai", "a Ming and Qing Dynasty street", "watery regions south of the Changjiang River". etc. As many as a million copies of films and TV films had been shot here. It is a great attraction for sightseeing and recreation.

Add: East Sea Farm, Nanhui County

Tel.: 58291225

Means of communication: Special bus

PROPOSED TOURS FOR NANHUI COUNTY

1st day: Shanghai Wildlife Zoo - Nationalities Grand View Garden - Xinchang Vegetable and Horticultural Garden

2nd day: East China Film and TV Amusement Park - Magnolia Holiday Resort - Pudong Marksman Shooting Ground

RECOMMENDED TRAVEL SERVICE

Shanghai China International Sighting Travel Service

SHANGHAI HUATING OVERSEAS TOURIST CO.

Add: F/4, 503 Wulumuqi Rd, N

Tel.: 62491234

Fax: 62485470,62482781

Post Code: 200040

SHANGHAI JINJIANG TOURS LTD.

Add: 191 Changle Road

Tel.: 64662828

Fax: 64662297

Post Code: 200020

SHANGHAI CYTS TOURS CORPORATION

Add: 2 Hengshan Road

Tel.: 64331826, 64331907

Fax: 64330507

Post Code: 200031

SHANGHAI CHINA INTERNATIONAL TRAVEL SERVICE CO., LTD

Add: CITS Building, 1277 Beijing Rd, W
Tel.: 62898899
Fax: 62894928
Post Code: 200040

SHANGHAI CHINA TRAVEL SERVICE

Add: 881 Yanan Rd, M
Tel.: 62478888, 62475770
Fax: 62475521
Post Code: 200040

6. CHONGMING

Chongming Island in the north of Shanghai city at the mouth of the Changjiang River is formed from the sand and mud washed up from the river. It is the third largest island in China, with a total area of 1,064 sq. km. It is fertile in soil, crisscrossed by rivers, luxuriant in vegetation, abundant in natural produce. It is an important base for Shanghai's agricultural, non-staple food and aquatic products and for export. Here, you will find a vast expanse of pastoral scenes. It is ready for development into a tourist area for convalescence and holiday resort. The Dongping Forest Park is the largest man-made forest in Shanghai, occupying an area of 353 hectares. It is an ideal summer resort for citizens in Shanghai. In the eastern part of the island is the Tuanjie River, where reeds and grass are luxuriant, water is clear and pure, fish and shellfish arc abundant. It is also a natural reserve for season birds, like the swans, red-crowned cranes, and wild ducks.

STUDY PALACE

The palace was first built in the Yuan Dynasty (1327) and has been turned into a museum now. There are well-kept ancient

architectures. It is a cultural relic under municipal protection.
Add: 696 Aoshan Road, Chongming County
Tel.: 59623827
Means of communication: No 5 tourist bus

GOLDEN AOSHAN HILL

Rebuilt during the Qing Dynasty (1668) and 2.5-km east of the city, has 9 peaks, the middle peak being the highest. There is a pagoda on top of the hill originally built to subdue the sea and hence named "Sea Subduing Pagoda"; on the walls are inscribed " calming". " silencing" and "stabilizing", all indicating sea subduing. By the side of the hill is a memorial hall of the national hero Tang Yicen.
Add: Chengqiao Town, Chongming County
Tel.: 50623200
Means of communication: No 5 tourist bus

TAN YICEN'S MEMORIAL HALL

Tang Yicen was the county magistrate in Chongming during the Ming Dynasty. In 1554, pirates invaded the island. Tang Yicen led his army in battle and drove the enemy out of the city. He himself was badly wounded and gave up his life. On his tombstone are inscribed the characters "A Martyr in Resisting the Enemy".

Add: Chengqiao Town, Chongming County
Tel.: 50623200
Means of communication: No 5 tourist bus

DONGPING STATE FOREST PARK

Located on Chongming Island, it is the largest forest park on plains in East China. Here you will a pastoral scene of an island, permeated with the fresh air of a great forest. Crossing the river and spending holidays in little wooden cottages one will find here a place of absolute peace and quietude. Swimming, water sports and sand beach volley ball all appeal to visitors with great interest.

Add: Chongming County

Tel.: 59641841 x 108

Means of communication: No 5 tourist bus

PROPOSED TOURS OF CHONGMING

Morning: Study Palace - Golden Aoshan Hill

Afternoon: Dongping State Forest Park

RECOMMENDED TRAVEL SERVICE

SHANGHAI HUATING OVERSEAS TOURIST CO.

Add: F/4, 503 Wulumuqi Rd, N

Tel.: 62491234

Fax: 62485470,62482781

Post Code: 200040

SHANGHAI JINJIANG TOURS LTD.

Add: 191 Changle Road

Tel.: 64662828

Fax: 64662297

Post Code: 200020

SHANGHAI CYTS TOURS CORPORATION

Add: 2 Hengshan Road

Tel.: 64331826, 64331907

Fax: 64330507

Post Code: 200031

SHANGHAI CHINA INTERNATIONAL TRAVEL SERVICE CO., LTD

Add: CITS Building, 1277 Beijing Rd, W

Tel.: 62898899

Fax: 62894928

Post Code: 200040

SHANGHAI CHINA TRAVEL SERVICE

Add: 881 Yanan Rd, M

Tel.: 62478888, 62475770
Fax: 62475521
Post Code: 200040

SHOPPING

In the course of historical changes, since the first half of the 20th century Shanghai has gradually developed into China's largest commercial city, with domestic and foreign trade prospering and communications well developed. Hundreds and thousands of businessmen have gathered in Shanghai. With shops standing rows upon rows people could get native, special and famous brand products from different places in China and imported general merchandise. After liberation, Shanghai is still China's largest industrial and commercial city. Shanghai's commerce is noted in the country and abroad for its old famous brands, high quality, great variety, complete specifications and new styles. Since the '90s Shanghai has undergone tremendous changes. It is now making its pace towards an international economic, trade and financial center. In the meantime, Shanghai's commerce is also working towards the standard of internationalization and modernization. Through several years of construction and development the modernization of Shanghai's commerce has developed rapidly. Now, there are many pluralistic shopping areas and large collections of commodities. Customers can not only shop in the beautifully arranged world-grade fashion shops but also get in the large shopping malls famous-brand commodities from places all over China or choose in the street stalls wear of foreign famous brands left as surplus from foreign trade companies. Shanghai offers commodities both Chinese and foreign, antique and modern, famous brands, special, new and quality goods in Shanghai or from other places in China and imported famous-brand goods. Shanghai has become really "a paradise for shoppers" much sought after by tourists.

(I) COMMERCIAL STREETS

There are in Shanghai several well-known commercial streets, each having its own position in the market, furnished with large and small shops of different categories and levels, offering beautifully arranged commodities and attentive service, catering to tourists from home and abroad.

1. NANJING ROAD - CHINA'S NO 1 COMMERCIAL STREET

Nanjing Road is the first commercial street in Shanghai and has always enjoyed the reputation of "China's No 1 Commercial Street". In the early 20th century, along with the setting up of the four famous big global department stores of"Wing On", "Sincere", "Sun Sun" and "Dai Sun", merchants from different trades began to choose this

favorable location to set up hundreds of large and famous shops. Since '20s, Shanghai became"ten miles of foreign glamour", glistening with red lights and festivity, the most prosperous commercial street in Shanghai. After liberation, through rearrangement and remolding, it has become a grand avenue of bustling commerce. With more than 600 shops standing on both sides it has long been known as "China's No 1 Commercial Street". In the past several years, it has changed to a new face, with old-brand stores and restaurants with increasing business and, on the other hand, new shopping malls have mushroomed, like the New World, Real Estates Plaza, Mozda, Manhattan Plaza, Wings and Sincere Companies, offering customers with modern and pleasant shopping environment. There are hundred-year old, famous-brand, specialty shops and "famous-brand houses" with distinctive individuality, fast food cafeterias filled with people's joyous laughter, the fragrance of coffee permeating the air and the sound of video games floating around. The special character of Nanjing Road Commercial Street is that it still keeps its leading position in the country's commercial trade as "China's No 1 Commercial Street." It will be built into the most accomplished commodity show room for products in Shanghai, the whole country and even in southeast Asian areas, by offering everything possible with commodities of different standards and prices and good service, catering to different levels of consumers.

Means of communication: Public buses 20, 37, 921, 18, 17,

22, 55, 21 and 23

SHANGHAI NO 1 DEPARTMENT STORE AND NEW BUILDING

Shanghai No 1 Department Store was set up on Oct. 20, 1949. It was the site of the former Dai Sun Company. There are 7 floors (including the basement) for business, with a total floor space of 23,000 sq.m. and more than 1,000 counters selling over 40,000 items of commodities in 60 categories. The 3,000 shop assistants serve every day 100,000 customers from places all over China. It has won the confidence from its customers with its large collection of commodities, reasonable prices and quality service. It is the largest department store in the country, most complete in varieties of commodities, largest number of customers and highest sales volume. It is famed as the "leader of general merchandise". In increasing its strength and expanding its business scale to meet the needs of modern consumers, a new No 1 Department Store building was erected in 1997 on the east side of the original building. The new building is 21-storied, connected to the old building with a total floor space of 100,000 sq.m. It is a new-type commercial center, combining shopping, recreation, catering, offices and exhibition into one, a brilliant star in Shanghai's commercial trade.

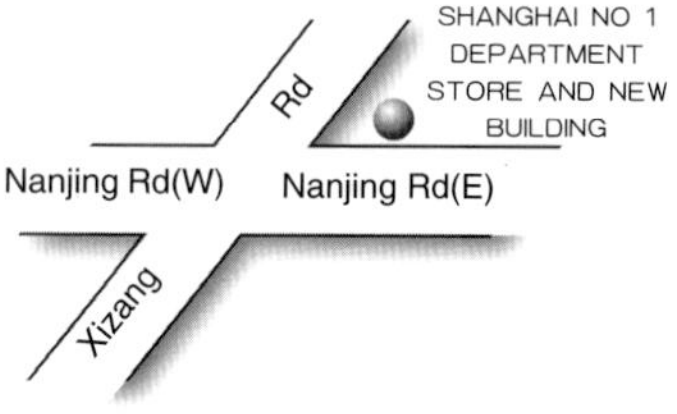

Add: 830 Nanjing Rd, E
Tel.: 63223344

HUALIAN COMMERCIAL BUILDING

Hualian Commercial Building was the former Wing On Company and renamed in 1996 as "Shanghai No 10 Department Store". In 1987, it was rebuilt into

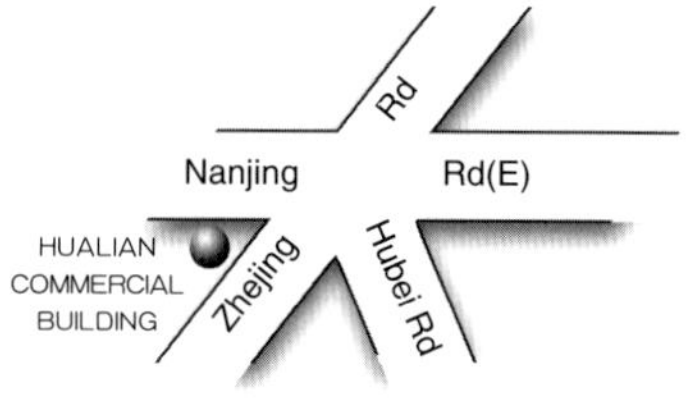

Hualian Commercial Building. In 1994, it was again rebuilt to become a large-scale modernized department store. It has ranked for several consecutive years in the third place in terms of sales volume among the country's general merchandise trade.

Add: 635 Nanjing Rd, E

Tel.: 63224466

NEW WORLD CO.,LTD.

New World Co.,Ltd. is opposite to Shanghai No 1 Department Store across the road. It is a newly built modernized department store on the west bank of the Huangpu River. It mainly sells medium and high grade general merchandise.

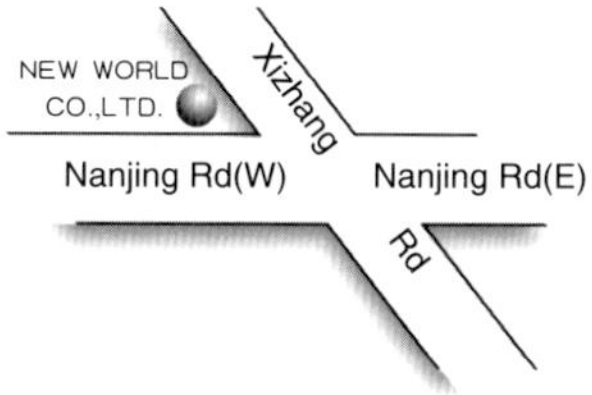

Add: 2 Nanjing Rd, W

Tel.: 63588888

SINCERE COMPANY

The former Sincere Company, one of the four big companies in Shanghai, was set up in 1914. In 1992, the Sincere Company in Hong Kong came to open its branch on Nanjing Road in the Manhattan Plaza under the name of "Sincere coming home". It has 6 floors for business, mainly engaged in selling medium and high-grade imported and joint venture commodities.

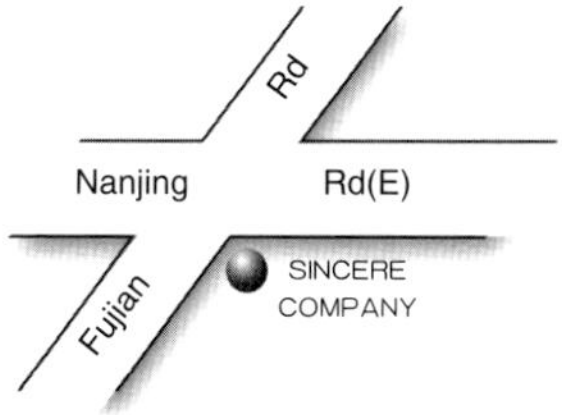

Add: 479 Nanjing Rd, E

Tel.: 63226888

FRIENDSHIP EUROPEAN COMMERCIAL CITY (EAST SEA COMMERCIAL CAPITAL)

The Friendship European Commercial City is a large-scale shopping center built according to the pattern of internationally fashionable, multi-purpose and multi-functional shopping mall. It was opened for business on June 1995. The whole building contains

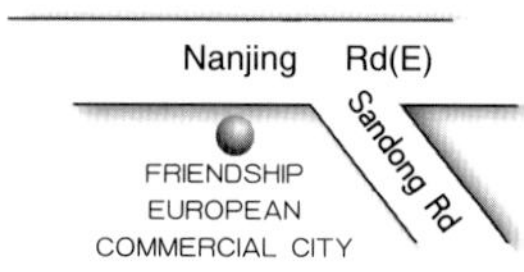

shopping, catering, recreation, leisure and business in one entirety.
Add: 490 Nanjing Rd, E
Tel.: 63511111

OVERSEAS CHINESE STORE

Established in 1961 the Overseas Chinese Store originally catering to overseas Chinese and their families, selling high-grade and famous brand high quality goods. It was opened to the general public in the '80s.
Add: 627 Nanjing Rd, E
Tel.: 63225508

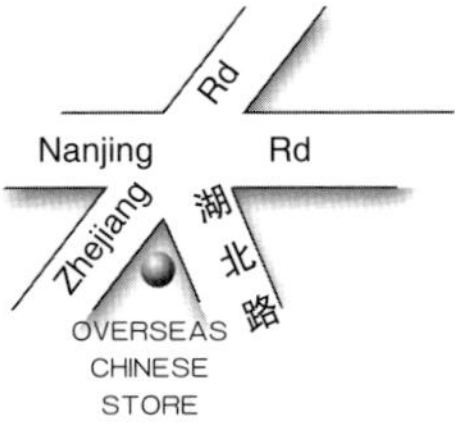

SHANGHAI FASHIONABLE CLOTHING CO.

Shanghai Fashionable Clothing Co. was the former Sincere Co. and changed its name in 1956. It is the largest specialized clothing store in Shanghai, selling more than 5,000 varieties in 140 categories of men's and women's clothing. It can be called "an aggregation of clothing".
Add: 690 Nanjing Rd, E
Tel.: 63225445

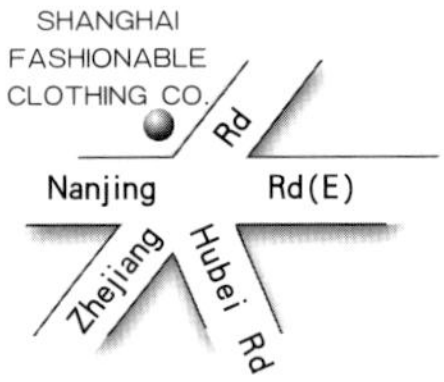

SHANGHAI NO 1 FOODSTUFF STORE

Shanghai No 1 Foodstuff Store was formerly the Sun Sun Co. and changed to its present name in 1956. It is the largest comprehensive foodstuff store in Shanghai, dealing in all kinds of foodstuff from different places in China and imported foodstuff.
Add: 720 Nanjing Rd, E
Tel.: 63222777

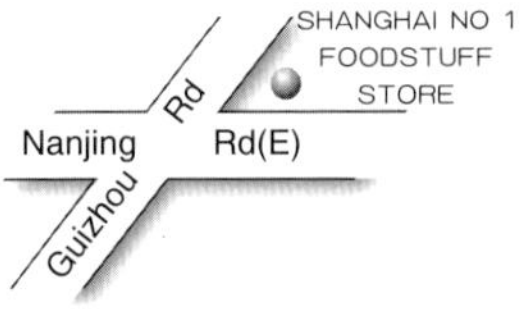

REAL ESTATES SQUARE

Add: 409 Nanjing Rd, E
Tel.: 63513828

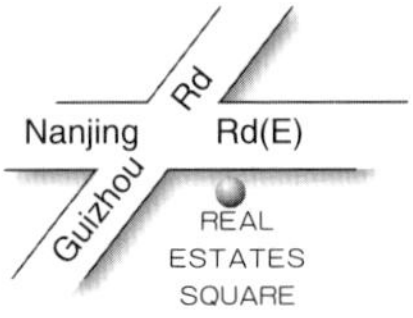

MANHATTAN PLAZA

Add: 463-477 Nanjing Rd, E

Tel.: 63222239

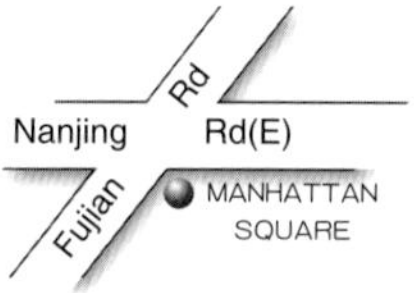

WINGS DEPARTMENT STORE, LTD.

Add: 869 Nanjing Rd, W

Tel.: 62582688

MOZDA COMMERCIAL BUILDING

Add: 889 Nanjing Rd, W

Tel.: 62588889

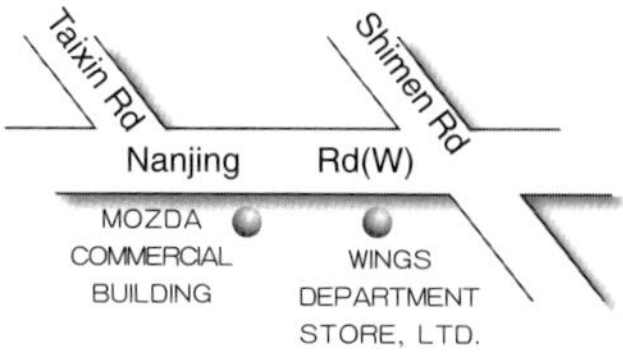

MEILONGZHEN SQUARE

Add: 1038 Nanjing Rd, W

Tel.: 62721111

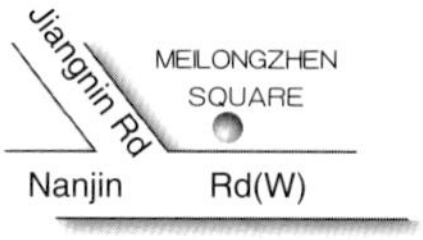

There are also other large-scale department stores on Nanjing Road, like the Super Fine Quality Commercial Building, Xiedaxiang Commercial Building, Baodaxiang Commercial Building, Huiluo, Zhonglian, Nanyang and Little Lusong Companies.

2. HUAIHAI ROAD - ELEGANT COMMERCIAL AND CULTURAL STREET

Huaihai Road and Nanjing Road are both tourist and shopping streets. Huaihai Road was formerly named Avenue Joffre. The 6 km-long street is a bustling but elegant street and can be compared to Ave. des Champs Elysees in Paris, the Fifth Avenue in New York, the Ginza in Tokyo, Wujie Road in Singapore. There are over 400 modernized shops on the most prosperous section of Huaihai Road, that is a 2.2 km-long commercial street from Shaanxi Road to Xizang Road. In the '90s, the remodeling of commercial establishments on Huaihai Road took place at the same time as the construction of the subway. The planning of the commercial street was aimed at a high starting point to cope with the status of an international metropolis.

Now, the buildings on both sides of the street look modern and graceful, with shops elegantly decorated in European and American classical style, in Chinese classical style, in new-trend European continental style and in trans-century metropolitan architectural style. Both the exterior and interior of the buildings send forth a strong

flavor of cosmopolitan culture and leisure. Huaihai Road has a collection of world's famous brands such as Printenps Shanghai, Maison Mode Department Store, Huating Isetan, displaying to visitors world-grade famous brands in all their beauty, attaining a world standard for shopping in Shanghai.

Means of communication: No 1 Subway Huangpi Road stop and Shaanxi Road stop and public buses 42, 926, 24, 126 and 911

SHANGHAI WOMEN'S ARTICLES STORE

Shanghai Women's Articles Store was the first of its kind specialized in selling articles for women. The store has a special counter for selling wear for middle-age professional women designed according to the characteristics of middle-age women. It also sells all kinds of fashionable clothing much appreciated by women from all circles. It has a collection of famous brand, high quality, new and special articles for women and high-grade imported articles. It also holds every month different kinds of special-topic sale, creating a unique commercial culture. Its over 1,000 sq.m.-business floor attracts large numbers of women consumers. It ranks the first among the 28 stores with annual sales volume above hundred million yuan and with unit sales volume.

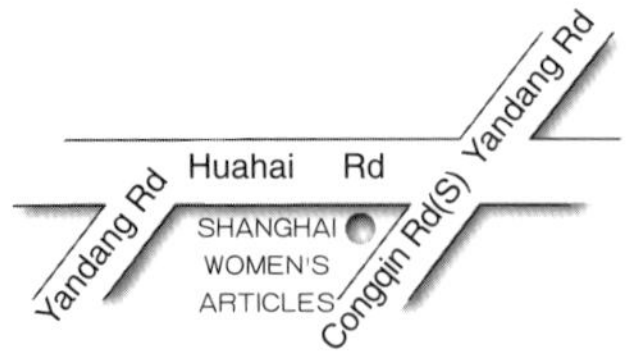

Add: 447 Huaihai Rd, M

Tel.: 63721595

INTERNATIONAL SHOPPING CENTER AND HUATING ISETAN CO.,LTD.

Set up on June 1993, the International Shopping Center, with a total floor space of 40,000 sq.m., consists of functions for shopping, catering, recreation and offices. It was a pioneer for modernized shopping center. It makes use of the pleasant atrium to create a unique layout of "a street within a street, a shop within a shop and a garden within a garden". The Huating Isetan Co.,Ltd., the Cordon Blue International Club and Fragrant Island Delicacies Plaza are all found here.

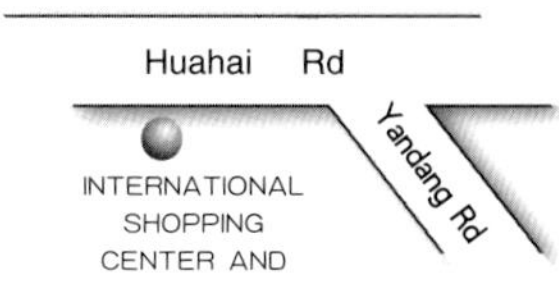

Add: 1-4 Floor No 527 Huaihai Rd, M
Tel.: 53061111

BASIC SHOPPING CENTER

Located at the crossroad of Huaihai Road and Shaanxi Road the Basic Shopping Center is managed by the Malaysian Basic Group. A supermarket is found in the basement. The 1st to 6th floors aboveground are for the sale of general merchandise. Its new and fashionable concept is expressed in the wear, leather goods, cosmetics and household necessities it offers. Here shoppers can have a rest while doing shopping in the Italian coffee shop, the Mcdonald or a southeast Asian snack bar. There is a restaurant "Chaojiang Spring" on the 7th floor and a Golden Age Night Club on the 8th floor, both enjoying good reputation in Shanghai. The Parkson, combining shopping, recreation and catering in one, is attracting Shanghai people and tourists from home and abroad with its multi commercial function, pleasant and dozy environment filled with the rhythm of modern life.

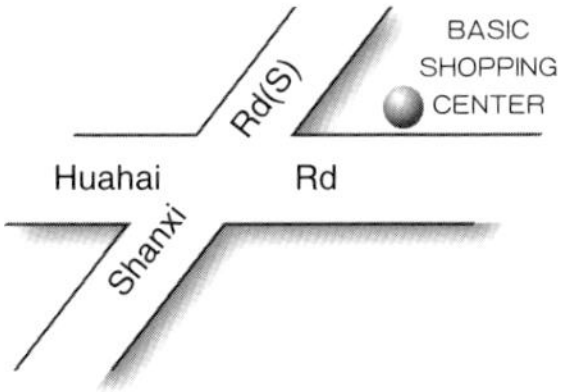

Add: 918 Huaihai Rd, M
Tel.: 64158818

SHANGHAI NO 1 DEPARTMENT STORE, LTD. HUAIHAI ROAD BRANCH

It is a retail store for general merchandise invested by Shanghai No 1 Department Store, Co., Ltd. opened for business on June 1993. It has a business floor of 5,500 sq.m. with a quietly elegant environment and managed by a modern system and complete with varieties of commodities.

Add: 523 Huaihai Rd, M

Tel.: 53061818

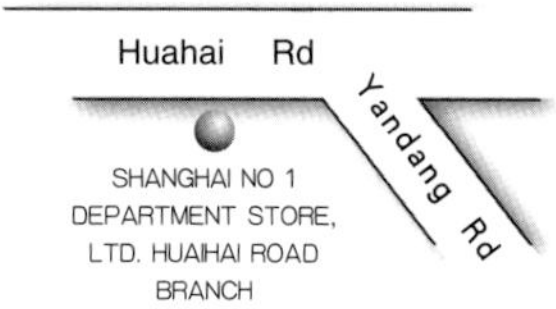

YIMIN COMMERCIAL BUILDING

Located in the middle section of Huaihai Road, Yimin Commercial Building mainly deals in general merchandise of daily use of 20,000 items in 150 categories of gold and jewelry, clocks and watches, ornaments, cosmetics, leather goods, men and women's clothing, bedding, sports goods, stationery and small household electric appliances. There is a local cuisine snack bar on the 5th floor, one of the earliest popular snacks bars in Shanghai, noted for its reasonable prices, great variety, genuine in taste and pleasant and cozy in environment.

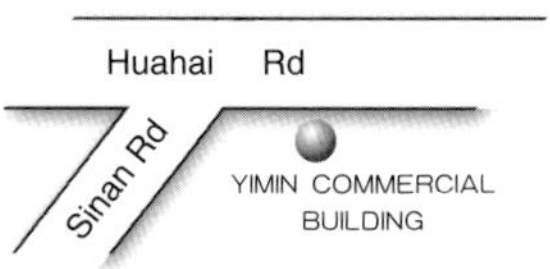

Add: 645–659 Huaihai Rd, M

Tel.: 53065075

SHANGHAI NO 2 DEPARTMENT STORE YONGXIN CO.,LTD.

Shanghai No 2 Department Store Yongxin Co.,Ltd. is a large-scale department store jointly run by Shanghai and Hong Kong. It is located in the center of Huaihai Road. With a magnificent and elegant exterior it is full of the modern flavor of the times. The interior is arranged beautifully and rationally with a great variety of new-style commodities at reasonable prices, which appeal

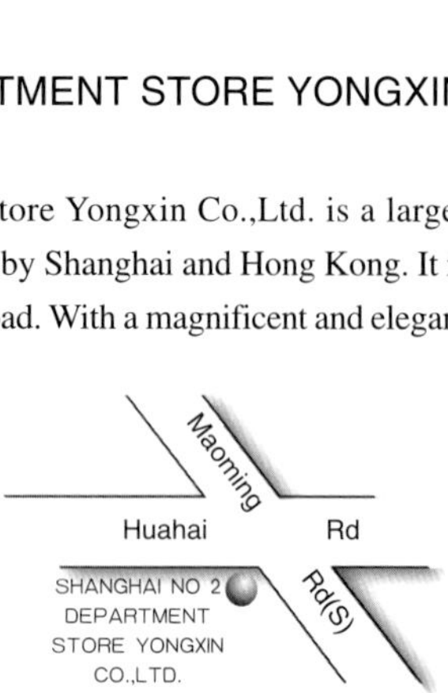

to customers of different levels. It is known as "a pearl of the general public".

Add: 887 Huaihai Rd, M

Tel.: 64732828

PACITIC DEPARTMENT STORE HUAIHAI BRANCH

pacitic Department Store is located on the Huaihai Road shopping street by No 1 Subway Huangpi Road stop. It is one of the large-scale department stores in Shanghai. It contains the functions of shopping, leisure and catering in one building, convenient in communications, elegantly peaceful in environment and good in service. It plays the lead in guiding the fashion and a model for new fashions, an ideal place for shopping.

Add: 288 Huaihai Rd, M

Tel.: 53068888

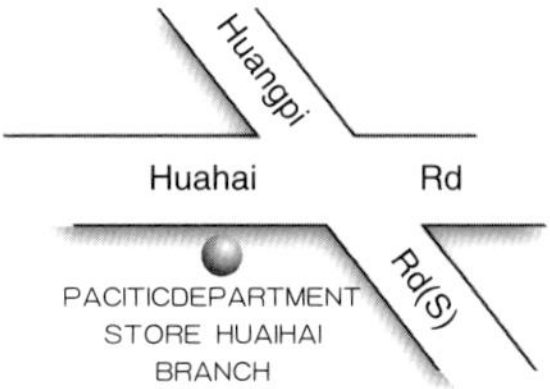

PRINTENPS SHANGHAI

Printenps Shanghai came from Paris. It is a building integrating the French classical architecture with modern lines. The exterior wall is decorated with bas-relief, bringing one's imagination to the side of River Seine. It is an aggregation for consumers in leading the fashionable trend of the art of life and a department store pioneering the international fashion. It has a collection of world-grade brands of clothing.

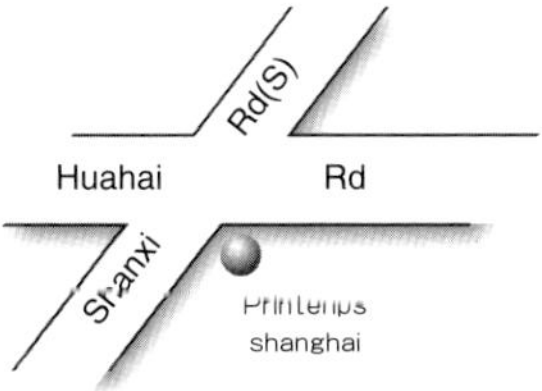

Add; 939-949 Huaihai Rd, M

Tel: 64310118

MAISON MODE

Add: 1312 Huaihai Rd, M

Tel: 64310100

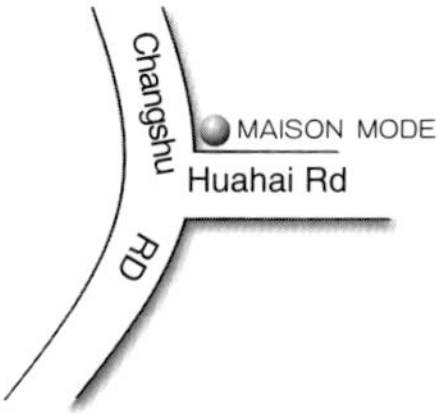

HONG KONG PLAZA

Add: 283 Huaihai Rd, M

Tel: 63863500

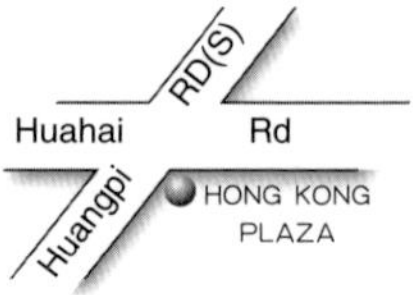

NEW HUALIAN COMMERCIAL BUILDING

Add: 755 Huaihai Rd, M

Tel: 64458000

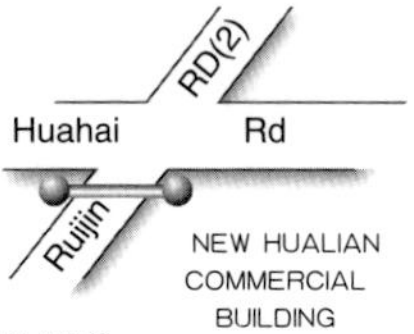

JINJIANG DICKSON CENTER

Add: 400 Changle Road

Tel: 64726888

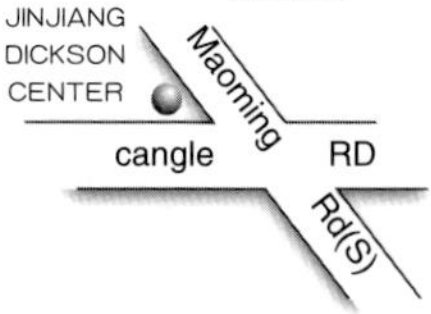

3.SICHUAN ROAD, NORTH - CHINA'S FAMOUS BRAND STREET

Sichuan Road, North, is the third largest commercial street next to Nanjing Road and Huaihai Road. It was the first street built after Shanghai was made an open port. It is located in the north of Suzhou Creek, traversing Hongkou District from south to north, with a total length of 3.7 km. In the '90s, it underwent large-scale renovation and was turned into today's modernized "commercial street for the general public" The rebuilt Sichuan Road, North, caters to consumers with high-quality commodities at medium and low prices, service with modern electronic technique, plus the humanistic sights in its surrounding areas, displaying a feature of modern cultural tourism and amusement facilities. With the introduction of many famous-brand stores it is attracting a great number of citizens and tourists from the country and abroad. There are four large commercial

buildings New Kaifu, Duolun, Kailun and Shanghai Spring. With the completion of many famous-brand stores it still emphasizes on the business of medium-price commodities, fully displaying its characteristic of its commercial individuality of serving the wage-class, different from the bustling Nanjing Road and the elegant Huaihai Road, in persisting its policy of serving the general public. It bases itself on China-made products and supporting the national industry. It has become a commodity center with the biggest collection of China-made famous brands with good quality and most complete in variety. "Take a walk in the other streets, but do shopping in Sichuan Road" is a catchword that appeals to customers' psychology for getting good-quality things at reasonable prices.

Means of communication: Public buses 13, 17, 21, 19, 70 and 18

SHANGHAI NO 7 DEPARTMENT STORE

Located at the crossroad of Sichuan Road and Haining road, Shanghai No 7 Department Store is a famous department store on Sichuan Road. In 1991 and 1992, it was commended as one of the best stores in business receipt. The store pursues the business policy of "high quality, serving the public and service in an all round way". It has established for itself the image of "a big store for the general public". It has 7 chain stores. It has jointly run with a foreign party in Goteborg, Sweden a "Swesia International Shopping Center".

Add: 887 Sichuan Rd, N

Tel.: 63249611

INTERNATIONAL COMMERCIAL BUILDING

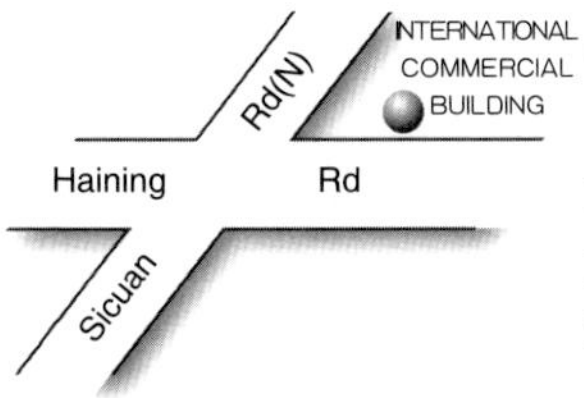

The International Commercial Building is opposite to the No 7 Department Store. It deals in 30,000 kinds of commodities. It is a department store, most complete in scale and first-grade facilities in Hongkou District. It pursues a policy of "high quality but reasonable price and an individuality in consumer service", to meet the needs of different levels of consumers, emphasizing on the needs of the wage-class.

Add: 358 Haining Road

Tel.: 63066518

FAR EAST ELECTRIC APPLIANCES COMMERCIAL BUILDING

Add: 840 Sichuan Rd, N

Tel.: 63562161

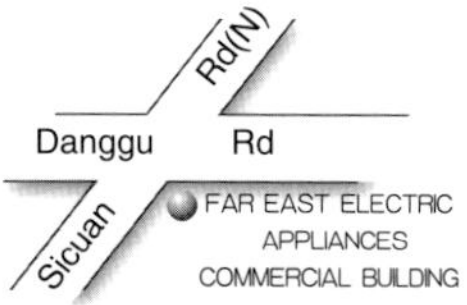

SHANGHAI NO 7 DEPARTMENT STORE EAST BUILDING

Add: 888 Sichuan Rd, N

Tel.: 63249611

FUDU COMMERCIAL CITY

Add: 518 Sichuan Rd, N

Tel.: 63931829

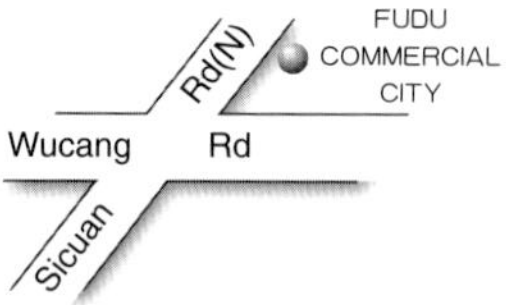

JIAMEI WOOLEN SWEATER CO.

Add: 496 Sichuan Rd, N

Tel.: 63252295

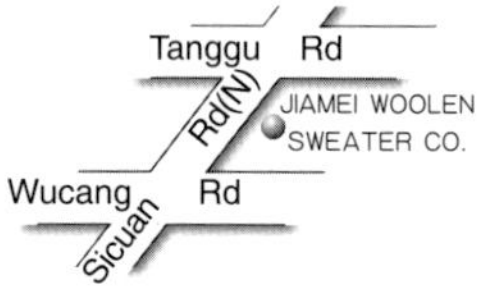

BOYANG DEPARTMENT STORE

Add: 1325 Sichuan Rd, N

Tel.: 63070746

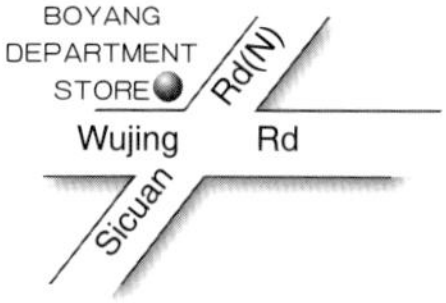

SHANGHAI SPRING DEPARTMENT STORE

Add: 521 Sichuan Rd, N

Tel.: 63570090

DONGBAO DEPARTMENT STORE

Add: 1666 Baoxing Rd, E

Tel.: 63561818x6105

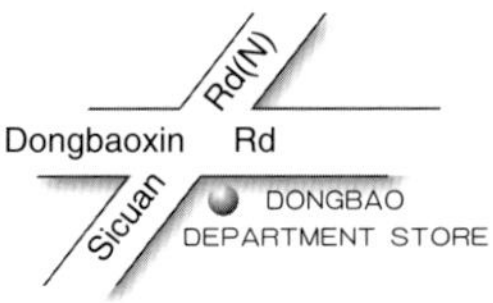

(II) COMMERCIAL CENTERS

1. IN THE SOUTH - YUYUAN TOURIST AND COMMERCIAL CITY

Yuyuan Tourist and Commercial City is located between the Yuyuan Garden and the City God Temple. The Old City God Temple area has been remolded in its first phase, still keeping its antique style. The shopping area has been expanded from its former 18,000 sq.m. to 80,000 sq.m. The shops known in the past as "a kingdom of small commodities" are now also selling large and medium commodities and specially noted for their complete collection of tourist souvenirs with local feature. Yuyuan Commercial City is a tourist shopping center, combining tourism, commerce and historic sites in one. In today's Yuyuan Commercial City tourists can find before them a number of Ming and Qing Dynasty imitation ancient buildings. Each building has upturned eaves and protruded roof corners, carved beams and painted columns, full of rich national flavor. The newly erected buildings have also adopted in their exteriors the style of Ming and Qing Dynasty gardens, but inside these imitation ancient buildings are modern shopping areas, with a feature of "antique exterior but modern interior" harmonizing with the original scenic sights and offsetting each other. It is now a tourist and shopping center offering the functions of shopping, tourism, catering and amusement.

Means of communication: Public buses 11, 42, 64, 66, 126 and 926

YUYUAN COMMERCIAL BUILDING

Add: 288 Fuyou Road

Tel.: 63732828

FUMIN STREET SMALL COMMODITIES CO.

Add: 225 Fuyou Road

Tel.: 63301690

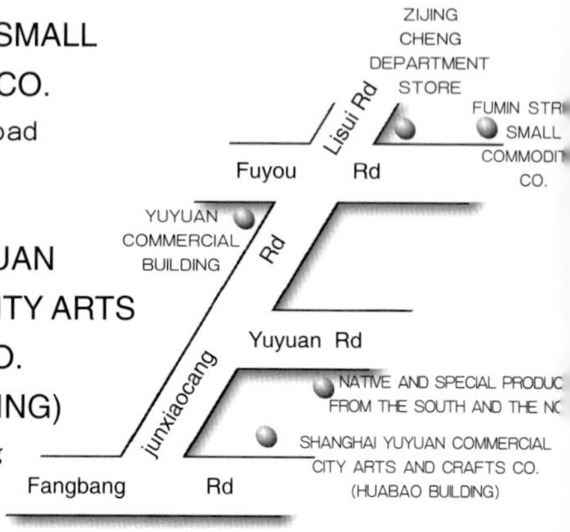

SHANGHAI YUYUAN COMMERCIAL CITY ARTS AND CRAFTS CO. (HUABAO BUILDING)

Add: 265 Fangbang Road, M

Tel.: 63559999

ZIJING CHENG DEPARTMENT STORE

Add: 81 Lishui Rd

Tel.: 63201818

NATIVE AND SPECIAL PRODUCTS FROM THE SOUTH AND THE NORTH

Add: 80 Yuyuan Road

Tel.: 63558011

2. IN THE WEST - XUJIAHUI COMMERCIAL CITY

Xujiahui Commercial City, located in the southwestern part of Shanghai, with Xujiahui Square as its center, occupies an area of 1.2 sq.km. it has been built in three stages with over 100 highrises and a total floor space of 2,000,000 sq.m.. among which 500,000 sq.m. are commercial facilities. At present, the commercial city is almost complete in scale, with a number of well-known shopping malls, restaurants and hotels, like the Oriental shopping Center,Pacitic Repantment Store Shanghai No 6 Department Store, Zhongxing Department Comercial Buildinhg, Huilian Commercial Building, Bainaohui (Center of computers), Daqian Gallery of Delicacies, Jianguo Hotel and Huating Hotel, all equipped with up-to-date commercial facilities. Here, visitors may experience the unique atmosphere of an oriental metropolis.

Means of communication: No 1 Subway Xujiahui stop and public buses 43, 15, 42, 50 and 56

ORIENTAL SHOPPING CENTER

Add: 8 Caoxi Rd, N
Tel.: 64870000

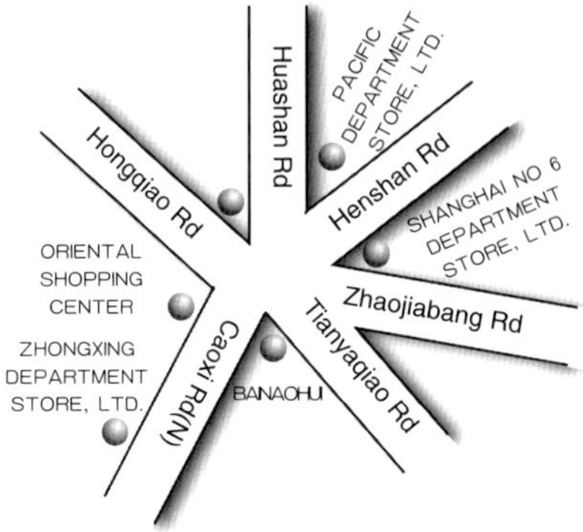

PACIFIC DEPARTMENT STORE, LTD.

Add: 932 Hengshan Road
Tel.: 64078888

SHANGHAI NO 6 DEPARTMENT STORE, LTD.

Add: 1068 Zhaojiabang Road
Tel.: 64071868

ZHONGXING DEPARTMENT STORE, LTD.

Add: 718 Caoxi Rd, N
Tel.: 64387420

BAINAOHUI

Add: 11 Caoxi Rd, N
Tel.: 64268888

3. IN THE NORTH - NEW RAILWAY STATION EVER BRIGHT CITY

New Railway Station Ever Bright City is a newly developed commercial city with Shanghai Railway Station as the center. It is still under construction. The Ever Bright City is on the site of a former most concentrated slum areas. In the past four years, with the introduction of foreign funds and a total investment of 18 billion yuan a planned construction of 3 million sq.m. floor space was taking

place on an area of 1.24 sq.km. At present, a number of modern commercial facilities, like the Japanese Jusco Department Store, Famous Brand Commercial Building, Huanlong Commercial Building, Yaxin Life Square, Xinya Square Hotel, Xinya Great Wall Hotel, Jiali Ever Bright City, East China Tourist and Commercial Building are completely changing the face of the area and turning it into an important commercial center in the city.
Means of communication: No 1 Subway Shanghai Railway Station stop and public buses 13, 18, 115, 95 and 104

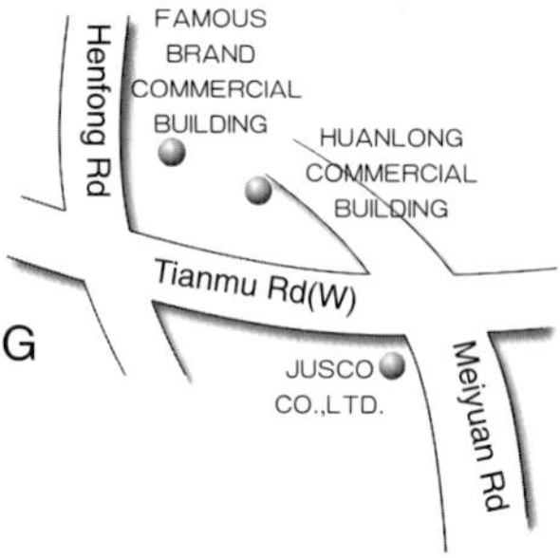

JUSCO CO.,LTD.
Add: 218 Tianmu Rd, W
Tel.: 63541110

FAMOUS BRAND COMMERCIAL BUILDING
Add: 228 Moling Road
Tel.: 63541118

HUANLONG COMMERCIAL BUILDING
Add: 360 Meiyuan Road
Tel.: 63172423

4. IN THE EAST - NEW SHANGHAI COMMERCIAL CITY

Located in the middle of Lujiazui Finance and Trade Zone, it is the largest commercial center in Pudong. It occupies an area of 14 hectares with a number of high-rises and a 600-m long pedestrian walkway. The commercial city was collectively invested with 8 billion yuan by the different commercial groups in Shanghai. The total floor space is 800,000 sq.m., of which 260,000 sq.m. are shopping areas. It is equipped with up-to-date facilities and managed by modern system with buried network piping, central heating, optical fiber communication and internet computerized. The Next-age Commercial Building within the commercial city is the first retail enterprise run by joint venture. It foretells the beginning of developing market jointly by Shanghai's commerce with international commercial groups.

Means of communication: Public buses 783, 785, 981, 01, 82, 86, 119, 773 and Tunnel line 3 and 4

NO 1 YAOHAN NEXT-AGE COMMERCIAL BUILDING

Add: 501 Zhangyang Road, Pudong

Tel.: 58301111

SHANGHAI TIMES SQUARE

Add: 500 Zhangyang Road, Pudong

Tel.: 58368888

SHANGHAI CLOTHING ARTICLES CENTER

Add: 655 Zhangyang Road, Pudong

Tel.: 58203587

(III)SPECIALTY STREETS, STREET MARKETS AND MARKETS

There are many special-featured streets and street markets in Shanghai. They are special for the commodities they deal in can form into market and trade. They have large collections of different brands of commodities of similar categories, available for the choice of customers. Some of the street markets and markets have far-reaching reputation. They attract both the domestic and overseas tourists.

FUZHOU ROAD CULTURAL STREET

A century ago, many bookstores and stationery shops were found on Fuzhou Road, which has ever since enjoyed the reputation of a cultural street. Now, about 30 bookstores and stationery shops have opened here, like China Science Bookstore, Shanghai Bookstore, Bookstore of Foreign Languages, and Ancient Bookstore. At the end of 1998, the 27-story Shanghai Book City was built and opened for business. There are many stationery shops and publishing house

business departments here. The street has become a cultural street known in the whole country.
Means of communications: No 1 Subway People's Square stop, public buses 17, 49, 123, 66 and 20

DONGTAI ROAD ANTIQUES STREET

Dongtai Road Antiques Market is a newly developed market of arts and crafts with some unique feature, dealing in old arts and crafts, including porcelain, jades, bronzes, wood articles, calligraphy and paintings, four treasures of the study (brushes, ink-sticks, ink-stones and xuan paper), embroideries, and miscellaneous articles. They mainly serve foreign consulate staff, tourists, domestic and overseas customers and arts and crafts lovers. The market has made a reputation in the country and abroad and been attracting crowds of visitors.
Means of communications: Public buses 17, 18 and 23

JIANGYIN ROAD BIRD AND FLOWER MARKET

Jiangyin Road Bird and Flower Market is the largest specialized bird and flower market in Shanghai. It is 200-m long with 100 simply built stalls. During the peak seasons of spring and autumn you can find over 300 stalls selling ornamental fish, flowers, birds, insects and plants, attracting bird and flower lovers for visit and exchanges.
Means of communications: Public buses 20, 37, 23 and 109

HUATING ROAD GARMENTS AND ORNAMENTS MARKET

Huating Road Garments and Ornaments Market is a quite popular private-run market. Since '80s many private businessmen have gathered here, dealing in clothes and small articles of ornaments. With its novel designs and styles, it has set the pace for leading the trend of fashions in Shanghai and attracted many young people who are after new fashions. It is now well-known both in the country and abroad. Here you will find many foreign visitors walking amidst new-styled clothing and ornaments.
Means of communications: No 1 Subway Changshu Road stop, public buses 15, 925 and 126

A LIST OF OTHER SPECIAL-FEATURED STREETS IN SHANGHAI

Shaoxing Road, a street of publishing houses
Duolun Road, a street of cultural celebrities
Jinling Road, a street of construction and decoration materials
Beijing Road, East, a street of hardware
Fuyou Road, a street of small articles
Xizang Road, a domestic tourists' street
Huanghe Road, a street of gourmet food
Zhapu Road, a street of gourmet food
Yunnan Road, South, a street of snack bars
Xiangyang Road, South, a street of electric appliances
Weihai Road, a street of automobile accessories
Zhongshan Road, North, a street of materials
East Damin Road, a street of shipping agencies
Wuyi Road, a market of fishing articles
Yuyuan Small Articles Market
Yishan Road, a market of building materials
Liulin Road, a market of woolen sweaters
Liuying Road, a market of lamps and lanterns
Wuyuan Road, a market of agricultural and non-staple products
Yongjia Road, a market of fresh flowers
Shiliupu fruit wholesale markets
Caoan Road, a market of light industrial and textile products
Ganshu Road, a market of lamps and lanterns
Liuhe Road Antiques Market
Lugong Stamp Trading Market
Wujiaochang, a market of plywood trade
Shanghai Business Center Household Electric Appliances Market
Golden Bay Tourist Trade Market
Hengda Ceramic Building Material Market
Fengze Stationery Wholesale Market
Golden Coast Lease Center

(IV) FEATURED AND SPECIALIZED STORES

1. ARTS AND CRAFTS/CULTURAL RELICS

Arts and Crafts Commercial Building

Add: 190–208 Nanjing Rd, W
Tel.: 63276530
Means of communications:
Public buses 20, 37 and 921

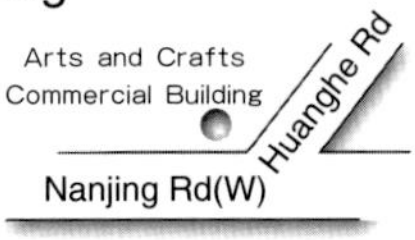

Jingdezhen Artistic Porcelain Co.

Add: 1185 Nanjing Rd, W
Tel.: 62530885
Means of communications:
Public buses 20, 37 and 921

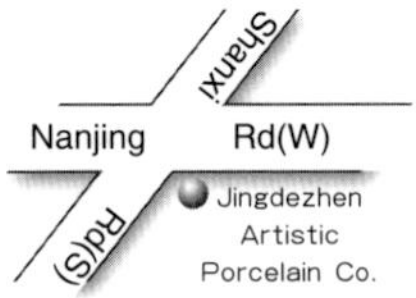

Cultural Relic Store

Add: 192–240 Guangdong Road
Tel.: 63212864
Means of communications:
Public buses 20, 55 and 65

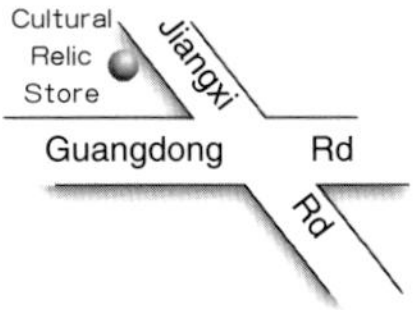

Shanghai Municipal Arts and Crafts Trade Fair Co.

Add: 1000 Yanan Rd, M
Tel.: 62790279
Means of communications: Public buses 71, 127 and 48

Yuyuan Commercial City Arts and Crafts Co.

Add: 265 Fangbang Rd, M
Tel.: 63559999
Means of communications: Public buses 11, 126 and 926

Lanxing Jewelry and Cultural Relic Firm

Add: 398 Changle Road
Tel.: 62551667
Means of communications:

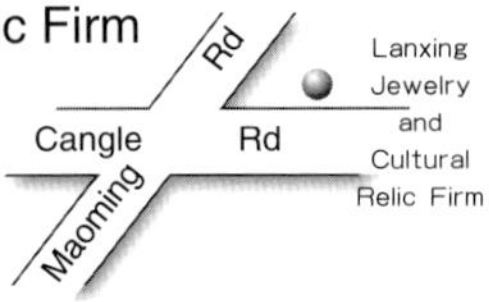

Public buses 125 and 926

Tiehuaxuan Purple Sand and Ceramics Store

Add: 68 Yuyuan Road
Tel.: 63559999x6154
Means of communications:
Public buses 11, 126 and 926

Fuguang Folk Arts and Cra

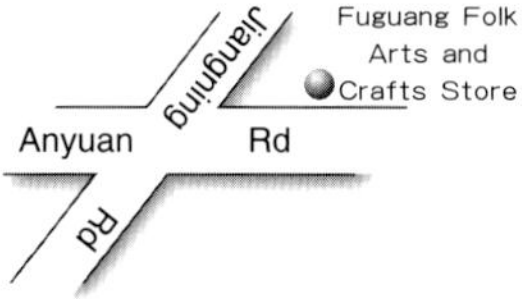

Add: 84 Anyuan Road
Tel.: 62660402
Means of communications:
Public buses 113 and 76

Duoyunxuan Painting Studio

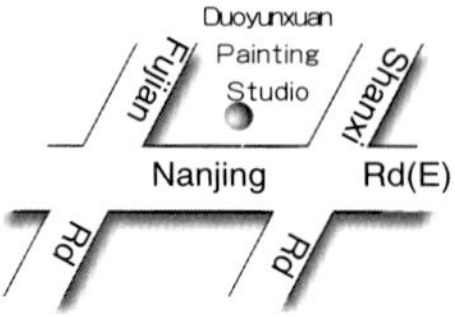

Add: 422 Nanjing Rd, E
Tel.: 63510063
Means of communications:
Public buses 20, 37 and 921

Shanghai Friendship Store

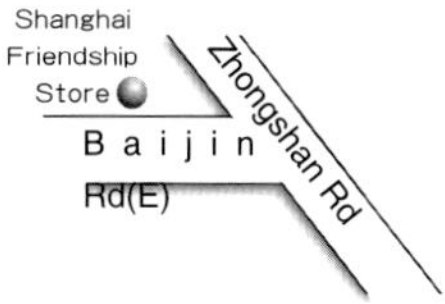

Add: 40 Beijing Rd, E
Tel.: 53080600
Means of communications:
Public buses 20, 921 and 37

2. BOOKSTORES/STATIONERIES

Shanghai Book City

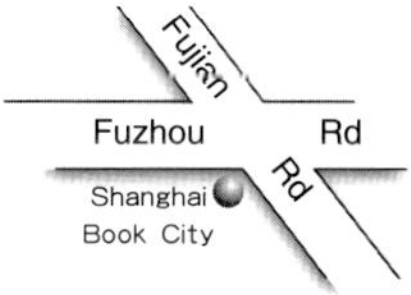

Add: 465 Fuzhou Road
Tel.: 63522222
Means of communications:
Public buses 49, 123 and 17

Xinhua Bookstore

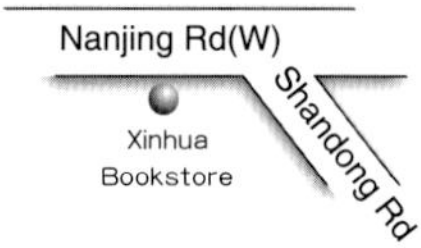

Add: 345 Nanjing Rd, W
Tel.: 63222964
Means of communications:
20, 921 and 37

Science Bookstore

Add: 221 Henan Rd, M

Tel.: 63234567

Means of communications:

Public buses 49. 123and 17

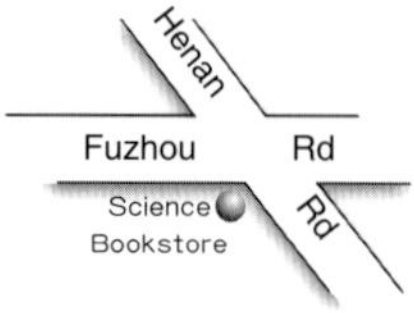

Art Bookstore

Add: 42 Huashan Road

Tel.: 62483080

Means of communications:

Public buses 15, 93 and 42

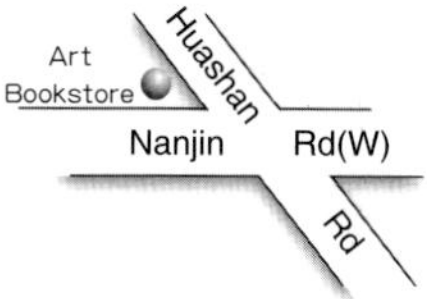

Foreign Languages Bookstore

Add: 390 Fuzhou Road

Tel.: 63223200

Means of communications:

Public buses 49, 123 and 17

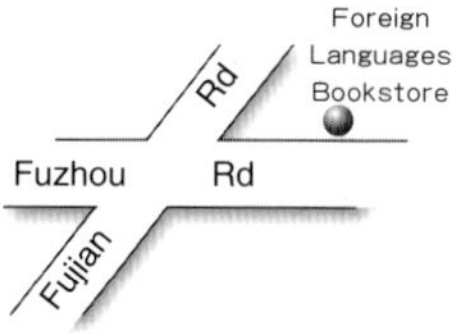

Shanghai Ancient Bookstore

Add: 424 Fuzhou Road

Tel.: 63224984

Means of communications:

Public buses 49, 123 and 17

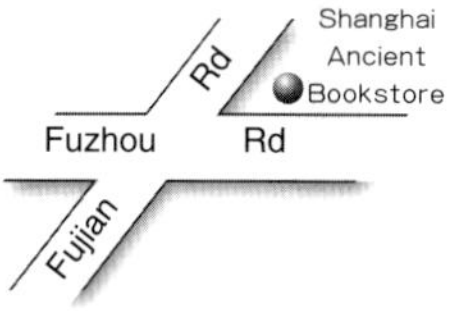

Music Bookstore

Add: 365 Xizang Rd, M

Tel.: 63223213

Means of communications:

Public buses 49, 123, 17 and 145

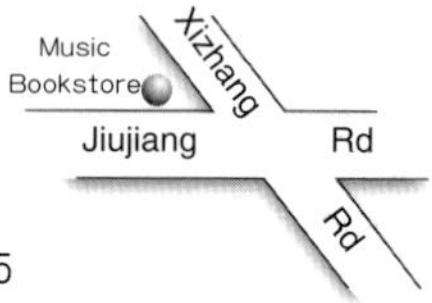

Reference Bookstore

Add: 856 Sichuan Rd, N

Tel.: 63246555

Means of communications:

Public buses 17 and 21

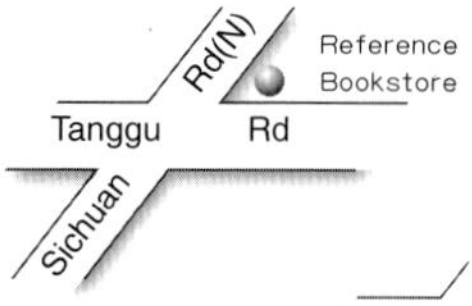

Liyunge Paper and Pen Store

Add: 35 Yuyuan Road

Tel.: 63289850

Means of communications: Public

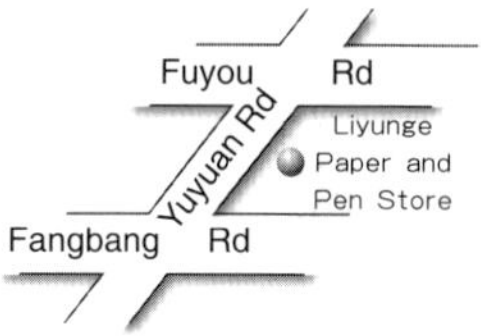

Old Zhou Hucheng Brush Store

Add: 90 Henan Rd, M

Tel.: 63297959

Means of communications:

Public buses 66, 17 and 49

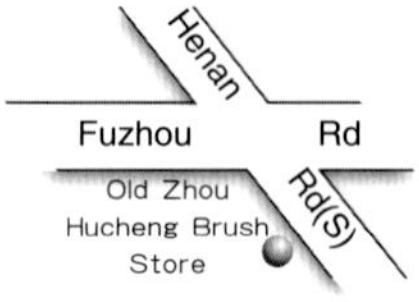

Yang Zhenhua Brush Store

Add: 290 Fuzhou Road

Tel.: 63223117

Means of communications:

Public buses 17, 49 and 123

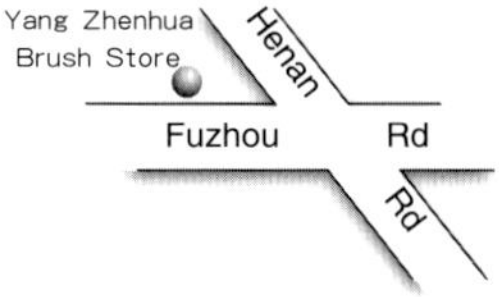

Shanghai-Hong Kong Sanlian Bookstore

Add: 628 Huaihai Rd, M

Tel.: 53064393

Means of communications:

Public buses 42, 926 and 911

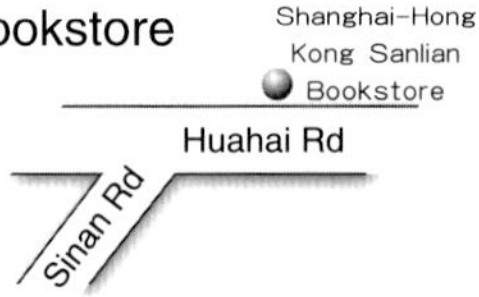

3. FABRICS/GARMENTS AND ORNAMENTS, HATS AND SHOES

Laojiefu Woolen and Silk Fabric Store

Add: 257 Nanjing Rd, E

Tel.: 63213221

Means of communications:

Public buses 20, 37 and 921

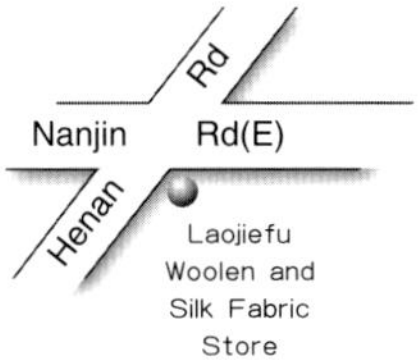

Sunlight Commercial building

Add: 580 Nanjing Rd, E

Tel.: 63220271

Means of communications:

Public buses 20, 37 and 921

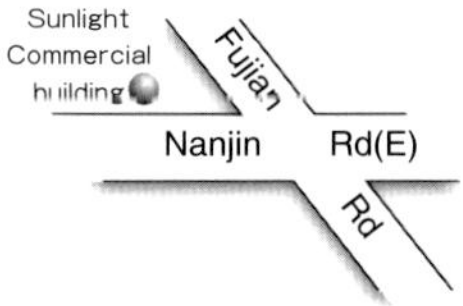

Hongxiang Fashionable Clothing Co.

Add: 723 Nanjing Rd, W

Tel.: 62178590

Means of communications:

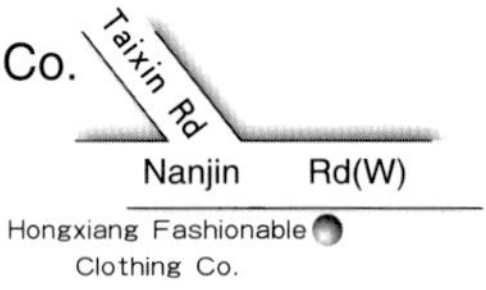

Public buses 20, 37 and 921

Hengyuanxiang Woolen Yarn Store

Add: 358 Jinling Rd, E

Tel.: 63268888

Means of communications:

Public buses 126 and 17

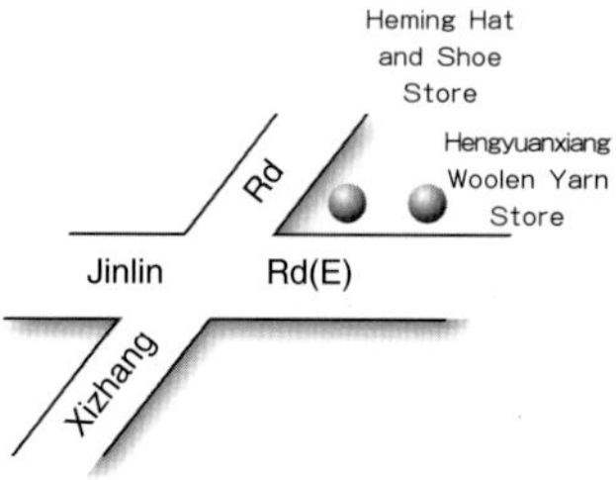

Heming Hat and Shoe Store

Add: 480 Jinling Rd, E

Tel.: 63877575

Means of communications:

Public buses 126 and 17

Peiluomen Western-style Clothes Store

Add: 580 Nanjing Rd, E

Tel.: 63226611

Means of communications:

Public buses 20, 37 and 921

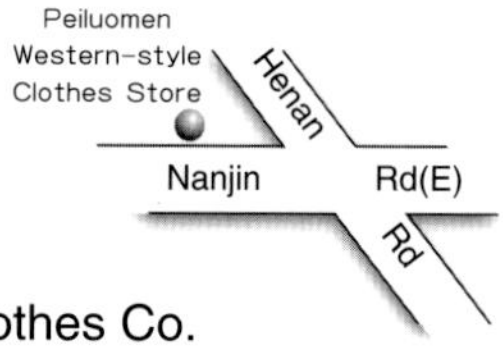

Hengsheng Western-style Clothes Co.

Add: 1135 Nanjing Rd, W

Tel.: 62728864

Means of communications:

Public buses 20, 37 and 921

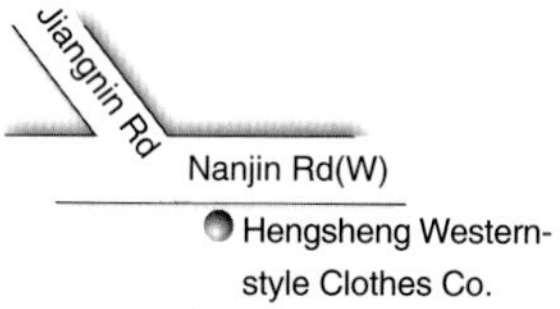

Shengxifu Hat Store

Add: 715 Hankou Road

Tel.: 63223240

Means of communications:

Public buses 20, 37 and 921

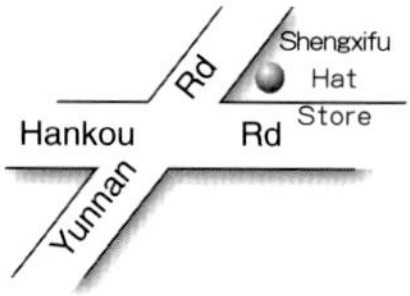

Pengjie Women's Clothing Store

Add: 154 Nanjing Rd, E

Tel.: 63234316

Means of communications:

Public buses 20, 37 and 921

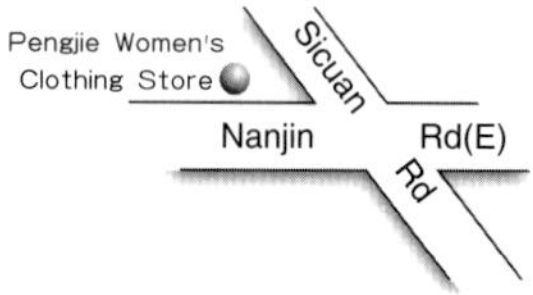

Gujin Brassiere Co.

Add: 867 Huaihai Rd, M

Tel.: 64733108

Means of communications:

Public buses 42, 24 and 926

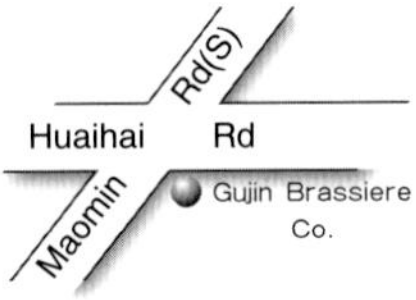

4. FOODSTUFF/NATIVE AND SPECIAL PRODUCTS

Wanyouquan Gured Meat Store

Add: 89 Donemen Road

Tel.: 63185049

Means of communications:

Public buses 55, 65 and 11

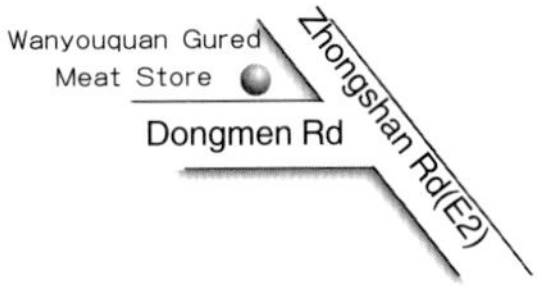

Sichuan-Hunan Seasoning Food Store

Add: 265 Jinling Rd, E

Tel.: 63556373

Means of communications:

Public buses 17, 66 and 126

Dafeng Native and Special Foodstuff Store

Add: 198 Xizang Rd, M

Tel.: 63226365

Means of communications:

Public buses 49, 123, 17 and 145

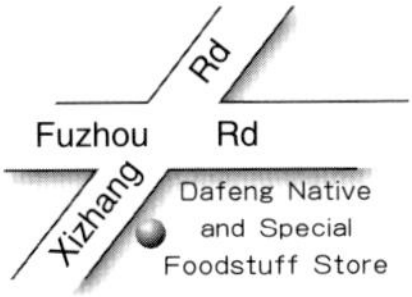

Guanshengyuan Foodstuff Store

Add: 555 Jinling Rd, E

Tel.: 63282473

Means of communications:

Public buses 126 and 17

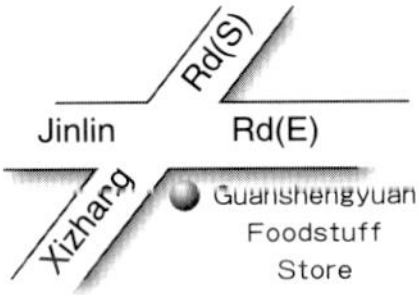

Laodachang Foodstuff Store

Add: 558 Huaihai Rd, M

Tel.: 63583537

Means of communications:

Public buses 42, 911 and 926

Linanju Foodstuff Store

Add: 149 Lane Shitan, Tianjin Road

Tel.: 63516108

Means of communications:

Public buses 20, 37 and 921

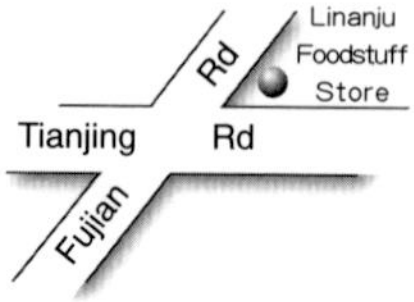

All-China Native and Special Foodstuff Store

Add: 491 Huaihai Rd, M

Tel.: 63721446

Means of communications:

Public buses 42, 911 and 926

Shaowansheng Store of Delicacies from South China

Add: 414 Nanjing Rd, E

Tel.: 63223907

Means of communications:

Public buses 20, 37 and 921

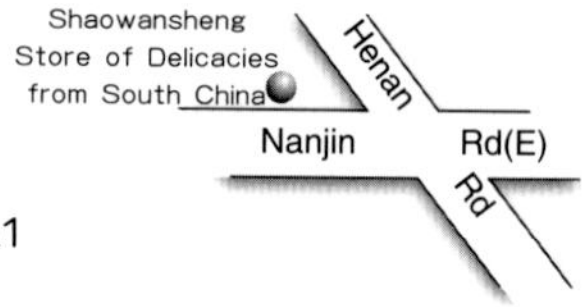

Five-flavored Broad Beans S

Add: 104 Yuyuan Road

Tel.: 63559999x1332

Means of communications:

Public buses 11, 126 and 926

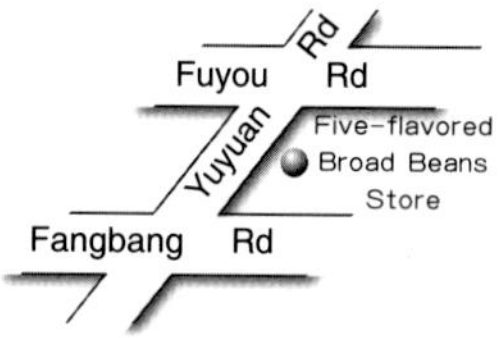

Yidinghao Foodstuff Store

Add: 2045 Sichuang Rd, N

Tel.: 56668947

Means of communications:

Public buses 17 and 21

5. SCISSORS/FANS

Zhang Xiaoquan Scissors Store

Add: 490 Nanjing Rd, E

Tel.: 63223858

Means of communications:

Public buses 20, 37 and 921

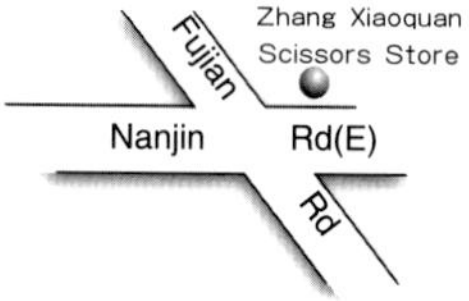

Wangxingji Fans Store

Add: 155 Xizang Rd, S

Tel.: 63260160

Means of communications:

Public buses 20, 37 and 921

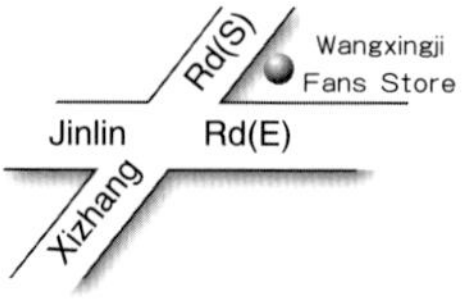

6. PHARMACEUTICALS

Shanghai No 1 Pharmaceutical Store

Add: 616 Nanjing Rd, E

Tel.: 63224567

Means of communications:

Public buses 20, 37 and 921

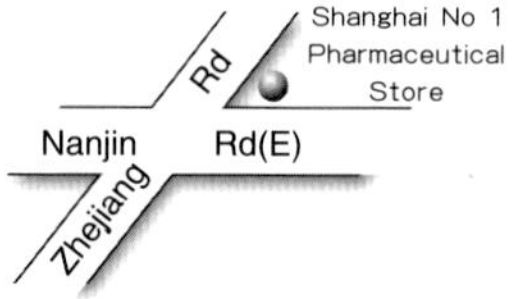

Leiyunshang Traditional Chinese Medicine Store (North Branch)

Add: 1384 Sichuan Rd, N

Tel.: 63243038

Means of communications:

Public buses 21 and 17

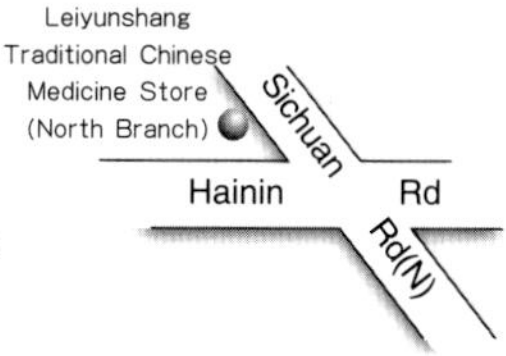

Huqingyutang

Traditional chinese Medicine Store

Add: 370 Xinzha Road

Tel.: 63276385

Means of communications:

Public buses 18, 21 and 15

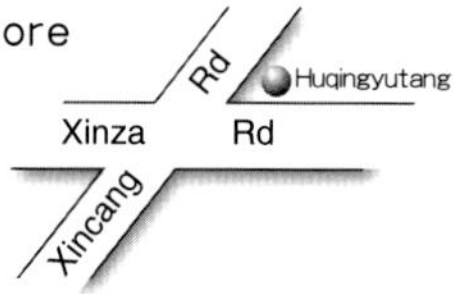

Leiyunshang Traditional Chinese Medicine Store (Western Branch)

Add: 719 Nanjing Rd, W

Tel.: 62552708

Means of communications:

Public buses 20, 37 and 921

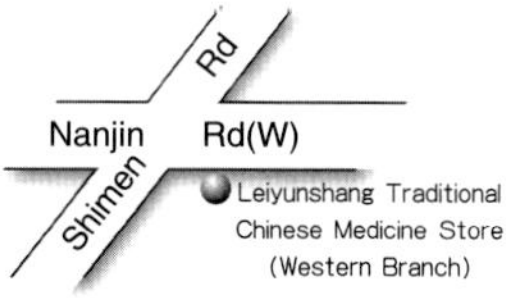

Caitongde Traditional Chinese Medicine Store

Add: 450 Nanjing Rd, E

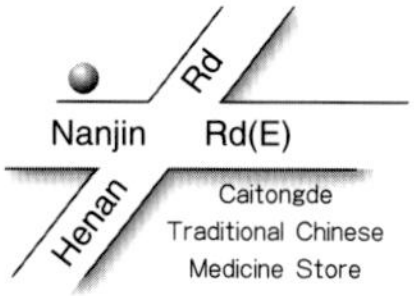

Tel.: 63221259

Means of communications: Public buses 20, 37 and 821

Tonghanchun Traditional Chinese Medicine Store

Add: 493-501 Yanan Rd, E

Tel.: 63866558

Means of communications:

Public buses 71, 127 and 145

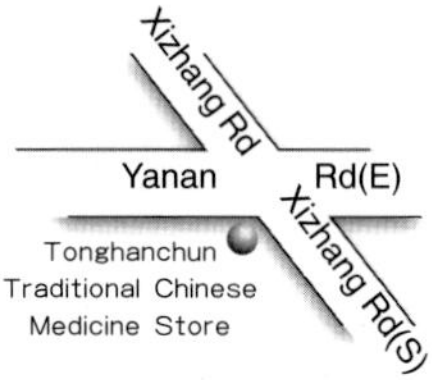

7. CLOCKS AND WATCHES/SPECTACLES

Shanghai Clock and Watch Store

Add: 478-492 Huaihai Rd, M

Tel.: 53826722

Means of communications:

Public buses 42, 911 and 926

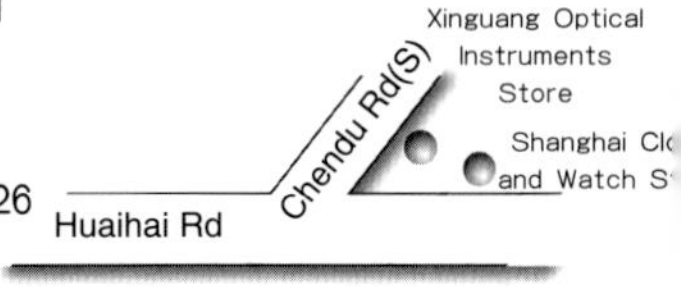

Xinguang Optical Instruments Store

Add: 538-540 Huaihai Rd, M

Tel.: 63275111

Means of communications:

Public buses 42, 911 and 926

Hengdali Clock and Watch Store

Add: 262 Nanjing Rd, E

Tel.: 63291514

Means of communications:

Public buses 20, 37 and 921

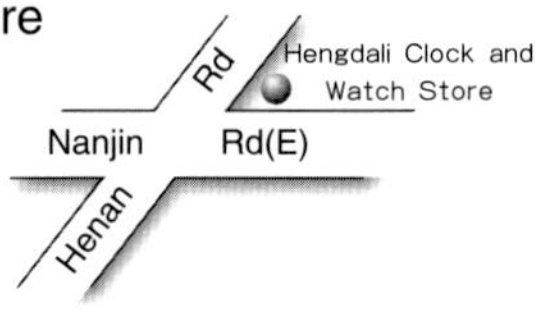

Wuliangcia Spectacles Store

Add: 191 Nanjing Rd, E

Tel.: 63514540

Means of communications:

Public buses 20, 37 and 921

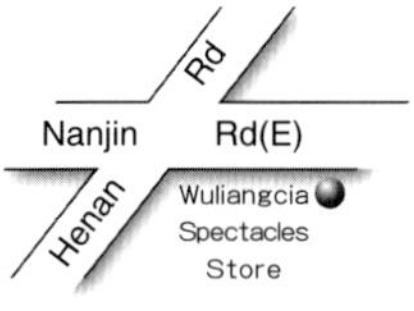

Maochang Spectacles Store

Add: 762 Nanjing Rd, E

Tel.: 63223839

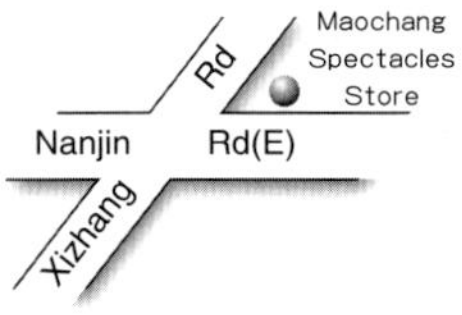

Means of communications: Public buses 20, 37 and 921

Paris Three Cities

Add: 1351 Sichuan Rd, N
Tel.: 63574345
Means of communications:
Public buses 17 and 21

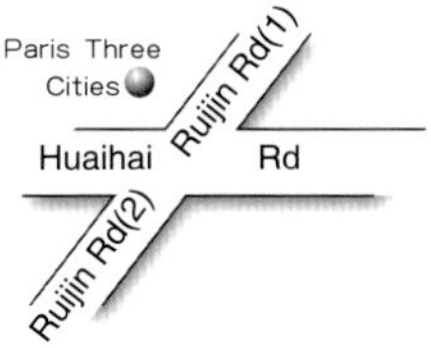

Hongxing Spectacles Store

Add: 598 Huaihai Rd, M
Tel.: 63840019
Means of communications:
Public buses 42, 911 and 926

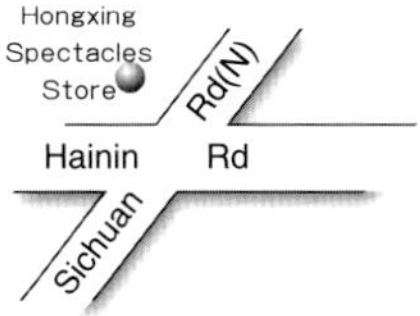

PROPOSED TOUR OF METROPOLITAN SHOPPING

One-day tour of metropolitan sightseeing and shopping
Morning: Visit Yuyuan Commercial City and lunch
Afternoon: Sightseeing on Huaihai Road and Xujiahui and dinner
Evening: Night view on Nanjing Road - China's No I Shopping Street and shopping

Two-day tour of metropolitan sightseeing and shopping

1st day:
Morning: Tour Sichuan Road, North, and lunch
Afternoon: Visit Pudong New Commercial City (No 1 Yaohan Next-age) and dinner
Evening: Night view on Nanjing Road -- China's No 1 Shopping Street and shopping
2nd day:
Morning: People's Square - Hong Kong Famous Brand Street - Huaihai Road and lunch
Afternoon: Tour Huaihai Road and Xujiahui Commercial City
Evening: Tour Yuyuan Commercial City

RECOMMENDED TRAVEL SERVICE
SHANGHAI HUATING OVERSEAS TOURIST CO.

Add: F/4, 503 Wulumuqi Rd, N

Tel.: 62491234
Fax: 62485470,62482781
Post Code: 200040

SHANGHAI JINJIANG TOURS LTD.

Add: 191 Changle Road
Tel.: 64662828
Fax: 64662297
Post Code: 200020

SHANGHAI CYTS TOURS CORPORATION

Add: 2 Hengshan Road
Tel.: 64331826, 64331907
Fax: 64330507
Post Code: 200031

SHANGHAI CHINA INTERNATIONAL TRAVEL SERVICE CO., LTD

Add: CITS Building, 1277 Beijing Rd, W
Tel.: 62898899
Fax: 62894928
Post Code: 200040

SHANGHAI CHINA TRAVEL SERVICE

Add: 881 Yanan Rd, M
Tel.: 62478888, 62475770
Fax: 62475521
Post Code: 200040

AMUSEMENT

Shanghai is China's largest industrial, commercial, financial, scientific and cultural center. In the '20s and '30s it used to be a very prosperous metropolis in the Far East, an ever bright city with glistening lights; its recreation trade had been flourishing and quite developed. Today, with the reform and opening to the outside world, Shanghai of the '90s is marching in the front of China's reform and opening up with a completely new face and is building up a new Shanghai of the 21st century. Shanghai's relaxing and recreation trade, after decades of lying low, began to develop continually with more vitality and in healthy forms to meet the recreational needs of Shanghai citizens and visitors from other parts of the country and abroad.

(I) THEME PARKS AND AMUSEMENT CENTERS

With the increase of the tempo of people in life and work of a modern metropolis, people yearn to embrace nature in holidays away from the hustle and bustle of the city. In recent years, many holiday resorts and amusement centers with the theme of "leisure" and "nature" have been developed. Pleasant natural scenery combined with modern cultural and recreational facilities help people to relax their body and mind after work, to breathe fresh air and stretch themselves to experience the pleasure of returning to nature.

DONGPING STATE FOREST PARK

Dongping State Forest Park is located in the mid northern part of Chongming Island - the third largest island in China. In 1997, it was commended as one of the "ten best tourist attractions" in Shanghai. The park, covering an area of 358 hectares, is the largest forest park in Shanghai and also the largest man-made forest on plains in China. The park, sending forth the fresh air of a forest, is full of natural scenery. Citizens, crossing the river, come to spend their holidays in leisurely pleasure. Water sports, swimming, sand beach volleyball, hunting in the forest offer people with enchanting pleasure. The forest convalescence center and little log cottages help to wipe out all people's fatigue and worries.

Add: Chongming County

Tel.: 59641592

Means of communication: No 5 tourist bus

CHANGXING ISLAND ORANGE ORCHARD

Changxing Island covers an area of 76.32 sq.km. It is reputed as a green jadeite for its "pure soil, pure air and pure water". The orchard is located in the middle of the island, occupying an area of 451.67 hectares. It is the largest production site of the "green food". There are rockeries, long corridors, a potted landscape garden, a Mongolian village with yurts, a horse track, a conch hall, and a hotel entertaining visitors with each of their own attractive characteristics. In autumn, amidst the ripe fruit in the orange orchard, visitors may feel the joy of a bumper harvest.

Add: Qianwei Farm, Changxing Island, Baoshan District

Tel.: 56850883

Means of communication: Public buses 51, 116 to Wusong Road Wharf and take the ferry

SHENSHAN STATE FOREST PARK

Shenshan State Forest Park, located in the city's near suburbs in the state's tourist holiday area, is a state-level forest park, consisting of 12 hill: the Eastern and Western Shenshan Hill, Tianma, Phoenix, Little Kunshan Hills etc.. The main rhythm of the park is "returning to nature". Along with the restoration of a number of cultural relics about a dozen of new tourist attractions and recreational facilities have been built to meet the needs of tourists. There are the Mind Rinsing Fountain, Dragon Riding Dam, Forest Bathing Ground, a Hundred-bird Garden, a Deer Farm, the Pearl-Protecting Pagoda and the Virtuous Priest Pagoda, all attracting peoeple with infinite charm. The scenery was built of bamboo and with bamboo in the main, flowers blooming and birds chirping, every spring all year round, quiet and peaceful, the park is an ideal place for tourists to spend their summer holidays.

Add: Sheshan State Tourist Area

Tel.: 57653328

Means of communication: No 1 tourist bus

WILDLIFE ZOO

Located in Sanzhao Town, Pudong, the Wildlife Zoo occupies an

area of 153 hectares and 35 km away from downtown. The zoo is arranged according to the living habits of the wild animals, imitating their natural habitat. It is divided into the herbivore free grazing area, the carnivore free preying area, the flamingo area, the scattered keeping area, the water foul lake and the precious animal enclosure area, all together 10,000 heads of 200 species. In the zoo visitors will feel as if they are in the kingdom of animals.
Add: Sanzhao Town, Nanhui County
Tel.: 58036000
Means of communication: No 2 tourist bus

GONGQING FOREST PARK

Located in the northeast of Shanghai and on the Huangpu River, it is the largest forest park in Shanghai downtown. There are over 300,000 trees of 90 species, hilly lawns, lakes and streams. It is divided into 3 scenic areas: the eastern part along the Huangpu River is the forest area; in the middle is the watery area with a water surface of 90,000 sq.m.; and the western part is the mountain and jungle area. Visitors can take a walk in the forests, angle in the lake and enjoy the barbecue in Mongolian yurts and appreciate the pleasure of nature.
Add: 2000 Jungong road
Tel.: 65740586
Means of communication: Public buses 75, 102, 124 and 841

AMERICAN DREAMLAND PARK

The American Dreamland Park is located in Huangdu Town, Jiading, 20 km from downtown, near the 312 state highway, 2 km from Shanghai-Nanjing Railway Huangdu stop and 3 km from the entry to Shanghai-Nanjing Freeway, very convenient in communications. It is a park expressing the style of an American theme park. The first stage of development covered 33 hectares of land, consisting of 5 themes: the colorful highway, the desolate West, the source of the European continent, wonderland of a fairy island and today's America. There are more than 50 tourist attractions and motorized games and over 100 actors staging and 20 interesting shows. Besides, there are 20 restaurants and souvenir shops and brightly lit night garden sending off fireworks. Visitors can enjoy themselves to their hearts' content and experience the leisurely pleasure of American life.

Add: 4498 Caoan Road, Huangdu Town, Jiading District

Tel.: 59598686

Means of communication: No 6 tourist bus B line

JINJIANG AMUSEMENT PARK

Jinjiang Amusement Park is a large-scale modern amusement park in Shanghai opened in the '80s. With its advanced recreational facilities, like the single-ring slide-car, water surfing, single-rail car, wooden horse merry-go-round, revolving chairs in the air, lotus pan, foot-peddled single track car, bumping cars, roller coaster, flying disc boat and laser shooting, attract a great number of tourists. Now, many new sports games have been added, such as high platform speed adjustable sliding, rock and roll sliding, 45℃ wave surfing, and massage pool. Visitors may choose their favorable items besides sightseeing and watching, finding pleasure in excitement and suspension and tempering their courage and increasing wisdom.

Add: 201 Hongmei Road

Tel.: 64364956

Means of communication: No 1 Subway Hongmei Road stop, public buses 50, 93 and Xumin line

CLCC OCEAN WORLD

CLCC Sea World is located inside the 80,000-seat Indoor Stadium. It has two levels. It is a large-scale amusement center combining water sports, sports, leisure, performance by sea animals, and catering in one. The sea world collects the best amusement items from Hong Kong Sea Park. There is an indoor theater, a man-made Hawaii waves and sand beach, 007 deep sea adventure submarine, a happy childhood children's swimming pool, extra wide water sliding channel and drifting in tropical jungle, plus many sea world sights.

Add: 666 Tianyaoqiao Road

Tel.: 64266066

Means of communication: No 1 Subway 80,000-seat Indoor, Stadium stop and public buses 15, 42, 926, 43 and 89

SHANGHAI FILM AND TV AMUSEMENT PARK

Many street scenes in Shanghai that have disappeared or are disappearing are reproduced here. Wooden wire posts, door and windwos frames are historical relics of appreciative value.

Add: 4915 North Songgong Rd, East Dun Town, Songjiang District

TEL.: 57601627

Means of communication: No 1 tourist bus

OCEAN WORLD

The Ocean World is located in Changfeng Park under the Silver Axe Lake, the largest lake in downtown Shanghai. It is the first aquarium with a new concept in Shanghai. There is a assimilated airport, a relic site of Peru's Inca ancient temple culture, Amazon valley, fisherman's cottage by the seaside, all of these are interesting attractions. In the ocean-bed world you can see many rare ocean-bed creatures and experience a world full of wonders.

Add: 451 Daduhe Road

Tel.: 52818888

Means of communication: Public buses 94, 837, 44, 67 and 754

SHESHAN STATE TOURIST HOLIDAY RESORT

Add: Sheshan Town, Songjiang District

Tel.: 57653328

Means of communication: No 1 tourist bus

SUNNY ISLAND INTERNATIONAL CLUB

Add: Taiyang Island, Shengang Town, Qingpu County

Tel.: 59830888

Means of communication: Special bus line

GREAT WORLD AMUSEMENT CENTER

Add: 1 Xizang Rd, S

Tel.: 63263760

Means of communication: Public buses 46, 145, 49 and 783

TROPICAL TEMPEST

Add: 78 Xinzhen Road

Tel.: 64783333

Means of communication: Special bus line

(II) PERFORMANCES AND MOVIES

Shanghai is an internationalized metropolis, having a number of performance troupes well-known both at home and abroad, such as Shanghai Symphony Orchestra, Shanghai Ballet Troupe, Shanghai Beijing Opera Troupe, Shanghai Drama Troupe, Shanghai Local Opera Troupe, Shanghai Shaoxing Opera Troupe, Shanghai Farce Troupe, Shanghai Acrobatics Troupe, and the Old Men Jazz Band in Peace Hotel. They often give performances of symphony, ballet, national folk dance, national folk music, acrobatics, magic show, opera and other plays and folk art forms. Besides, famous performance groups, singers and orchestras from abroad often come to perform in Shanghai and make performance tours in our country. Thus, Shanghai's performance market is always very active. Shanghai citizens have the opportunity of enjoying all kinds of art performances, adding much an atmosphere of refined art to people's leisure and recreational life.

The movie house is also a place for people to spend their leisure time and enjoy themselves. There are several dozens of movie houses in Shanghai located in every corner of the city. Those located in downtown, having been remodeled and equipped with up-to-date movie facilities, are producing greater effect in the appreciation of the movies. Every year, the famous movies made in the country and imported from abroad are attracting a great number of movie goers.

SHANGHAI FILM CITY

Add: 160 Xinhua Road

Tel.: 62806088

Means of communication: Public buses 48 and 76

GRAND CINEMA

Add: 216 Nanjing Rd W

Tel.: 63274260

Means of communication: Public buses 20, 37 and 921

YONGLE PALACE

Add: 308 Anfu Road

Tel.: 64312961

Means of communication: Public buses 48 and 113

PINGAN DYNAMIC MOVIE HOUSE

Add: 1193 Nanjing Rd, W

Tel.: 62473007

Means of communication: Public buses 20, 37 and 921

SHANGHAI GRAND THEATER

Add: 190 Huangpi Rd, N

Tel.: 63875480

Means of communication: Public buses 46, 71, 49 and 127

SHANGHAI MUSIC HALL

Add: 523 Yanan Rd, E

Tel.: 63869153

Means of communication: Public buses 46, 71, 49 and 127

MAJESTIC THEATER

Add: 66 Jiangning Road

Tel.: 62174409

Means of communication: Public buses 112, 13 and 20

LYCEM THEATER

Add: 57 Maoming Road

Tel.: 62178530

Means of communication: Public buses 42 and 126

CHINA THEATER

Add: 704 Niuzhuang Road

Tel.: 63517839

Means of communication: Public buses 20, 37 and 921

TIANCHAN OPERA CENTER YIFU THEATER

Add: 701 Fuzhou Road

Tel.: 63514668

Means of communication: Public buses 17, 49 and 123

SHANGHAI CENTER THEATRE

Add: 1376 Nanjing Rd, W

Tel.: 62798663

Means of communication: Public buses 20, 37 and 921

OLD MEN JAZZ BAND

Add: 20 Nanjing Rd, E

Tel.: 63216888x6210

Means of communication: Public buses 20, 37, 22 and 55

SHANGHAI CIRCUS CITY

Add: 2666 Gonghexin Road

Tel.: 66527550

Means of communication: Public buses 46, 95, and 114

DRAMA INSTITUTE EXPERIMENTAL THEATER

Add: 670 Huashan Road

Tel.: 62485600

Means of communication: 48, 113 and 71

(III) TEA HOUSES AND STORY-TELLING AND BALLAD SINGING THEATER

Shanghai's tea houses began in the early years of Qing Emperor Tongzhi's reign. The Mid-lake Pavilion Tea House in Yuyuan Garden, Songyuan Garden and Wangyiji Tea House have always enjoyed popularity. Beginning from the 20th century, affected by the social customs of the Western countries and Japan, music tea-booths and open- air tea stalls began to take place in Shanghai. Shanghai's story-telling and ballad-singing theaters have a long history. Shanghai people, especially the elderly, love to listen to stories and ballads. At present, such theaters are decreasing in number. However, the middle-aged and the elderly still love to stay in tea houses or story-telling and ballad-singing theaters, enjoying themselves over a cup of tea and chatting with friends.

MID-LAKE PAVILION TEA HOUSE IN CITY GOD TEMPLE

Add: 257 Yuyuan Road

Tel.: 63736950

Means of communication: Public buses 11 and 126

WANGYIJI TEA HOUSE

Add: 38 Jinling Rd, M

Tel.: 63866155

Means of communication: Public buses 126, and 926

SONGYUAN TEA HOUSE

Add: 1667 Gonghexin Road

Tel.: 56334409

Means of communication: Public buses 46, 95 and 114

TIANTIANWANG TEA ART CEREMONY HOUSE

Add: 48 Lane 1088 Yuyuan Road

Tel.: 62125758

Means of communication: Public buses 20 and 57

RED STAR BALLAD SINGING THEATRE

Add: 1357 Sichuan Rd, N

Tel.: 63065161

Means of communication: Public buses 18 and 21

XIZANG BALLAD SINGING THEATRE

Add: 704 Niuzhuang Road

Tel.: 63225270

Means of communication: Public buses 20 and 14

(IV) AMUSEMENT IN FASHION

1. A STREET FOR LEISURELY ENJOYMENT - HENGSHAN ROAD

Hengshan Road in Shanghai is only 2-km long, but on both of its sides are several dozens of big and small amusement facilities. It is, therefore, known as a street of leisurely enjoyment. The street is an avenue with European atmosphere. There are luxuriant French planes on both sidewalks and many buildings of European-style architecture of the '20s and '30s. In the evening, many well-dressed people and young people in fashionable clothing come here to take a walk, play chess or cards in the tea club, have a drink in the bar, while listening to music, spend some time in the bowling room or discotheque, enjoying themselves freely.

Add: Hengshan Road

Means of communication: No 1 Subway Hengshan Road stop and public buses 15 and 93

2. BUNGI

Bungi is a challenging sport. It is a game of tieing oneself to a piece of string to face death. Once introduced into China it has attracted the interest of many courageous people. On July 1998, Shanghai Jinjiang Amusement Park built the first diving tower in Shanghai, 25-m high. There is a thick protecting mattress on the ground. Though every jump costs 88 yuan, it still attracts many young people. Among them the majority are tourists. A leap is an adventure that is exciting and thrilling. It is a game for the brave.

Add: 201 Hongmei Road

Tel.: 64364956

Means of communication: No 1 Subway Hongmei Road stop and public buses 50, 93 and Xu-Min bus line

3. KARTING CAR

In Shanghai driving a karting car gives an impression of a fashionable game to many young people. This sport was introduced to China in 1995 and it has developed rapidly. In 1998, there were already 29 karting race courses in Shanghai. Among them the Fushida and Magnolia race courses have been approved for C-grade international races. The car gives a feeling that you are riding speedily 4-mm from the ground, twice of the normal speed, just like driving a F-1 race car, giving you much excitement and thrill. The number of such race courses are increasing in number and the prices are reducing enabling many of the general public to experience the pleasure of excitement.

SHANGHAI FUSHIDA RACING KART CO.,LTD.

Add: Binghai Tourist Holiday Resort

Tel.: 58291000x646

Means of communication: Special bus line

SSC KARTING CLUB, LTD.

Add: 666 Tianyaoqiao Road

Tel.: 64265180

Means of communication: No 1 Subway Indoor Stadium stop and public buses 42, 926 and 49

FUZDA KARTING CAR CLUB

Add: 880 Zhongshan Rd, N 1

Tel.: 65316800

Means of communication: Public buses 139, 502 and 217

SHANGHAI JIANGCHENG CAR RACING CENTER

Add: 3055 Zhoujiazui Road

Tel.: 65180759

Means of communication: Public buses 8 and 22

DISC KART KARTING HALL

Add: 326 Aomen Road

Tel.: 62775641

Means of communication: Public buses 112, 40 and 76

GENERAL PROSPEROUS KARTING HALL

Add: 777 Wuyi Road

Tel.: 62346138

Means of communication: Public buses 70, 57 and 96

4. CLIFF CLIMBING

Cliff climbing is a very challenging sport. It is a perfect

combination of strength and suppleness. It is necessary for the climber to have a strong physique, strength in the muscles of his arms, fingers, legs, feet and waist and more important, to have pliability, flexibility and concert. For this reason it attracts many people to challenge themselves and try their own strength.

OUTDOOR IMITATION CLIFF CLIMBING AMUSEMENT PARK

Add: Dongping State Forest Park in Chongming
Tel.: 59641592
Means of communication: No 5 tourist bus

5. INTERNET BAR

American president Clinton visited the 3C +T Internet Bar while in Shanghai and made it more popular. The internet has shortened the distances among people. On the network you can look up unformation, dispatch and receive mail, do shopping, play games or chat freely with friends in another part of the world. Many white-collared staff and students are attracted to the bar with quiet and pleasant environment and music in accompaniment. To enter the network to broaden one's mind is now a fashion in Shanghai.

UNIVERSAL INTERNET CLUB

Add: 555 Jiangsu Road
Tel.: 62521188
Means of communication: public buses 01, 44 and 77

6. BLACK TEΛ HOUSE

Shanghai's traditional tea houses provide room for the middle-aged and the elderly. Recently, black tea houses have been molded into a new fashion, integrating the oriental tradition with Western taste for the young people. In a pleasant and peaceful environment, listening to popular music, tasting black tea or other drinks, or chatting, playing cards or chess with friends brings one into a world of peace and free thinking.

HAVEN

Add: 859 Nanjing Rd, W

Tel.: 62729590

Means of communication: Public buses 20, 37 and 921

HUMBLE HOME

Add: 10 Hengshan Road

Tel.: 64746547

Means of communication: No 1 Subway Hengshan Road stop

7. GOLF

Golf is a sport much favored by people, especially by social celebrities and successful businessmen. It is not only a keep-fit sport in fashion but also provides a good place for social contacts. In recent years, some American, Japanese, Hong Kong and Taiwan businessmen, seeing the promising prospects of golf as a sport in Shanghai, have invested funds to build golf courses. At present, there are several first-grade golf courses opened to the public. For those who love the sport it is a an enjoyment to have such exercise in an open field.

SUNNY ISLAND INTERNATIONAL GOLF CLUB

Add: Sunny Island, Shengang Town, Qingpu County

Tel.: 59830888

Means of communication: Special bus line

TOMSON GOLF CLUB

Add: 1 Longdong Road

Tel.: 58338888

Means of communication: Special bus line

ORIENTAL PARIS GOLF COUNTRY CLUB

Add: 277 Yangzi Road, Nanxiang Town, Jiading District

Tel.: 59126888

Means of communication: Special bus line

SHANGHAI GOLF CLUB

Add: Plot No 12 Shuangtang Village, Tanghang Town, Jiading District

Tel.: 59950111

Means of communication: Special bus line

SHANGHAI GOLF COUNTRY CLUB

Add: Xinyang Village, Zhujiaqiao Town, Qingpu County

Tel.: 59728111

Means of communication: Special bus line

SHANGHAI LINKS GOLF COUNTRY CLUB

Add: 1600 Lingbai Road, Pudong

Tel.: 58975899

Means of communication: Special bus line

(V) GYMNASTIC CLUBS

In a modern metropolis like Shanghai people are busy at work all day. In their spare time they would like to relax themselves and do some exercises. To meet the needs of people who care for their health gymnastic clubs have come into being. Here, people not only can have physical training, relax their body and mind, but also experience the pleasure of different kinds of keep-fit exercises. At present, there are many such clubs in Shanghai. Many of the stadiums and gymnasiums are now opened to the public. At weekends and in the evenings, in gymnastic clubs, tennis courts and badminton fields many white-collared staff and young people are found. To go to gymnastic clubs to have physical training is a fashion in people's daily life. There is an increasing number of people taking part in such activities.

PHYSICAL LADIES' CLUB

Add: 311 Shandong Rd, M

Tel.: 63297529

Means of communication: Public buses 20, 37 and 921

INTERNATIONAL HEALTH CITY

Add: 301 Yichuan Road

Tel.: 56058888

Means of communication: Public buses

PUDONG SHOOTING AMUSEMENT CO.,LTD.

Add: East Binhai Township, Nanhui County

Tel.: 58058234

Means of communication: Special bus line

SHANGHAI INTERNATIONAL GOLF CENTER

Add: 516 Hengshan Road

Tel.: 64155588

Means of communication: No 1 Subway Hengshan Road stop and Public bus 15

SHANGHAI HIGH POINT BOWLING SPORTS CO.,LTD.

Add: 456 East Jiangwan Road

Tel.: 56711111

Means of communication: Public buses 70, 51 and 18

LAILAI PALACE BOWLING ROOM

Add: 765 Wuyi road

Tel.: 62345657

Means of communication: Public buses 69 and 71

QUYANG BOWLING ROOM

Add: 789 Quyang Road

Tel.: 65423906

Means of communication: Public buses 116 and 100

TONGLING BOWLING ROOM, LTD.

Add: 15 Lane 123 Caoxi Road

Tel: 64685858

Means of communication: Public buses 54, 43 and 42

SHANGHAI FECC INTERNATIONAL YACHT CLUB, CO., LTD.

Add: 8500 Huqingping Highway

Tel.: 62762472

Means of communication: Special bus line

XIANGSHAN REDUCING HEALTH CENTER

Add: 8 Lane 622 Huaihai Rd, M

Tel.: 63854352

Means of communication: Public buses 911, 926 and 42

(VI) METROPOLITAN NIGHT LIFE

Shanghai is an internationalized metropolis full of vitality. Shanghai's night life is also very enchanting. There are a number of bars, discotheques, karaoke (KTV) rooms, and night clubs with first-grade facilities and elegantly peaceful environment. After a day's work, people in threes and fours have a drink and chat with friends to relax their body and mind, or enjoy themselves in discotheques or KTV rooms and fill the evening with youth and vitality.

1. DISCO

REAL LOVE DISCO

Add: 10 Hengshan Road

Tel.: 64746830

Means of communication: Public buses 15 and 49

TIMES DISCO PLAZA

Add: Fl/7-8 No 550 Huaihai Rd, M

Tel.: 63275566

Means of communication: Public buses 126, 925 and 42

NEW YORK DISCO PLAZA

Add: 146 Huqiu Road

Tel.: 63215611

Means of communication: Public buses20, 37 and 22

GALAXY AMUSEMENT DISCO PLAZA

Add: 888 Zhongshan Rd, W

Tel.: 62755888x2380

Means of communication: Public buses 127, 71 and 57

K · K DISCO PLAZA

Add: 588 Kaixuan Road

Tel.: 62127318

Means of communication: Public buses 57, 71 and 73

YANGYANG DISCO PLAZA AMUSEMENT CLUB

Add: 1127 Yanan Rd, M

Tel.: 62481691

Means of communication: Public buses 71, 57 and 127

2. KARAOKE HALLS

QIANGUI KTV

Add: 208 Chongqing Rd, S

Tel.: 63741111

Means of communication: Public buses 926, 42 and 126

POP MUSIC CITY

Add: 169 Xizang Rd, S

Tel.: 63866666

Means of communication: Public buses 135, 783, 126, 17 and 18

HAPPYLAND KTV

Add: 401 Changshou Road

Tel.: 62777788

Means of communication: Public buses 13, 40 and 112

EUROPEAN STAR TONGLING KTV

Add: 111 Caoxi Road

Tel.: 64271188

Means of communication: Public buses 15, 49, 42 and 926

3. NIGHT CLUBS

CAESAR'S PALACE

Add: 2000 Yanan Rd, W

Tel.: 62753388

Means of communication: Public buses 71, 57 and 127

LITAI CLUB

Add: 120 Henan Rd, M

Tel.: 63245273

Means of communication: Public buses 66 and 49

97 NIGHT CLUB

Add: 65 Yanan Rd, W

Tel.: 62481688

Means of communication: Public buses 71, 127 and 48

CORDON BLUE INTERNATIONAL CLUB

Add: 527 Huaihai Rd, M

Tel.: 53069999

Means of communication: Public buses 926 and 42

VENUS CLUB

Add: 301 Huashan Road

Tel.: 62488888

Means of communication: Public buses 113 and 48

CAESARS CLUB

Add: Fl/6 No 328 Nanjing Rd, E

Tel.: 64871818

Means of communication: Public buses 20, 37 and 021

NEW RAINGOW CLUB

Add: 35 Loushanguan Road

Tel.: 62757888

Means of communication: Public buses 127 and 57

INTERNATIONAL SEAMEN'S CLUB

Add: 60 Huangpu Road

Tel.: 63251500

Means of communication: Public buses 22 and 37

HONG KONG CITY AMUSEMENT CLUB

Add: 630 Sichuan Rd, M

Tel.: 63235304

Means of communication: Public buses 22, 19 and 37

YING-MEI JINGJI PALACE AMUSEMENT CLUB, LTD.

Add: 77 Songshan Road

Tel.: 53067789

Means of communication: Public buses 126, 42 and 108

GOLDEN AGE

Add: Fl/8 No 918 Huaihai Rd, M

Tel.: 64159587

Means of communication: Public buses 926, 42 and 24

CATERING

Chinese culinary art is a wonder in Chinese nation' s brilliant culture with a long, far-reaching history. Shanghai is China's largest economic center. A hundred years ago, since Shanghai was made an open port, hundreds and thousands of businessmen gathered in Shanghai and the city has ever since been alive with prosperity. The development of economy and culture has brought along the flourishing of the catering business. Restaurants of different styles of food came along with the people from different areas. There are 17 different styles of food in Shanghai, including Beijing, Sichuan, Guangdong, Fujian, Hunan, Shandong, Yangzhou, Shanghai, Suzhou, Hangzhou, Ningbo, Anhui, Henan, Chaozhou, Muslim and the vegetarian, plus those serving German, Russian, French food and those of Japanese and Korean cuisine and barbecue and southeast Asian food. Shanghai has become a center with the collection of Chinese delicacies. Among the Chinese culinary styles,Shanghai cooking is varied and colorful, absorbing the good points of the different styles. The chefs trained in Shanghai are broad in vision and quick-witted, under the influence of the local culture, are able to learn the strong points from others to offset their own weaknesses and make a comprehensive study of others'skills to form a school of their own, to enable the different food styles and to gain a solid footing in Shanghai, while creating their typical courses, forming a Shanghai style with the characteristics of Shanghai culture. Shanghai's catering market, with its strong workforce , chefs with excellent culinary skill, cozy and pleasant catering environment and quality service, supporting the good image of an international metropolis, has made "eating in Shanghai" an attractive item to tourists in experiencing Shanghai's charm.

(I) CHINESE CUISINES

1. SHANGHAI-STYLE FOOD

Shanghai food is also called Shanghai food. Its selection of raw materials is very meticulous and quality, first grade. Its preparation emphasizes on the control of flames and heavy flavor with original gravy and original taste, thick in gravy and bright in color, mellow and fresh to the palate. It is not only popular in Shanghai but also in other big cities like Beijing and Guangzhou and much appreciated by customers. The major reason is that it has drawn the strong points from other styles of food and created a school of its own. Shanghai food developed from informal feasts, food stalls, small restaurants and home-made daily meals in the countryside. But, it has continually absorbed the good points from other cuisines to upgrade its quality. Once it has matured, it has established a style of its own, a style that suits both the refined and popular taste, and simple meals good for rich dinners.

SHANGHAI OLD TOWN RESTAURANT

The most famous Shanghai-food restaurants are the Old Town Restaurant and Dexingguan Restaurant. Shanghai Old Town Restaurant was set up in the City God Temple area during Qing Dynasty, more than 100 years from now. It is the first local-food restaurant in Shanghai. It is well-known for preparing fresh fish, shrimps, crabs and eels. In cooking it pays attention to the control of flames, rich flavor, original gravy and original taste, thick in gravy and bright in color, mellow and delicious to the palate. The restaurant's dishes are typical of Shanghai-style food. Through long-time study and practice it adopts different ways of cooking for different raw materials and for different parts of the material. By absorbing the good points from Suzhou, Zhejiang and Anhui food, emphasizing on rich flavor with original gravy and original taste, it keeps the food fragrant, crispy, fresh and tender without losing the nutrients, thus enriching the flavor of Shanghai food to form a special Shanghai cuisine. Its specialties are the eight-jeweled duck, pork rib in prickly ash and salt, squirrel-shape yellow croaker.

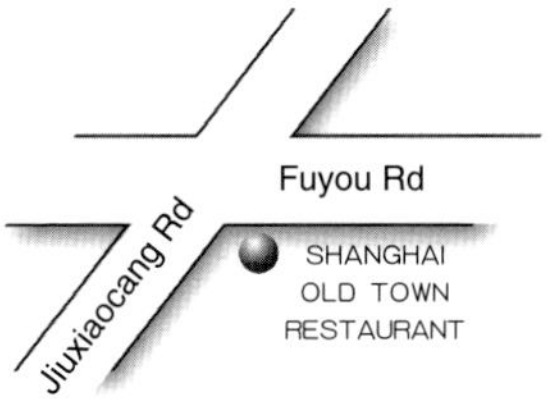

Add: 242 Fuyou Road
Tel.: 63282782
Means of communication: Public buses 11, 24 and 64

DEXINGGUAN RESTAURANT

Dexingguan was set up in 1883, 100 years from now. This old-brand restaurant was first set up at Shiliupu. The chef was a Shanghai local. In the early days, all the Shanghai-style restaurants served only such popular dishes as the salty port in bean-curd soup, chicken and duck's blood soup, pork braised in brown sauce. Now, the restaurant prepares special dishes with well selected raw materials, such as chicken, meat, shrimps and fish of good quality. Known for its quality dishes, its business is prosperous. The restaurant is specially good at preparing traditional Shanghai-style dishes, thick in gravy, bright in color, heavy in oil and rich in flavor. Its well-known sea cucumber cooked with shrimp roe is its invention, attractive in color, tender and mellow, but not greasy. It is very nutritious and highly commended by customers. Its menu is designed in favor of Shanghai people's palate, while absorbing the good points from Pudong local folk cooking to improve and upgrade its dishes. Its specialties are fish fin, fresh pork and salted pork cooked with bamboo shoot, and fish lip with shrimps.

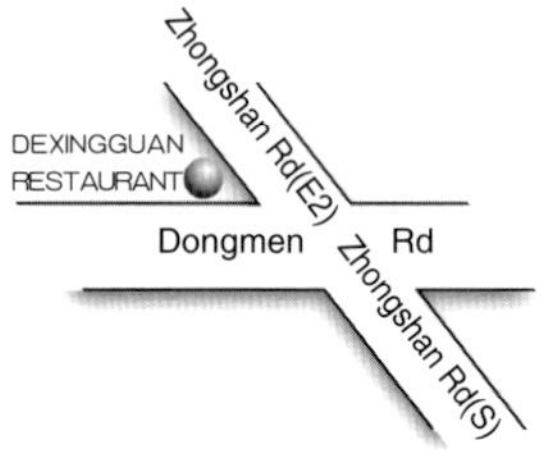

Add: 29 Dongmen Road

Tel.: 63281426

Means of communication: Public buses 11, 55, 64 and 65

2. BEIJING FOOD

Beijing food has a history of 1,000 years. To Shanghai people Beijing food is known for its roast duck. Besides the traditional dish of roast duck prepared from stuff-fed duck, there is also a famous dish of plain boiled pork enjoying a good reputation. Beijing food is composed of local flavor and that from Shandong, each has its own characteristics in raw material and way of cooking. Its main cooking ways are frying, stir-frying, quick-frying, roasting and stewing. The dishes taste crispy, fragrant, tender and delicious. Besides the roast duck there are such specialties like the sliced fish in brewery rice, and fish in vinegar and pepper. There are also recently developed imperial dishes known as “fang shan”, attracting much interest in customers.

YANYUNLOU RESTAURANT

Beijing food was first introduced to the south to suit the palate of Beijing people in Shanghai. Now, Beijing-style restaurants add sugar in preparing the dishes to suit the palate of Shanghai people and thus have formed a special Beijing-style food in Shanghai. The oldest Beijing-food restaurant is Yanyunlou with a history of 50 years. Its specialty is roast duck, which is less fat than that in Quanjude in Beijing, but bright in color and crispy in skin, suitable to the palate and habit of Shanghai people. In the ’50s it had already established its fame for its excellent culinary skill and a menu of variety of dishes. Yanyunlou’s “four kinds of vegetable treasures” and “steamed fine-threaded bread” are much favored by Shanghai diners.

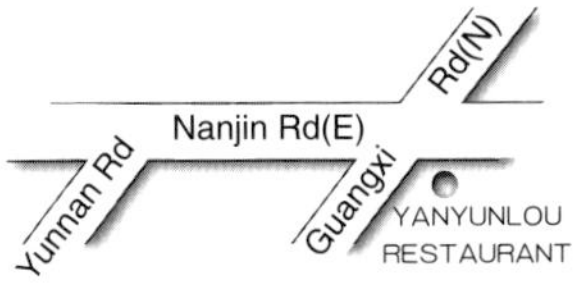

Add: 288 Guangxi Rd, N
Tel.: 63223298
Means of communication: Public buses17, 20, 37 and 49

BEIJING HOTEL

Beijing Hotel’s special dishes are roast duck, pig’s intestine, sliced chicken in egg white and newly developed dishes of fresh scallop in shells .

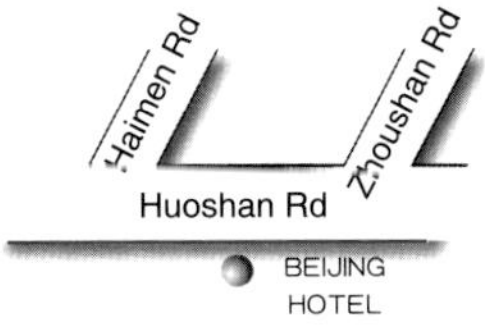

Add: 68 Huochan Road
Tel.: 65416693
Means of communication: Public buses 13, 15, 19, 25, 28, 37 and 47

YANJINGLOU RESTAURANT

Yanjinglou Restaurant’s traditional specialties are beef quick-fried in soybean paste, lamb quick-fried with scallion, and young chicken in oil. It has absorbed the culinary skill from Tianjin food. Another specialty is the meat dumpling, which is called by people "goubuli".

Add: 1029 Huaihai Rd, M

Tel.: 64726855

Means of communication: Public buses 26, 42, 911 and 926

3. GUANGDONG FOOD

Guangdong food was introduced into Shanghai in the early days. In the early 20th century, Cantonese people moving into Shanghai were increasing in number and so was the number of Cantonese restaurants. The selection of raw material and the way of cooking for Cantonese food were quite unique, especially it has drawn the cooking skill from the Western food, which has added much vigor into the Cantonese food. The dishes prepared by famous chefs look neat and fresh. They are substantial and rich in content, much appreciated by Shanghai diners. Today, apart from the old-brand Cantonese restaurants, like Xin Ya and Xinghualou, there came into being many new Cantonese-style restaurants, totaling a few dozens. Thus, Cantonese food has been raised to a new level among the catering trade in Shanghai.

Xin YA CANTONESE RESTAURANT

Located on Nanjing Road, East, Xin Ya Cantonese Restaurant is a famous old-brand Cantonese restaurant in Shanghai. It has a strong technical workforce. The dishes prepared by famous chefs are crispy, smooth, fresh, light and tender. The restaurant serves different kinds of Cantonese cuisines and snacks. To suit the palate of Shanghai customers it has employed chefs from Guangzhou to create new dishes, emphasizing on original gravy and original taste, retaining the special flavor of Cantonese food, while coping with the food habits of Shanghai diners. Its specialties are stir-frying shrimps, roast piglet, braised winter melon, crispy mandarin fish, and steamed barbecued meat dumpling.

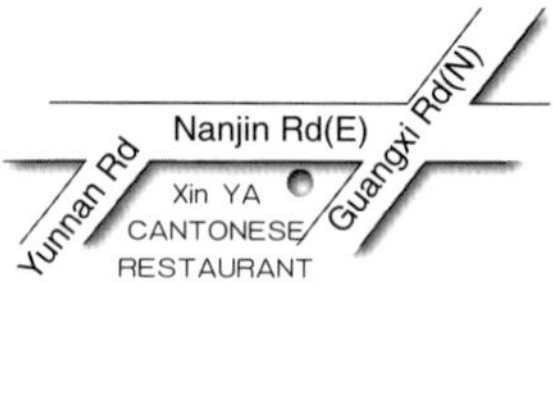

Add: 719 NANJING Rd, E

Tel.: 63517788

Means of communication: Public buses 18, 20, 37 and 902

XINGHUALOU RESTAURANT

Xinghualou has a history of 150 years. It is known for its genuine Cantonese dishes and Cantonese-style moon cakes. The specialties are sliced fish in cream and beef in oyster sauce. The restaurant is specially famous for its moon cakes with a history of 70 years. The moon cake is beautiful in appearance, bright in color, soft and smooth, and sweet to the taste. Every Mid-Autumn Festival customers line up in long queues to buy moon cakes. It is a busy time for the restaurant with crowds of customers. Its moon cakes are the best gifts for the season.

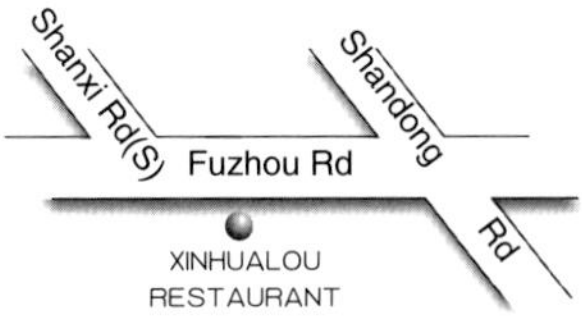

Add: 342 Fuzhou Road

Tel.: 63553777

Means of communication: Public buses 17, 49, 123 and 66

4. SICHUAN FOOD

Sichuan food has a history of 100 years since it was introduced into Shanghai. "Hot" is the specialty of Sichuan food. Shanghai people are not used to taking hot food. Therefore, in order to take root in Shanghai the Sichuan restaurants have to adapt themselves to the habit of Shanghai diners and modify their dishes.

JIEERJING

Set up in 1927, Jieerjing Sichuan Restaurant is also an old-brand restaurant. Here diners can find all typical Shanghai-style Sichuan dishes. Its specialties are stir-fried pork fillet, kidney in hot fish gravy, fried shrimp cake and "Mapo" bean-curd.

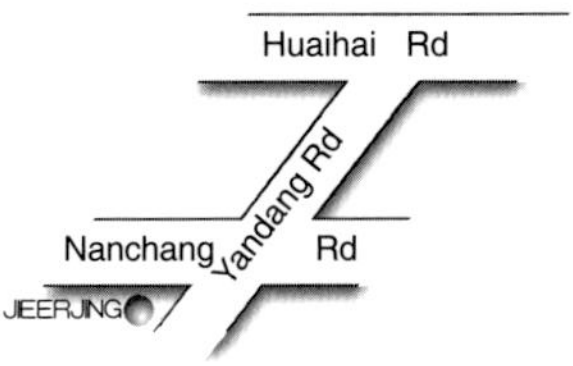

Add: 82 Yandang Road

Tel.: 63581004

Means of communication:

Public buses 24, 42, 911 and 926

MEILONGZHEN

Meilongzhen Restaurant combines Shanghai food flavor in Sichuan cooking, forming Shanghai-style Sichuan food. Its specialties are "longan" bean-curd and celery shredded quail.

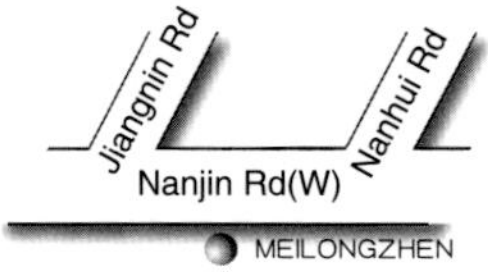

Add: 22 Lane 1081 Nanjing Rd, W

Tel.: 62566705

Means of communication: Public buses 20, 23, 37 and 112

LUYANGCUN

Luyangcun Restaurant is a specialty old-brand restaurant in Shanghai, specialized in preparing Sichuan and Yangzhou dishes. It was set up in 1936. Its specialties are minced meat in crab meat sauce, stir-fried shredded beef and braised winter melon with white fungus.

Add: 763 Nanjing Rd, W

Tel.: 62537221

Means of communication: Public buses 20, 23, 37 and 112

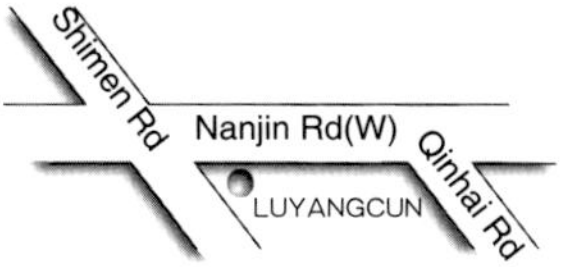

5. YANGZHOU FOOD

Yangzhou food is one of the Jiangsu food series. It is also called Huaiyang food, combining the three styles of Yangzhou, Zhenjiang and Huaian food, representative of Yangzhou style. It is special in its own feature in meticulous selection of raw material, skilful in cooking, fine in cutting, different ways of cooking for different material, beautiful in shape and color. The ways of cooking are braising, covered-boiling, warming, steaming, roasting, stewing, frying, deep-frying, stir-frying and smoking. It pays attention to add delicious soup in cooking.

YANGZHOU RESTAURANT

The predecessor of the restaurant was the "Mo Youcai Kitchen" set up by three Mo brothers in the '50s at the crossroad of Jiangxi Road and Ningbo Road. Its culinary art is first-grade and dishes are delicious. Its specialties are five-flavored kidney, pine nut shredded fish, stewed fish head, popular far and wide. Many celebrities of the art circle like Mei Lanfang, Yu Zhenfei, Zhou Xinfang had been its regular diners. In the early '70s, it was moved to Nanjing Road, and officially named Yangzhou Restaurant. In the last decades, the founders and their students developed, rearranged and created many typical Yangzhou dishes and have contributed greatly to the food culture in China. Its specialties are shredded bean-curd cooked with chicken and ham, crucian carp in creamy soup, crystal salted meat and lotus seed in honey.

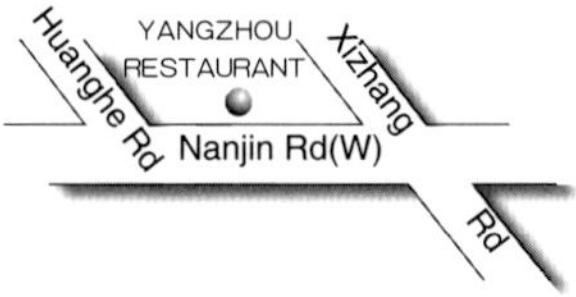

Add: 72 Nanjing Rd, W
Tel.: 63587988
Means of communication: 18, 20, 37 and 46

LAOBANZHAI

Laobanzhai Restaurant is the oldest restaurant still serving Yangzhou food in Shanghai. Its dishes are light and palatable, much appreciated by Shanghai diners. Its traditional specialty is minced meat in crab meat sauce, soft, heavily flavored, tender and fat but not greasy. It is highly commended by diners. It also serves steamed meat dumplings, noodles in anchovy soup and noodles stewed in preserved vegetable.

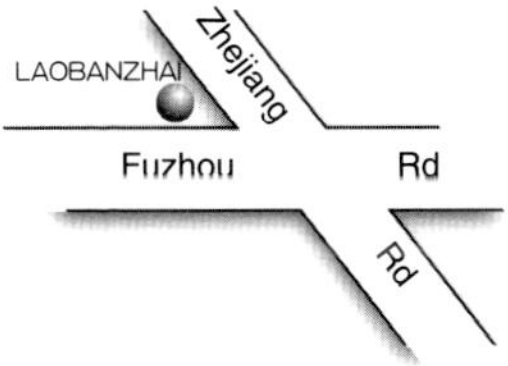

Add: 600 Fuzhou Road
Tel.: 63517868
Means of communication: Public buses 17, 49 and 123

6. SUZHOU AND WUXI FOOD

It is the combined name of Suzhou and Wuxi food. Wuxi food is related to Shanghai local food and has absorbed some of the characteristics of Shanghai food. Suzhou food is also similar to Wuxi food. It emphasizes on beautiful shape and variety.

PEOPLE'S RESTAURANT

The People's Restaurant located on Nanjing Road, West, is much recommended for its Suzhou-Wuxi food. It is specialized in stewing in brown sauce, quick-frying, covered boiling, and plain steaming. Its famous dish is the stewed chicken. Other specialties are five-flavored shark's fin, yellow croaker rolls, and stir-fried crab roe. It also serves such Suzhou floury snacks as steamed meat and crab roe dumplings, and shrimp spring rolls. The chefs have developed the "hundred fish feast" by using 48 kinds of sea and fresh water fish to prepare 120 kinds of fish dishes. It is really an invention!

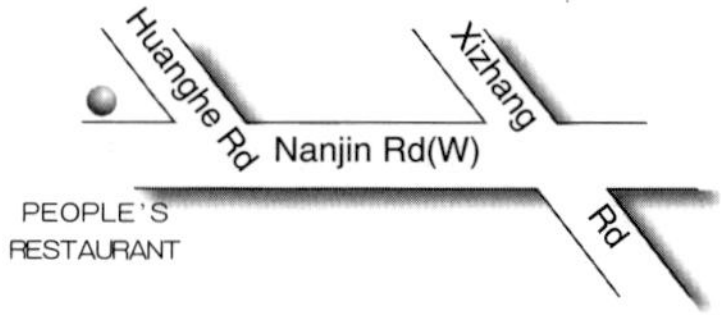

Add: 226 Nanjing Rd, W
Tel.: 63273511
Means of communication: No 1 Subway People's Square stop and public buses 18, 20, 23 and 37

7. ANHUI FOOD

Anhui food was introduced into Shanghai at an earlier date. During the Ming and Qing Dynasties many merchants came from Huizhou to do business in Shanghai. After Shanghai was made an open port, it had become an important place for business by Anhui merchants. At one time, Anhui food ranked the top in Shanghai's catering trade. However, with the changes of times and under the competition by other styles of food, it is no longer the favorite.

DAFUGUI RESTAURANT

Dafugui Restaurant always keeps the spcialty of Anhui cooking. Its famous dish is the boneless duck's web cooked with shrimps, called "pearls on the palm". It is tender, fragrant and delicious as a special dish of Anhui-style food. Traditional specialties familiar to Shanghai diners are, pheasant cooked with green bean sprouts,

Huizhou meat balls, stir-fried chopsoy and assorted dish.
Add: 1465 Zhonghua Road
Tel.: 63770322
Means of communication: Public buses 11, 18, 23 and 24

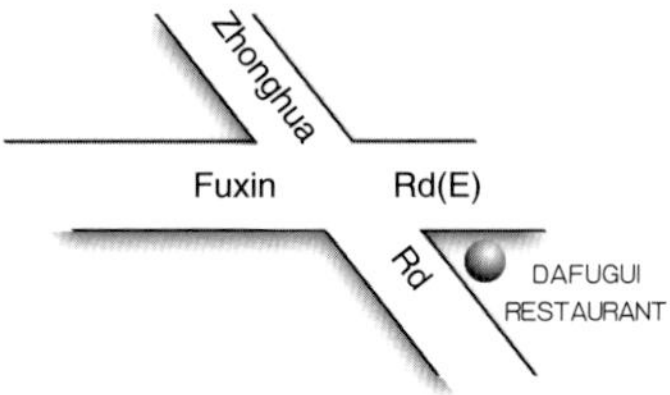

8. ZHEJIANG FOOD

Zhejiang food is mainly represented by Hangzhou and Ningbo food. It is quite popular in Shanghai. Hangzhou food is light and fresh. Famous traditional West Lake dishes are much favored by Shanghai people. Ningbo food is favored by many diners. In the past, many Ningbo people came to make a living in Shanghai. At present, there are still several hundred thousands of Ningbo people in Shanghai. Ningbo food specialized in its native folk style is much appreciated by diners.

WEST LAKE RESTAURANT

Hangzhou food in Shanghai is represented by West Lake Restaurant. The restaurant attracts diners with its famous dishes, like the West Lake water shield soup, West Lake fish in vinegar sauce, steamed pork in lotus leaf, and sliced fish in egg white. There is a special dish called "Dongbo meat", bright in color, tender and fragrant, fat but not greasy.

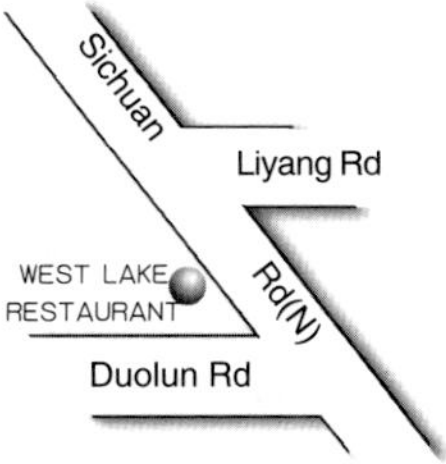

Add: 1805 Sichuan Rd, N
Tel.: 56662415
Means of communication: Public buses 18, 21 and 47

9. CHAOZHOU FOOD

In recent years, the once silent Chaozhou food has suddenly become popular in Shanghai. There are several restaurants serving Chaozhou food in Shanghai, such as the Sea Palace, Spring on Chao

River, Fuling Palace Chaozhou Restaurant and Night Shanghai, crowded with diners.

SEA PALACE CHAOZHOU RESTAURANT

The Sea Palace Chaozhou Restaurant serving unique innovated dishes to suit Shanghai diners' palate. Its specialties are Chaozhou fish balls, fish dumpling soup, chestnut paste in lard, stir-fried squid, all prepared in its traditional way. They are the best dishes in Chaozhou-style food.

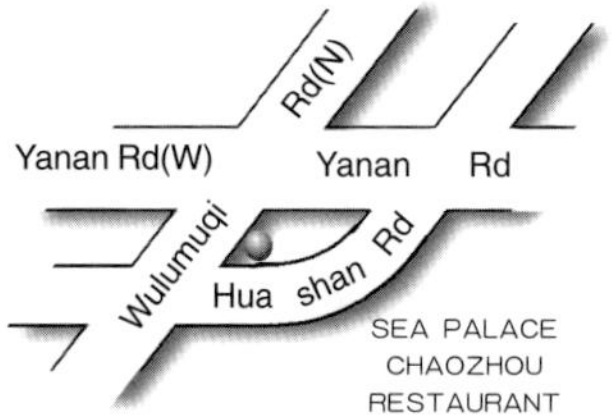

Add: 505 Wulumuqi Rd, N

Tel;: 62481388

Means of communication: Public buses 71, 127 and 925

10. HUNAN FOOD

SANXIANG HOTEL YANGGUANG RESTAURANT

Hunan food is one of the 8 major styles of food in China.It is heavy and spicy.

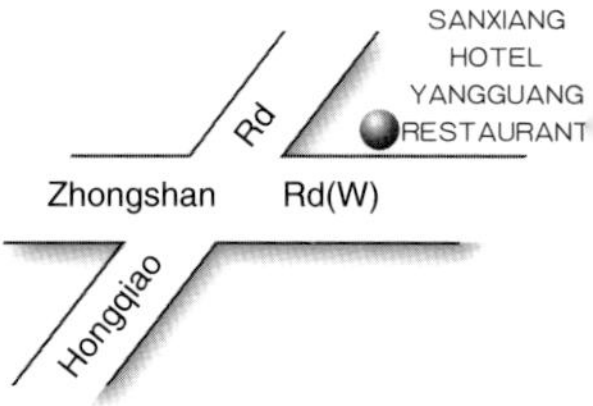

Add: 1243 Zhongshan Rd, W 2

Tel.: 62752468

Means of communication: Public buses 12, 17, 18 and 135

11. MUSLEM FOOD

HONGCHANGXING

Muslem restaurant has a history of 1200 years in Shanghai. Hongchangxing is the first restaurant serving Muslem food. It was set up in 1913, known as mainly selling floury food and pot-stewed lamb. Later, it added to its menu lamb and beef dishes and was renamed Hongchangxing Lamb Restaurant, specially serving lamb chafing dish. The lamb is tender and delicious without smell of mutton. It is a unique specialty. It is a favorite dish in winter and the

best choice for lamb-lovers.
Add: 288 Guangxi Rd, N
Tel.: 63529700
Means of communication: Public buses 20 and 37

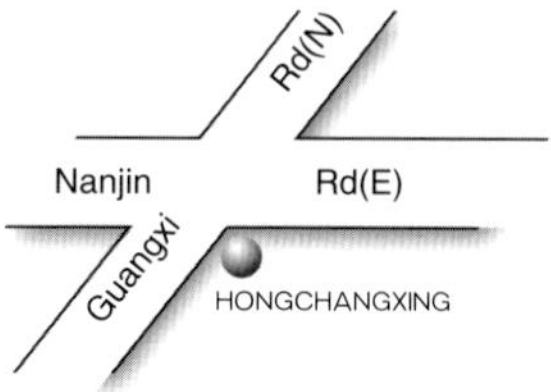

12. VEGETARIAN FOOD

GONGDELIN VEGETARIAN RESTAURANT

Shanghai Gongdelin Vegetarian Restaurant was set up in 1922, founded and managed by Zhao Yunshao, disciple of Monk Weijun, Buddhist preacher in City God Mountain Changji Temple in Hangzhou. At first, it only served vegetarian food in temples. Later it was opened to the public. Gradually it had a school of its own. It is special in meticulous selection of raw materials, skilful in preparing, varied in kinds and tastes. Its dishes in imitation of meat and fish look genuine.

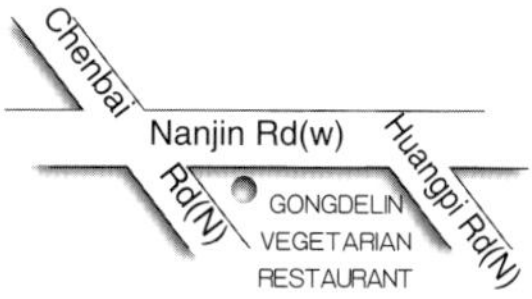

Add: 445-453 Nanjing Road, West
Tel.: 63270218
Means of communication: Public buses 20, 21, 37 and 920

LONGHUA HOTEL VEGETARIAN FOOD

Longhua Hotel is a 3-star hotel featured by Buddhist culture. It has a peaceful and pleasant environment, furnished in simple antiquity. It is popular for the vegetarian dishes prepared by famous chefs. It uses fresh vegetable, fruit, mushroom, bamboo shoot, glutin and soybean products as raw material to prepare dishes in imitating meat and fish. Vegetarian dishes cooked in the way of preparing meat dishes are much appreciated by both Chinese and foreign diners.

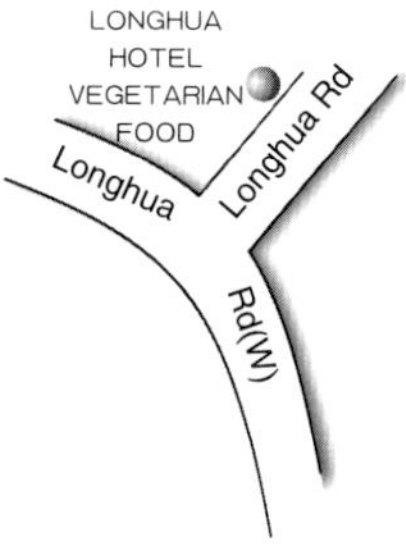

Add: 2787 Longhua Road
Tel.: 64570570
Means of communication: Public

buses 44, 73, 87 and 104

13. SHANGHAI SPECIALTY RESTAURANTS

XIAO SHAOXING PLAIN BOILED CHICKEN

Xiao Shaoxing plain boiled chicken is a famous specialty of Xiao Shaoxing Restaurant, founded in 1943. It has been popular for half a century and is still much favored. It is called "a top in China". The restaurant's special skill accumulated in the last 50 years has turned out a plain boiled chicken of best quality. The raw material is yellow-feathered chicken from Pudong. The chicken is fed at regular hours, kept at regular places and with designated fodder, keeping the original nutrition and taste of the chicken meat. The careful selection of raw material and skilful cooking turns out a chicken, crispy in skin, tender in meat, delicious in flavor and beautiful in shape. It has become an indispensable cold dish in a banquet, much appreciated by diners. Its chicken porridge and chicken and duck's blood soup are its specialties.

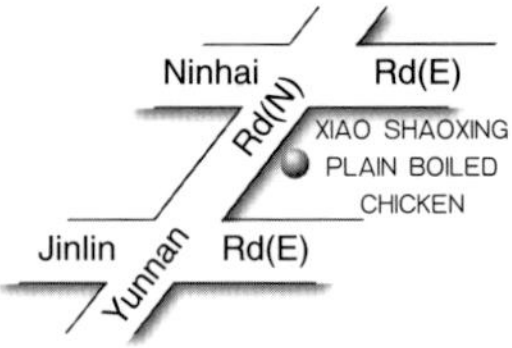

Add: 118 Yunnan Rd, S
Tel.: 63732890
Means of communication: Public buses 17, 49, 71 and 135

XIAO JINLING SALTED DUCK

The duck is prepared from a lean-type duck with special condiment and skillfully cooked. The salted duck is tender but not greasy, properly salted, unique in style. The product has won the title of fine quality food from the state and a super prize in China's Consumer Goods Exposition. In 1997, it was commended as China's famous snack by the National Culinary Art Association. It is well appreciated by Chinese and overseas customers.

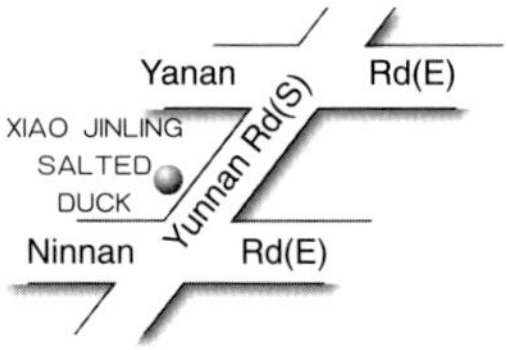

Add: 28 Yunnan Rd, S
Tel.: 63283737
Means of communication: Public

buses 17, 49, 71 and 135

WANGBAOHE CRAB FEAST

Known as "king of crabs and ancestor of wine", Wangbaohe Restaurant was founded 250 years ago. It is one of the first restaurants in Shanghai, specially serving "Wangbaohe wine and fresh water crabs". It has a cozy and pleasant environment, featured for its oriental national character. In serving the crab dish in its traditional way, the restaurant has developed a "chrysanthemum crab feast". The chrysanthemum feast is noted for its uniqueness, novelty and excellence and has enjoyed a good reputation over the past decade known at home and abroad.

Add: 603 Fuzhou Road

Tel.: 63517609

Means of communication: Public buses 17, 49 and 123

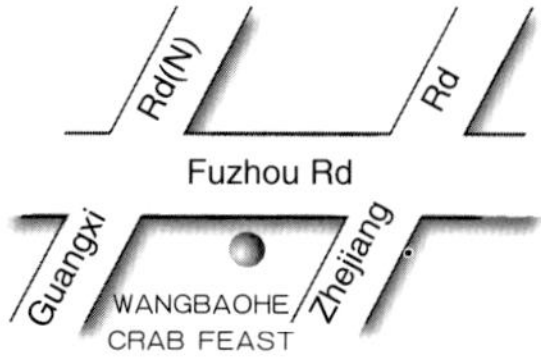

(II) SHANGHAI LOCAL- FLAVOR SNACKS

Shanghai's local-flavor snacks is one of China's major snacks. Shanghai snacks are great in variety, varied in flavor, plus skillful in preparation, beautiful in shape, and delicious in taste, known as the top in China. Shanghai snacks have been developed and upgraded from local snacks, absorbing the essence of snacks from different places. They are great in variety and suitable to the palate of people both from the south and from the north. The most popular 4 kinds of snack are flat-bread, deep-fried twisted dough, soybean milk and fried rice cake. They regularly serve all kinds of flat-bread, steamed dumpling, stuffed dumpling, jiaozi, noodle soup, wenton soup, rice cake, porridge, soup and thick soup. There are different tastes of snacks-fragrant, crispy, sour, hot, bitter, sweet and salty, suitable to the palate of different consumers. There are a number of popular snacks, unique in style. Among these there is the Nanxiang meat dumpling, Wufangzhai and Shendacheng's rice cake, Xuandelai's pork rib new year cake, Laobanzhai's glutinous rice shaomai, Qiaojiashan's meat zongzi, Lubolang's shredded turnip shortcake, Dahuchun's fried meat dumpling, baked shortcake, Xinghualou's moon cake, Gongdelin's vegetarian and the recently developed Xin Ya big meat dumpling. Popular snacks by street peddlers are the baked sweet potato, egg boiled in tea and brown sauce, deep-fried shredded turnip cake, and deep-fried stinking preserved bean-curd, all appealing to the palate of people. Besides, Shanghai has also introduced snacks from different places in China, such as rice noodle from Yunnan, bread in mutton soup from Xian, barbecued lamb string, hand-made noodle from Lanzhou, knife-chopped noodle from Shaanxi, which diners can find in every corner.

1. SPECIALTY SNACK BARS

LUBOLANG (GREEN WAVE PAVILION)

Lubolang is located beside the nine-twist bridge in the Old City God Temple area opposite to the Mid-lake Pavilion. It faces the bustling downtown in the south and the scenic garden in the north. The restaurant is furnished in an antique style, quiet and peaceful. It serves Shanghai local flavor dishes, especially popular for its snacks. It has hosted many state leaders from abroad. Its specialties are steamed dumpling with crab meat, steamed jiaozi with meat and vegetable, cake with date paste filling and eye-brow shortcake.

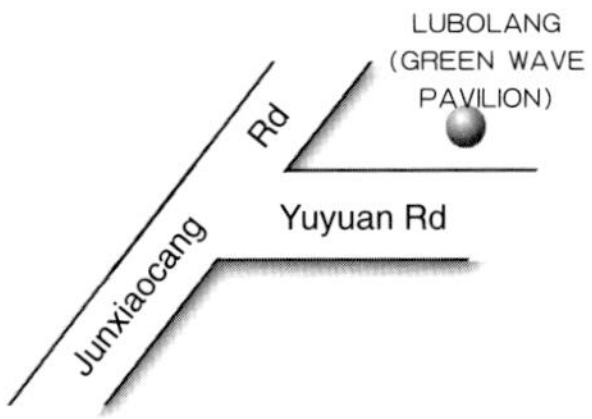

Add: 131 Yuyuan Road

Tel.: 63737020

Means of communication:Public buses 11, 65 and 126

WUFANGZHAI

Located at 391 Nanjing Road, East, Wufangzhai is the first snack bar in Shanghai serving Suzhou-style rice cakes. It has a history of 100 years. It serves rice cakes for all four seasons, birthday cakes and birthday floury peaches, and Suzhou-style floury snacks, which are much appreciated by customers. Its most popular specialty is lotus root cooked with

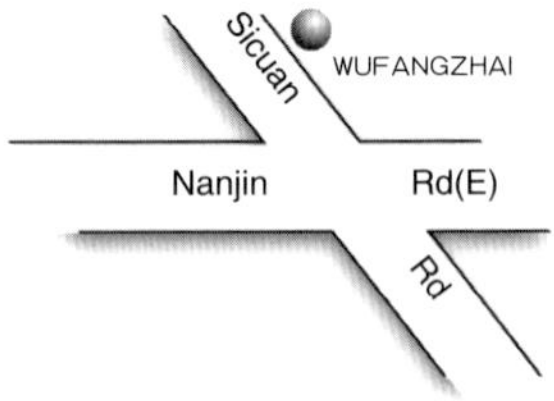

sugared sweet osmanthus.

Add: 136 Sichuan Rd, M

Tel.: 63216647

Means of communication: Public buses 20 and 37

CANGLANGTING HOUSE OF DELICACIES

Canglangting mainly serves floury snacks and rice cakes. It is meticulous in the selection of raw material and in preparation. It is known in Shanghai for its culinary art. Its specialties of three kinds of shrimp noodle soup, shrimp and crab noodle soup are specially popular.

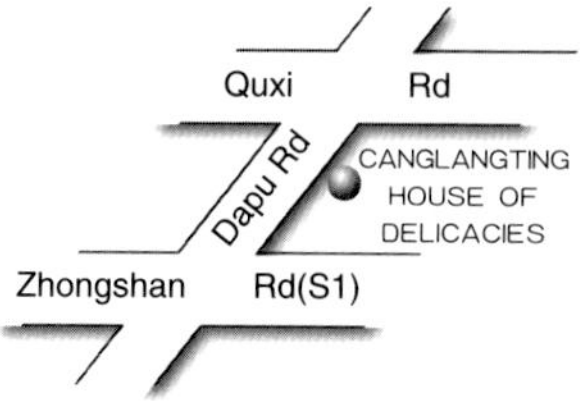

Add: 455 Dapu Road

Tel.: 63043515

Means of communication: Public buses 17, 128, 43 and No 1 Tunnel line

SHENDACHENG

Located at 636 Nanjing Road, East, Shedacheng Snack Bar is a famous 100-year old store. It mainly serves rice cakes. Its specialties are glutinous rice dumpling, green-weed rice cake, zongzi, shrimp wenton soup and steamed dumpling with shrimp filling.

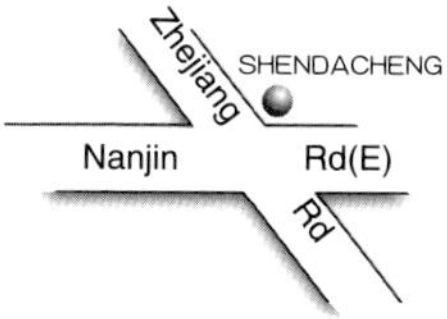

Add: 636 Nanjing Rd, E

Tel.: 63225615

Means of communication: Public buses 20 and 37

QIAOJIASHAN

Located at 336 Xiangyang Road, South, Qiaojiashan has a history of 80 years. Its specialties are glutinous rice dumpling, eight-jeweled rice, zongzi, spongy cake, cat-ear noodle soup and rice cake of three kinds of delicacies.

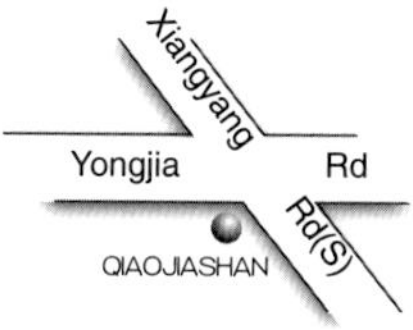

Add: 336 336 Xiangyang Road, South

Tel.: 64374174

Means of communication: Public

buses 42, 911 and 926

WANGJIASHA

Wangjiasha is a snack bar located at 805 Nanjing Road, West. It mainly serves fresh port shortcake, shortcake filled with bean puree, fried chicken meat dumpling and noodles baked on two sides.

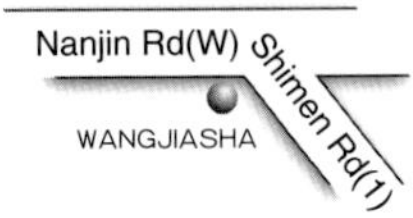

Add: 805 Nanjing Rd, W

Tel.: 62586373

Means of communication: Public buses 20, 37 920 and 23

2. SHANGHAI LOCAL-FLAVOR SNACK SQUARE

NINTH FLOOR IN NEW WORLD COMMERCIAL CITY

Add: 2 Nanjing Rd, W

Tel.: 63584199

Means of communication:

Public buses 20, 37 and 921

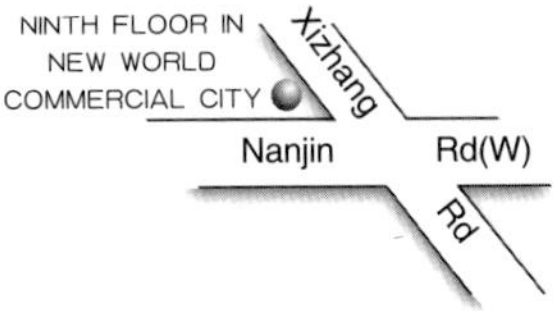

FIFTH FLOOR IN PACIFIC DEPARTMENT STORE HUAIHAI BRANCH

Add: 333 Huaihai Rd, M

Tel.: 53068888

Means of communication:

Public buses 42, 109, 926 and 911

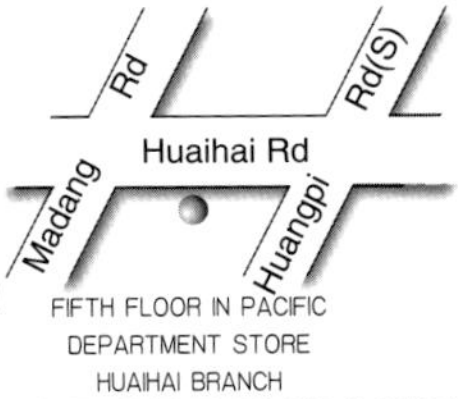

FIRST FLOOR IN DAQIAN HOUSE OF DELICACIES

Add: 1117 Zhaojiabang Road

Tel.: 64871177

Means of communication:

Public buses 43, 15 and 72

EIGHTH FLOOR IN PACIFIC DEPARTMENT STORE

Add: 932 Hengshan Road

Tel.: 64078888

Means of communication:Public buses 43, 15 and 72

NINTH FLOOR IN FIRST YAOHAN NEXT-AGE COMMERCIAL BUILDING

Add: 501 Zhangyang Road
Tel.: 58301111
Means of communication:
Public buses 01, 783 and 785

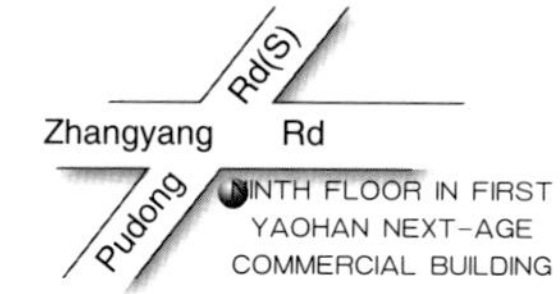

EIGHTH FLOOR IN SHANGHAI NO 1 DEPARTMENT STORE EAST BUILDING

Add: 800 Nanjing Rd, E
Tel.: 66323344
Means of communication:
Public buses 20, 37 and 911

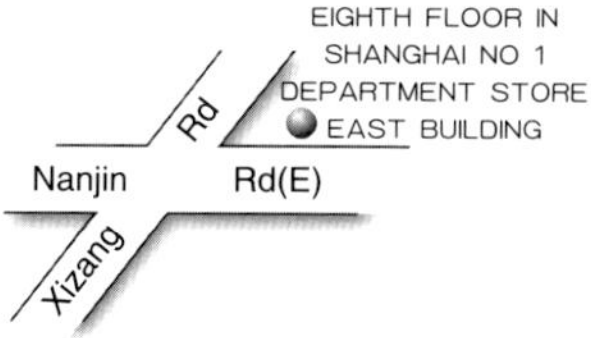

FIFTH FLOOR IN SHANGHAI NO 7 DEPARTMENT STORE EAST BUILDING

Add: 888 Sochuan Rd, N
Tel.: 63249611
Means of communication:
Public buses 18 and 21

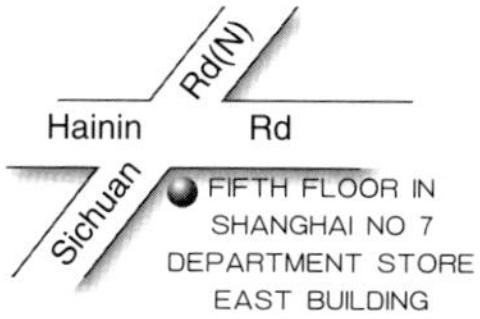

SIXTH FLOOR IN BASIC SHOPPING CENTER

Add: 918 Huaihai Rd, M
Tel.: 64158818
Means of communication:
Public buses 42, 926 and 911

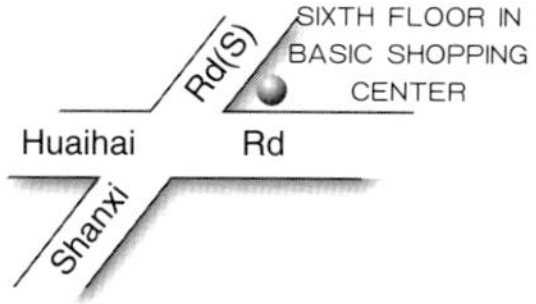

FIFTH FLOOR IN YIMIN COMMERCIAL BUILDING

Add: 647-659 Huaihai Rd, M
Tel.: 63564562
Means of communication:
public buses 42, 926 and 91

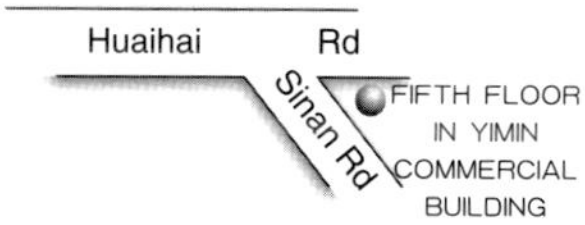

(III) WORLD CUISINES

Since 1840, after the Opium War, Shanghai was forced to open as a trading port, foreign priests and businessmen came in crowds. Along with them came the Western food. Through a hundred years' development and evolution, Western food, like the local food from different places in China, has undergone changes by absorbing the essence of Western culinary art and developing the different characteristics of different countries and formed into 5 major styles: the French, Amerian, Russian, German and Italian. It has enriched the character of the local food. In recent years, local cuisines and delicacies from different countries have been introduced into Shanghai, as well as those from Taiwan, Hong Kong, Macao, Korean barbecue, Japanese shousi and courses, Indonesian satai, Singaporean pork rib tea, Thailand's fried rice, India's curry rice, Italian spaghetti and pisa, American Mcdonald and Kentucky chicken and Californian beef noodle, filling Shanghai food market with beautiful colors and fragrance and greatly stimulating Shanghai's food market. The renewal and upgrading of the concept of food is very significant. In today's food market in Shanghai there is so much vitality never seen before and such a vast space for development. Shanghai people can freely have a taste of different flavors of food from different countries and enjoy themselves with all the delicacies.

1. WESTERN RESTAURANT

RED HOUSE WESTERN RESTAURANT

Located on Shaanxi Road, South, the Red House Western Restaurant is the most popular western restaurant among all the Western restaurants in Shanghai. It was set up in 1935, 60 years from now. It was formerly run by an Italian named Chzlovise. It was painted all brightly red on the doors and window frames and outside walls, and hence called the "Red House". It is known for serving French food. It is much appreciated by diners not only for its specialty Western-style food but also for its peaceful and pleasant environment. Many foreign state leaders and celebrities had also visited it on their visit to Shanghai. The restaurant has a number of famous chefs, who prepare genuine French dishes integrating Chinese traditional menu. Its specialties are baked clam, baked snail, river snail, French onion

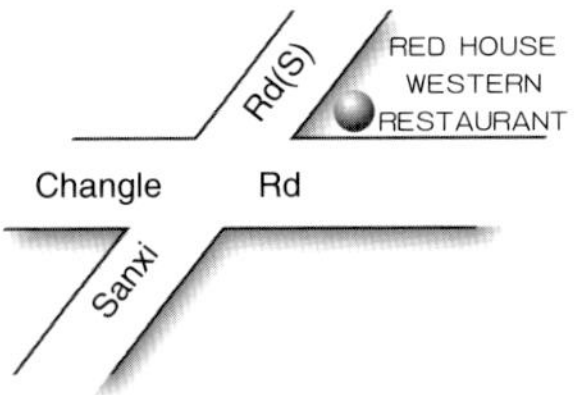

soup, all much appreciated by diners.
Add: 37 Shaanxi Rd, S
Tel.: 64374902
Means of communication: Public buses 48, 24, 71 and 49

DEDA WESTERN RESTAURANT

Deda Western Restaurant, located at the crossroad of Nanjing Road and Sichuan Road, has a history of 100 years. It serves German-style food, famous for its beef steak. Other specialties are fillet steak, Hamburger steak, French steak, Hungarian chicken, Italian baked fish and salad.

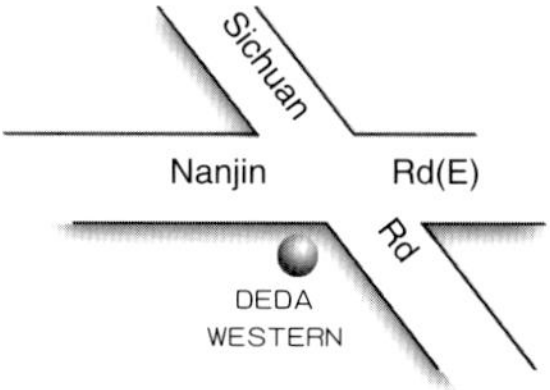

Add: 359 Sichuan Rd, M
Tel.: 63213810
Means of communication: Public buses 20, 37, 22, 65 and 66

SHANGHAI WESTERN RESTAURANT (RED HOUSE BRANCH ON HUAIHAI ROAD)

Located on Huaihai Road, West, Shanghai Western Restaurant, with a history of 50 years, mainly serves Italian food.

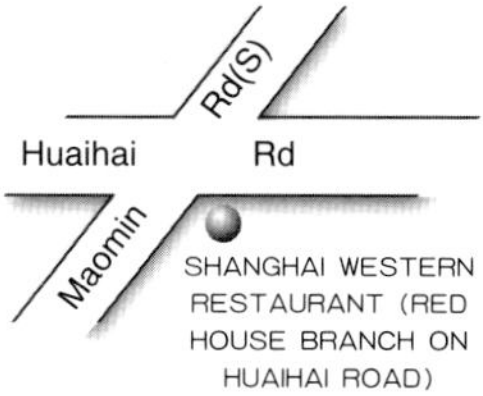

Add: 845 Huaihai Rd, M
Tel.: 64313293
Means of communication: Public buses 42, 126 and 926

Apart from these traditional Western restaurant with a long history, since '80s the foreigners coming to Shanghai has been growing in number, western restaurants are found in many 5 and 4-star hotels. Comparing with the traditional Western restaurants, these restaurants pay attention to keeping the original flavor and environment and atmosphere for diners. The chefs are usually foreigners, more suitable to the palate of foreign diners. In the meantime, many restaurants serving local cuisine food of different Asian countries and other areas in the world have been set up in Shanghai, thus turning Shanghai into a center of world delicacies.

2. JAPANESE FOOD

There are about 200 Japanese restaurants in Shanghai. The higher-standard Japanese restaurants are found in tourist hotels. Japanese food is also much appreciated by Shanghai diners. There is a number of Japanese restaurants in downtown areas. It is famous for its fresh and light food. The most popular are raw fish and sushi. Other specialties are Teppanyaki, Sukiyaki and Soba. Japanese Shabu is also very popular.

OKURA JAPANESE RESTAURANT IN GARDEN HOTEL

Add: 58 Maomin Rd, S
Tel.: 64151111x5216
Means of communication:
Public buses 126, 926 and 42

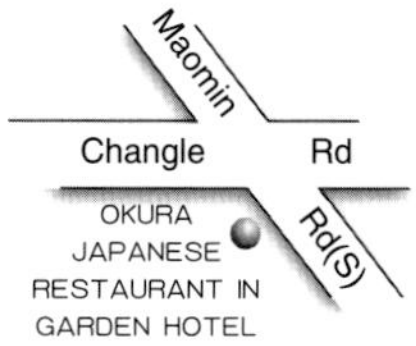

BEIHAI JAPANESE RESTAURANT

Add: 3667 Zhongshan Rd, N
Tel.: 62850066
Means of communication:
Public buses 69, 224, and 909

KANAKYU JAPANESE RESTAURANT IN SHANGHAI HOTEL

Add: 505 Wulumuqi Rd, N
Tel.: 62480088x6319
Means of communication:
Public buses 71. 127 amd 925

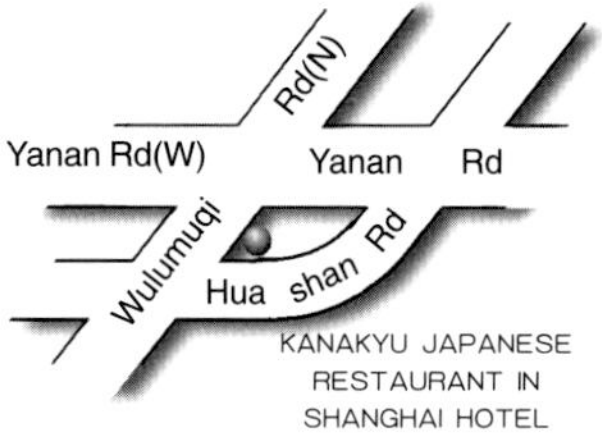

KAMACACHI JAPANESE RESTAURANT IN INTERNATIONAL EQUITORIAL HOTEL

Add: 65 Yanan Rd, W
Tel.: 62481688x2341
Means of communication:
Public buses 71, 127 and 925

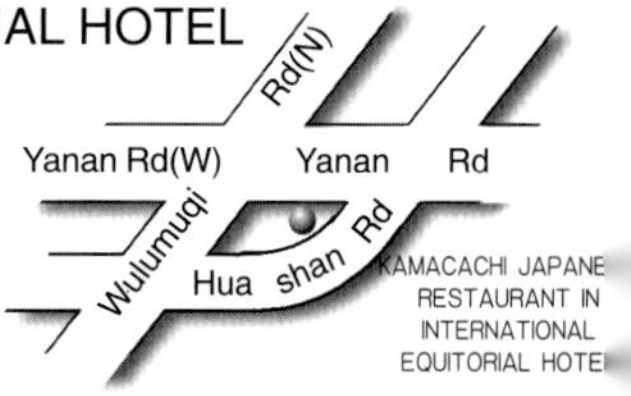

GINZA JAPANESE RESTAURANT IN WORLD CONVENTION HOTEL

Add: 2106 Hongqiao Road
Tel.: 62703388x1902
Means of communication:
Public buses 48, 57, 925 and 911

ITOYA

Add: 111 Ruijin Rd, 1
Tel.: 63184722
Means of communication:
Pubblic buses 42, 926, 126 and 24

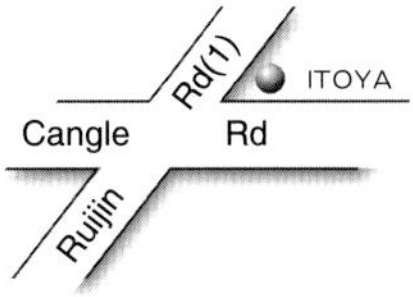

YAMATO

Add: 136 Maomin Rd, S
Tel.: 64339056
Means of communication:
Public buses 93, 49 and 42

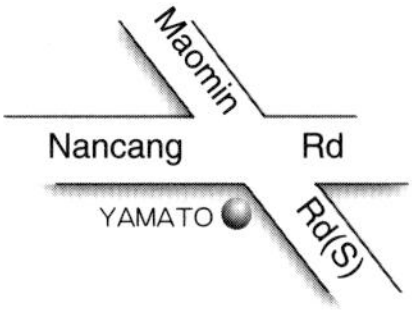

SUMO SUSHI

Add: 668 Lane Huaihai Rd, M
Tel.: 53069136
Means of communication:
public buses 42, 926 and 911

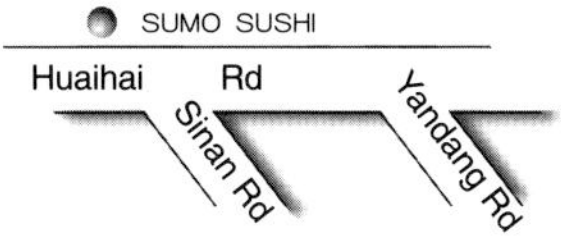

3. KOREAN FOOD

Korean food is popular for its barbecue. It usually uses beef, but, sometimes, it also uses chicken and fish. It is always accompanied by pickles as appetizers. Pickles, kelp soup, rice and jinsen tea together make up a rich Korean dinner.

SEOUL RESTAURANT

Add: 2000 Yanan Rd, W
Tel.: 62753388x3033
Means of communication:
Public buses 48, 57, 911 and 925

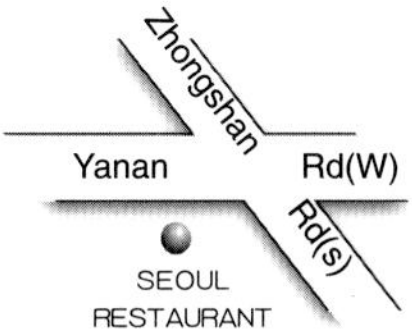

HANJIANG RESTAURANT

Add: 888 Zhongshan Rd, W
Tel.: 62755888x2942
Means of communication:
Public buses 48, 73, 57 and 831

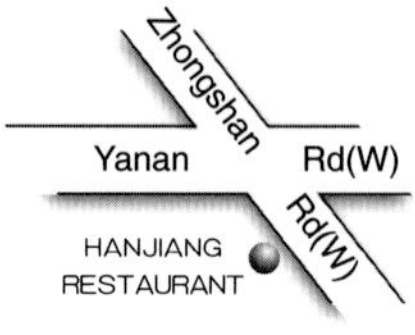

GOLDEN BRIDGE KOREAN RESTAURANT

Add: 2077 Yanan Rd, W
Tel.: 62709082
Means of communication:
Public buses 57, 911 and 925

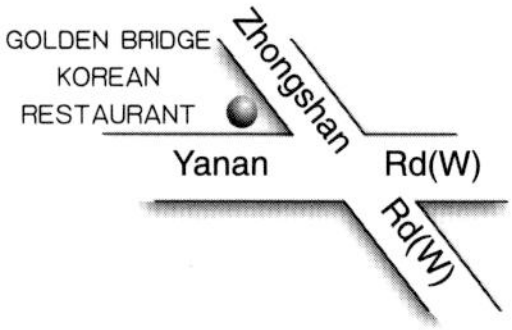

ARIRANG RESTAURANT CO,.LTD.

Add: 28 Jiangsu Rd, N
Tel.: 62527146
Means of communication:
Public buses 01, 44 and 62

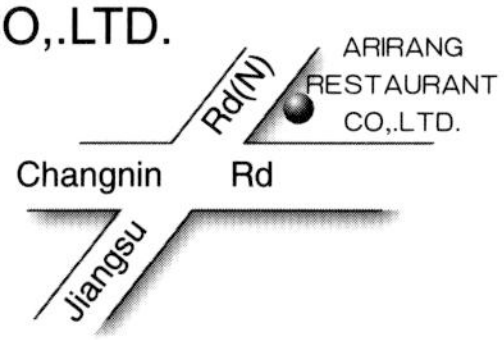

4. INDIAN FOOD

Indian food is noted for its curry. The specialties are Tikka, Tandoori, Naan, Puri, baked fish, baked chicken, curry mutton and vegetable. The most popular is the fried curry rice added with spices.

BOMBAY RESTAURANT

Add: 59 Maomin Rd, S
Tel.: 62582582x9301
Means of communication:
Public buses 126, 926 and 42

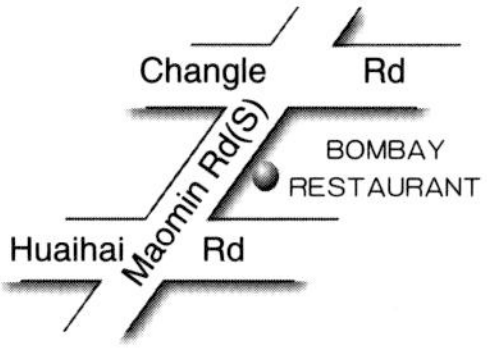

5. FRENCH FOOD

The romantic French are always proud of their food. They pay much attention to food and regard it as an art. French courses are very meticulously prepared. Famous courses are barbecued food and French onion soup. Deserts are shortcake, egg and cream shortcake and ice-cream.

BUND WESTERN RESTAURANT

Add: 161 Changle Road
Tel.: 64151188x80303
Means of communication:
Public buses 126, 42 and 911

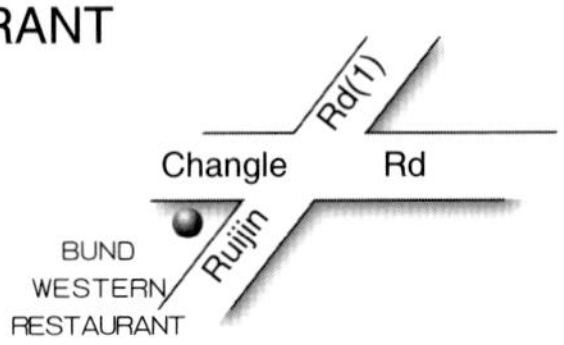

PARK 97

Add: 2 Gaolan Road
Tel.: 63180785
Means of communication:
Public buses 17, 24, 41 and 128

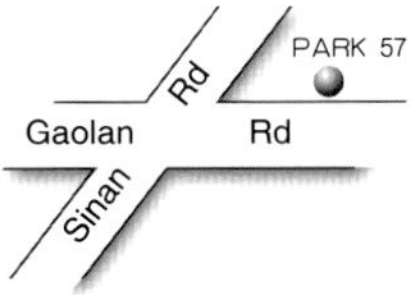

6. ITALIAN FOOD

The most popular Italian food are spaghetti and pisa. Besides, there are the seasoned rice and seafood, a great variety of thick soup and cold dishes.

CAPPUCCINO RESTAURANT

Add: 65 Yanan Rd, W
Tel.: 62481688x2384
Means of communication:
Public buses 911, 925, 71 and 127

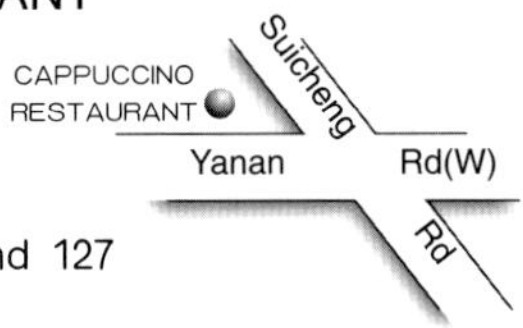

DA VINCI RESTAURANT

Add: 250 Huashan Road
Tel.: 62480000x8622
Means of communication:
Public buses 48, 113 and 44

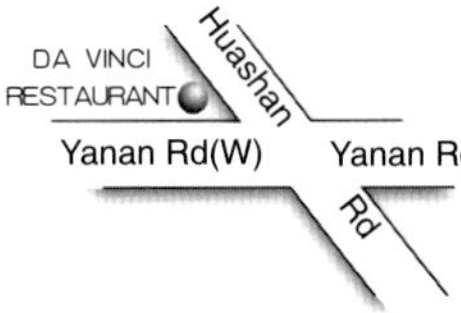

7. CONTINENTAL AND AMERICAN FOOD

ROCKS RESTAURANT

Add: 1376 Nanjing Rd, West
Tel.: 62798133
Means of communication:
Public buses 37, 20 and 921

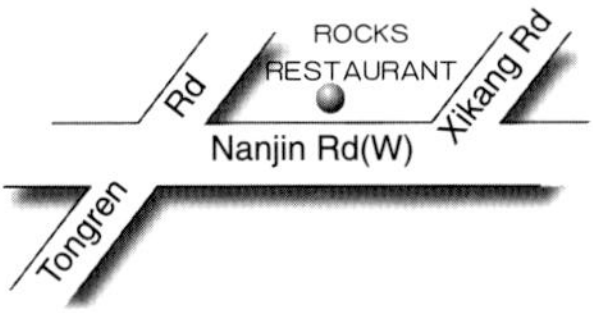

CHAMPS ELYSEES RESTAURANT

Add: 505 Nanjing Rd, E

Tel.: 63515888x4405

Means of communication:

Public buses 37, 20 and 921

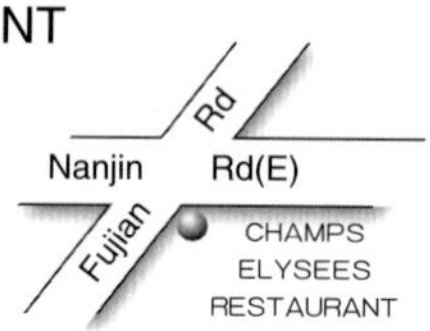

AMERICAN FRIDAY RESTAURANT

Add: 10 Hengshan Road

Tel.: 64734602

Means of communication:

No 1 Subway Hengshan Road stop public buses 15 and 49

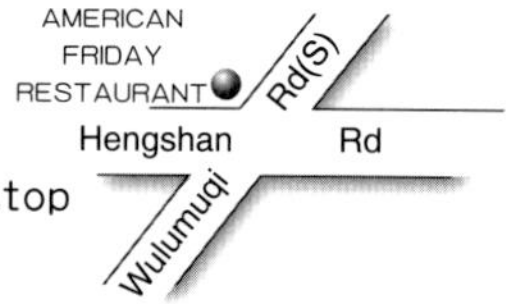

8. SOUTHEAST ASIAN FOOD

SUMMER PAVILION RESTAURANT

Add: 1376 Nanjing Rd, W

Tel.: 62798888x4770

Means of communication:

Public buses 37, 20, 921 and 24

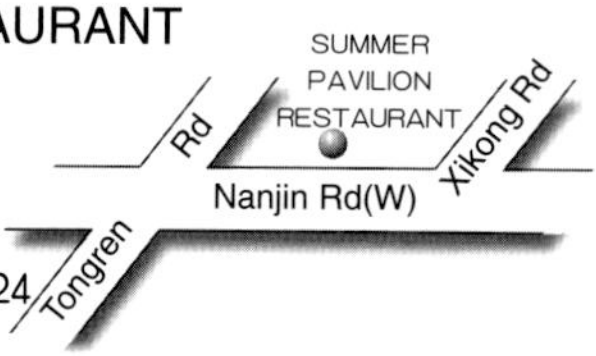

DONNA CAFE, BAR AND RESTAURANT

Add: 129 Yanan Rd, W

Tel.: 62493292x80208

Means of communication:

Public buses 71, 127 and 48

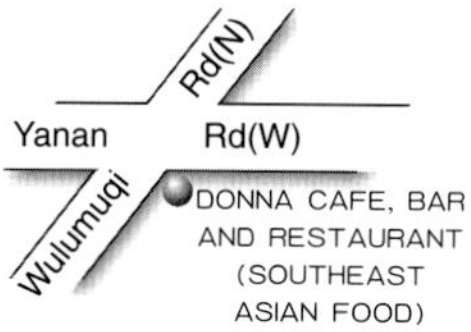

SINGAPORE THAT VILLAGE SHARKS FIN

Add: 660 Xinhua Road

Tel.: 62801000

Means of communication:

Public buses 48 and 71

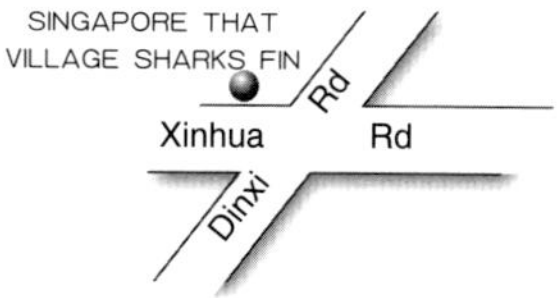

(IV) WESTEN FAST FOOD

Apart from large numbers of Chinese and Western restaurants, in recent years, along with the mingling of the Western culture, fast food has become very popular in Shanghai. Kentuckys and

Mcdonalds chains have mushroomed in Shanghai's bustling downtown. Pisa Huts, Haagen Dazs, Hardrock, and Friday Restaurant are favorite places for young people.

Kentucky (Service hours 10:00-22:00)

Huangpu Restaurant　Add: 66–69 Xizang Rd, MR
Huaihai Restaurant　Add: 627–641 Huaihai Rd, M

Mcdonald (Service hours 8:00-23:00)

Huaihai Road Restaurant　Add: 588 Huaihai Rd, M
Jingansi Restaurant　Add: 16–24 Wanhangdu Road
Nanjing Road, East, Restaurant　Add: 588 Nanjing Rd, E
88 Club Restaurant　Add: 88 Nanjing Rd, W

Pizza Hut (Service hours 8:30-22:00)

Xizang Road Branch　Add: 2nd Floor 700 Xizang Rd, M
88 Club Branch　Add: 2nd Floor Nanjing Rd, W

ACCOMMODATION

Shanghai, as China's largest city and a window of China's reform and opening to the outside world, attracts large numbers of domestic and overseas tourists for sightseeing and spending their holidays. However, before the reform and opening up Shanghai was poor in tourist facilities. In 1978, there were only 8 hotels that could cater to foreign tourists, namely, Jinjiang Hotel, Peace Hotel, Shanghai Mansions (including Pujiang Hotel), Park Hotel, Overseas Chinese Hotel, Jingan Hotel, Hengshan Hotel and Dahua Hotel with around 1,000 guest rooms. Since its reform and opening up, Shanghai has made great efforts in developing tourist hotels and facilities. Beautiful high-risers serving as hotels have come up one after another. In the meantime, international, trans-national hotel groups began to build or manage hotels with their own funds or as joint ventures, so that hotel facilities and service have been upgraded at big strides. At present, there are more than 100 star-rated hotels designated as tourist hotels that cater to foreign tourists with over 30,000 guest rooms. In Pudong New Area, a number of high-standard hotels have been built, thus greatly improving Shanghai's environment for investment and tourism. At the same time, in meeting the needs of tourists, Shanghai also built some economy-class hotels, such as "Jinjiang Star" and "Metropolitan Hotel". These are much appreciated by tourists. Shanghai's hotels have provided tourists a comfortable environment for rest and pleasure with their first-grade facilities and excellent service.

(I) 4-STAR AND 5-STAR DELUXE HOTELS

As an international metropolis, Shanghai, through several decades of development, now owns a number of high-class hotels with deluxe facilities and excellent management. There are now over 20 4-star and 5-star hotels, among which some are managed by international, trans-national hotel groups, who have brought along their up-to-date hotel management experience and contributed to the promoting of China's hospitality trade to world standard and upgraded the image of Shanghai's service trade. These high-grade hotels have greatly improved Shanghai's environment for investment and tourism.

1. 5-STAR HOTELS ☆☆☆☆☆

OKURA GARDEN HOTEL ☆☆☆☆☆

Garden Hotel, located by the well-known Huaihai Road, occupies an area of 37,000 sq.m., including a garden of 28,000 sq.m. The hotel is invested and managed by a Japanese group. It has 500 guest rooms, including 22 presidential suites and royal suites. Since its opening it has been awarded every year by the China National Tourism Administration as the "best hotel in the country" for its "best facilities, best food and beverage, and best service" as its principle of operation. It has also been appraised as one of the 45 best hotels in the world by the world-famous monthly journal "Organization of Investment".

Add: 58 Maoming Road

Tel.: 64151111

Means of communications: No 1 Subway Shaanxi Road, South, stop, public buses 126, 925 and 48

JINJIANG TOWER ☆☆☆☆☆

Shanghai Jinjiang Tower is a 5-star deluxe hotel managed by the Chinese. It is located in downtown Shanghai, near the bustling commercial street-Huaihai Road. The hotel consists of a 43-story main building and 5-story apron building, with different types of guest rooms, including 2 Chinese-style and Western-style presidential suites, 46 high-class suites, different restaurants, coffee rooms, bars and multi-functional halls, totaling 19 in number. Since its opening for business it has hosted state leaders from 150 countries. Many large-scale international conventions have been held here and many important agreements for international cooperation and investment projects have been signed here. It has been regarded popularly as a state guesthouse and been appraised as one of the 10 new scenic sights in Shanghai. In 1996, it was awarded the "5-star diamond prize", the highest prize for good service by the American Fine Quality Service Science Association. It was the first of its kind in Shanghai that had won this prize.

Add: 161 Changle Road

Tel.: 64151188

Means of communications: No 1 Subway Shaansi Road, South, stop, public buses 126, 925 and 48

PORTMAN RITZ-CARLTON ☆☆☆☆☆

Located on Nanjing Road, West, in downtown Shanghai, Portman Ritz-Carlton Hotel was formerly the Portman Shangri-la Hotel. In 1998, the world-known hotel management group, Ritz-Carlton, took over the management. The hotel was designed by the world-grade Portman Architects Firm. It is 50-story high, with 600 guest rooms of different types. President Clinton stayed in the hotel's presidential suite when he visited Shanghai in 1998.

Add: 1376 Nanjing Rd, W

Tel.: 62798888

Means of communications: Public buses 37, 20 and 76

HILTON SHANGHAI ☆☆☆☆☆

Located in bustling downtown, Jingan Hilton is a 5-star hotel set up by the internationally well-known Hilton Hotel Chain Group. It has 775 gracefully decorated guest rooms, including 48 deluxe suites and 21 presidential suites. It is complete in all room facilities, in food and beverage, business center, gym and convention service.

Add: 250 Huashan Road

Tel.: 62480000

Means of communications: Public buses 15, 127 and 71

SHANGHAI JC MANDARIN ☆☆☆☆☆

JC Mandarin Hotel, located on Nanjing Road, West, opposite to the Portman Ritz-Carlton, is a 5-star hotel with 600 guest rooms, 6 Chinese and Western restaurants and bars, 6 large and small meeting rooms and complete with business center, recreational and relaxing facilities.

Add: 1225 Nanjing Rd, W

Tel.: 62791888

Means of communications: Public buses 20, 37 and 76

HUATING HOTEL AND TOWERS ☆☆☆☆☆

Huating Hotel and Towers is a 5-star hotel largest in scale in Shanghai for hosting businessmen and tourists. It has a total floor space of 10,000 sq.m. with 1008 guest rooms of different types, including high-class villa-type suites of British, French, Japanese and Thai and different nationality styles, standard suites, double rooms and single rooms. It provides simultaneous interpretation equipment in its international convention hall. It is also complete in business center, recreational and relaxing facilities.

Add: 1200 Caoxi Rd, N

Tel.: 64391000

Means of communications: Public buses 43, 50, 42, and 926

THE WESTIN TAIPINGYANG ☆☆☆☆☆

It is located in Hongqiao Economic Development Zone, neighboring the International Exhibition Center and World Trade Center. The hotel owns 578 guest rooms, including 39 deluxe suites. It offers the most accomplished facilities and quality service.

Add: 5 Zunyi Rd, S

Tel.: 62758888

Means of communications: Public buses 57, 127 and 911

NEW ASIA TOMSON HOTEL ☆☆☆☆☆

Located on Zhangyang Road in the bustling New Shanghai Commercial City in Pudong, the 5-star hotel offers services of business, residence, convention, food and beverage, sports and keeping-fit, and holiday leisure. It has 422 gracefully furnished and cozy rooms, an extra large multi-functional hall and large and small meeting rooms. It is an ideal place for holding business meetings, wedding and birthday banquets and private parties. It is equipped with up-to-date gymnastic and recreational facilities, providing an environment for leisure and relaxation.

Add: 777 Zhangyang Road, Pudong

Tel.: 58318888

Means of communications: Public buses 983 and 980

JIN MAO GRAND HYATT HOTEL ☆☆☆☆☆

It is located in the middle of Lujiazui Finance and Trade Zone in Pudong on the 53-87 floors of China's No 1 high-riser, the Jin Mao Tower. It is the top of China's deluxe hotels. It is complete with deluxe suites, deluxe guest rooms, restaurants, snack bars, banquet halls, an amusement center, a jazz bar, a coffee room, a wine gallery, a descotheque, karaoke rooms, a recreational center, a swimming pool, a sauna bath, a gym, a convention center, equipped with simultaneous interpretation and audio-visual facilities. Guests staying there can enjoy the best service and a beautiful bird's-eye view of the city.

Add: 2 Century Avenue, Pudong

Tel.: 50491234

Means of communications: Public buses 81, 82 and 980

SHANGRI-LA HOTEL ☆☆☆☆☆

The newly completed Shangri-la Hotel with 612 guest rooms was designed according to the standard of a 5-star hotel. It is located beside the Huangpu River. Staying there, guests can enjoy the beautiful view on both banks of the river. It is managed by Shangri-la, the "best hotel group in Asia", and offers guests with the best hotel facilities and service.

Add: 33 Fucheng Rd, Pudong

Tel.: 68828888

Means of communications: Public buses 81, 82 and 980

2. 4-STAR HOTELS ☆☆☆☆

PEACE HOTEL ☆☆☆☆

It is located on the Bund at Nanjing Road, Shanghai's financial and commercial center, opposite to the newly developing Pudong New Area and the Oriental Pearl TV Tower. The hotel has a long history and a fine reputation. It consists of the southern and northern buildings of European architecture. The southern building was formerly the Palace Hotel built in 1906, designed in the architectural style of the Italian Renaissance. The northern building was formerly called Sassoon House. It is a British-style architecture, with granite walls and a cone-shape roof. There are 394 guest rooms, including suites of Chinese, British, French, Italian, German, Indian and Spanish styles. In recent years, it has been completely renovated and, apart from keeping its original style, all the rooms have been furnished with imported high-class furniture, electronic door locks, modern bathroom toiletry. Business and executive rooms are equipped with direct telephone lines, fax machines, and digtial-controlled communication facilities.

Add: 20 Nanjing Rd, E

Tel.: 63216888

Means of communications: Public buses 20, 55 and 123

JIN JIANG HOTEL ☆☆☆☆

Located on Maomin Road in downtown Shanghai and occupying an area of 10,000 sq.m., it is a well-known garden-type hotel. Since its opening to business, it has hosted 300 state leaders and government officials from 100 countries. It has won high comments from guests with its accomplished services. There are 515 guests rooms complete in facilities. It provides a modernized business center, a shopping arcade and a recreational center.

Add: 59 Maoming Rd, S

Tel.: 62582582

Means of communications: Public buses 71, 57 and 126

CROWNE PLAZA SHANGHAI ☆☆☆☆

It is one of the best managed hotels operating in China by the International Holiday Group. It occupies an area of 5,400 sq.m. The main building is 26-story with 496 finely decorated guest rooms. The rooms are installed with 25-channelled TV sets, self-aid coffee and tea-making utensils, DDD and IDD telephones, international internet and E-mail service, individually-controlled central air-conditioning, clocks, radios, private safes, wall-hanging hair blowers and mini bars. There are restaurants of different styles, 24-hour business center, facilities for recreation and relaxing in meeting the needs of guests.

Add: 388 Fanyu Road

Tel.: 6280888

Means of communications: Public buses 76, 48 and 911

HOLIDAY INN PUDONG ☆☆☆☆

It is the first hotel in Pudong managed by an international group. It was designed according to the standard of a 4-star hotel. It offers delicious food to guests, whether they dine in parties or individually.

There are finely decorated guest rooms, meeting halls complete in facilities, a specially managed gymnastic center, a swimming pool, a jaccuzzi and a business center.
Add: 899 Dongfang Road, Pudong
Tel.: 58306666
Means of communications: Public bus 980

HOTEL NIKKO LONGBAI SHANGHAI ☆☆☆☆

The hotel is only 5-minute drive from Shanghai Hongqiao International Airport. It provides safe and comfortable living environment. There are Chinese, Japanese and Western restaurants, bars, karaoke rooms, banquet halls and 24-hour room service. The guest rooms are air-conditioned, equipped with DDD and IDD direct dialing telephones, mini bars, color TV sets, shower and baths, a gymnastic center, a tennis court, a golf practice course, a sauna bath, a beauty parlor, a shopping arcade, laundry service, a business center and Japanese-speaking service attendants.
Add: 2451 Hongqiao Road
Tel.: 62689111
Means of communications: Public buses 48, 91 and 831

HOTEL SOFITEL SHANGHA’ ☆☆☆☆

The hotel is located in Shanghai's financial, trade, cultural, shopping and amusement center. A 10 minutes' walk will bring one to the Bund to appreciate the beautiful view on both banks of the Huangpu River and facing Pudong New Area in the distance on the opposite bank. The hotel has 400 rooms, including 68 gracefully decorated suites equipped with up-to-date facilities. The food and beverage, recreational and gymnastic facilities and business center all cater to guests with excellent service.
Add: 505 Nanjing Rd, E
Tel.: 63515888
Means of communications: public buses 14, 10 and 37

JIAN GUO HOTEL ☆☆☆☆

The 4-star hotel is located in Shanghai's bustling commercial area, Xujiahui. There are 475 guest rooms. Floors 19 to 23 are executive floors. There is an executive club, named Tianyuan Garden, for businessmen to relax and hold business talks. The guest rooms are elegantly furnished and complete in facilities. There are Chinese and Western restaurants, bars, coffee rooms and multi-functional meeting halls, totalling 29 in number.

Add: 439 Caoxi Rd, N

Tel.: 64399299

Means of communications: No 1 Subway Shanghai Stadium stop, public buses 15, 43 and 93

INTERNATIONAL EQUATORIAL HOTEL ☆☆☆☆

It is located in Shanghai's bustling Jingansi area, next to Hilton Hotel. It has 526 cozily and gracefully furnished guest rooms, different restaurants, a coffee room, a bar, a snack bar, a gymnastic center, a sauna bath, and a bowling room. It offers guests with attentive and excellent service.

Add: 65 Yanan Rd, W

Tel.: 62481688

Means of communications: Public buses 71, 127 and 15

RADISSON SAS LANSHENG HOTEL ☆☆☆☆

Located in the northeast corner of Shanghai, the hotel is the first of a chain hotel Radisson SAS Group specially permitted to run in China. It has 405 guest rooms, including 39 suites. All the rooms are elegantly furnished and complete in facilities, especially in the bathrooms decorated with marble and fitted with both shower and bath, all of a first-grade establishment in Shanghai. There is a sea food restaurant, a coffee room, a bar, a snack bar, a gym, a sauna bath, a bowling room and a badminton court, offering guests with attentive and meticulous service.

Add: 1000 Quyang Road

Tel.: 65428000

Means of communications: 116, 139 and 123

WORLDFIELD CONVENTION HOTEL ☆☆☆☆

Located in Hongqiao Economic Development Zone and occupying an area of 30,000 sq.m., the hotel is the first of its kind in Shanghai catering specially to international conventions and exhibitions. It owns 3 large-scale meeting halls, a 700-seat banquet hall, a 600-

seat multi-functional lecture hall and a 600-seat conference hall. There are also 15 large and small meeting rooms available for business activities and 370 spacious and well furnished guest rooms, complete with all necessary facilities and services.

Add: 2106 Hongqiao Road

Tel.: 62703388

Means of communications: Public buses 48, 57 and 911

YANGTZE NEW WORLD HOTEL ☆☆☆☆

The 4-star hotel is located in Hongqiao Economic Development Zone. It has 553 guest rooms of different types, all equipped with individually controlled central air-conditioning and up-to-date facilities and services. It provides quality service to businessmen and tourists with its business center, private meeting rooms, ticket booking, limousines, executive suites and recreational facilities for guests to spend their leisure time.

Add: 2099 Yanan Rd, W

Tel.: 62750000

Means of communications: Public buses 57, 127 and 911

JING AN HOTEL ☆☆☆☆

Jing An Hotel, located in downtown Shanghai, is a Spanish architectural building with a history of 70 years. It has 230 guest rooms of different types, different restaurants, bars, multi-functional halls and gymnastic and recreational facilities, offering guests with quality service.

Add: 370 Huashan Road

Tel.: 62481888

Means of communications: Public buses 15, 71 and 127

OCEAN HOTEL ☆☆☆☆

Located near the Bund, the hotel provides guests with a wide view of the Huangpu River. It has 370 guest rooms, all elegantly furnished and uniquely designed. There are 2 executive floors. All the suites and rooms are complete with necessary facilities for the convenience and comfort of guests on business or tours.

Add: 1171 East Damin Road

Tel.: 65458888

Means of communications: Public buses 37 and 135

RAINBOW HOTEL ☆☆☆☆

The 4-star hotel, located in Hongqiao Economic Development Zone, has a 3l-story main building with 650 guest rooms of different types, different restaurants, bars, multi-functional halls and health and recreational facilities, offering guests with quality service.

Add: 2000 Yanan Rd, W

Tel.: 62753388

Means of communications: Public buses 57, 127 and 911

GALAXY HOTEL ☆☆☆☆

Located in Hongqiao Economic Development Zone, the hotel has 840 guest rooms of different types and restaurants serving different local flavors, bars and a number of recreational facilities, totaling 15 in number.

Add: 888 Zhongshan Rd, W

Tal: 62755888

Means of communications: Public buses 57, 127 and 911

PARK HOTEL ☆☆☆☆

Located in downtown Shanghai, it is a well-known hotel with a long history. It has 175 standard rooms and executive suites, Chinese and Western restaurants, banquet halls, meeting rooms and recreational facilities for guests to spend their leisure time and relax themselves.

Add: 170 Nanjing Rd, W

Tel.: 63275225

Means of communications: No 1 Subway People Square stop, public buses 37, 20 and 921

BAOSHAN HOTEL ☆☆☆☆

Baoshan Hotel under Baogang Group is a 4-star hotel located in Baoshan Iron and Steel Complex area. It has hosted many state leaders, government officials and VIPs of the financial circle from different countries. The hotel is beautifully designed and decorated, complete with restaurants, banquet halls, meeting rooms, a bussiness center and recreational facilities.

Add: 1813 Mudanjiang Road

Tel.: 56698888

Means of communications: Public buses 53, 116 and 531

SHANGHAI MANSIONS ☆☆☆☆

Shanghai Mansions, formerly named the Broadway Mansions, is one of old and famous hotels in Shanghai. Standing by the Huangpu River and Suzhou Creek, at the side of the Waibaidu Brigde, it has a favorable location. From its top floors one can have a good view of the scenery on both banks of the river. It has 234 rooms and restaurants of different.

Add: 20 North Suzhou Road

Tel.: 63246260

Means of communications: Public buses 22, 37 and 55

(II)OTHER STAR-RATED HOTELS

Apart from the above high-class hotels, there are also other star-rated hotels in meeting the needs of different guests. They totally nearly 100, which are basically managed by ourselves. They also offer guests with quality service and provide good places for comfort and rest.

1. 3-STAR HOTEL ☆☆☆

BAO LONG HOTEL ☆☆☆

Add: 180 Yixian Road

Tel.: 65425425

Means of communications: Public buses 51, 52 and 116

CITY HOTEL ☆☆☆

Add: 5-7 Shaansi Rd, S

Tel.: 62551133

Means of communications: Public buses 57, 127 and 113

DONG HU HOTEL ☆☆☆

Add: 70 Donghu Road

Tel.: 64158158

Means of communications: Public buses 44, 45 and 94

EAST CHINA HOTEL ☆☆☆

Add: 111 Tianmu Rd, W

Tel.: 63178000

Means of communications: No 1 Subway Railway Station stop, public buses 95, 113 and 116

HENGSHAN HOTEL ☆☆☆

Add: 534 Hengshan Road

Tel.: 64377050

Means of communications: No 1 Subway Hengshan Road stop, public buses 15 and 42

GOLDEN BRIDGE HOTEL ☆☆☆

Add: 1370 Jinqiao Road

Tel.: 58990890

Means of communications: Public buses 783, 792 and No 6 Tunnel line

JINJIANG Y.M.C.A. HOTEL ☆☆☆

Add: 123 Xizang Rd, S

Tel.: 63261040

Means of communication: Public buses 18, 108 and 46

JINSHAJIANG HOTEL ☆☆☆

Add: 801 Jinshajiang Road

Tel.: 62578888

Means of communication: Public buses 94 and 67

LONGMEN HOTEL ☆☆☆

Add: 777 Hengfeng Road

Tel.: 63170000

Means of communication: No 1 Subway Railway Station stop and public Buses 95, 113 and 114

MAGNOLIA HOTEL ☆☆☆

Add: 1251 Siping Road

Tel.: 65026888

Means of communication: Public buses 55, 61 and 115

NEW ASIA HOTEL ☆☆☆
Add: 422 Tiantong Road
Tel.: 63242210
Means of communication: Public buses 21, 19 and 17

NEW GARDEN HOTEL ☆☆☆
Add: 1900 Hongqiao Road
Tel.: 62426688
Means of communication: Public buses 57, 127 and 911

QIAN HE HOTEL ☆☆☆
Add: 650 Yishan Road
Tel.: 64700000
Means of communication: Public buses 93 and 89

SHANGHAI HOTEL ☆☆☆
Add: 505 Wulumuqi Road
Tel.: 62480088
Means of communication: Public buses 71, 127 and 15

OLYMPIC CLUB
Add: 1800 Zhongshan Rd, S 2
Tel.: 64391399
Means of communication: Public buses 15, 43 and 93

PACIFIC HOTEL ☆☆☆
Add: 108 Nanjing Rd, W
Tel.: 63276226
Means of communication: No 1 Subway People Square stop and public buses 37, 20 and 921

SILK ROAD HOTEL
Add: 777 Quyang Road
Tel.: 65549988
Means of communication: Public buses 116, 139 and 123

YANAN HOTEL ☆☆☆
Add: 1111 Yanan Rd, M
Tel.: 62481111

Means of communication: Public buses 71, 127 and 57

2. 2-STAR HOTELS

AUGUST FIRST GUESTHOUSE ☆☆

Add: 888 Quyang Road

Tel.: 65535288

Means of communication: Public buses 116, 139 and 123

BAILEMEN HOTEL ☆☆

Add: 1728 Nanjing Rd, W

Tel.: 62488686

Means of communication: Public buses 15, 21 and 94

EAST ASIA HOTEL ☆☆

Add: 680 Nanjing Rd, E

Tel.: 63223223

Means of communication: Public buses 20, 37 and 921

LIANG LIANG HOTEL ☆☆

Add: 77 Zhongshan Rd, S

Tel.: 63743969

Means of communication: Public buses 55, 22 and 65

SEA GULL HOTEL ☆☆

Add: 60 Huangpu Road

Tel.: 63251500

Means of communication: Public buses 55, 22 and 37

PUJIANG HOTEL ☆☆

Add: 15 Huangpu Road

Tel.: 63246388

Means of communication: Public buses 55, 65 and 37

SEVEN HEAVENS HOTEL ☆☆

Add: 627 Nanjing Rd, E

Tel.: 63220777

Means of communication: Public buses 37, 20 and 921

3. 1-STAR HOTELS

CHANGYANG HOTEL ☆

Add: 1800 Changyang Road

Tel.: 65434890

Means of communication: Public buses 22 and 137

SOUTH CHINA HOTEL ☆

Add: 55 Caoxi Sicun, Longcao Road

Tel.: 64705888

Means of communication: Public buses 93, 925 and 48

WEST GARDEN HOTEL ☆

Add: 2384 Hongqiao Road

Tel.: 62687840

Means of communication: Public buses 48, 57 and 911

JIAOYUAN HOTEL ☆

Add: 170 Huoshan Road

Tel.: 65412160

Means of communication: Public buses 22, 37 and 28

YUNFENG HOTEL ☆

Add: 1700 Beijing Rd, W

Tel.: 62560469

Means of communication: Public buses 112 and 21

(Ⅲ)POPULAR INNS, HOTELS AND HOSTELS

Apart from the above hotels catering to foreign tourists there are many popular hotels, inns and hostels in Shanghai. These are not so well furnished as the star-rated hotels, but they also provide comfortable lodging at reasonable prices, therefore, they are appreciated by a great many general tourists. The recently built Hotel of Jinjiang Star and Metropolitan Hotel chain are very good economy-class hotels. They provide a clean and neat environment with basic facilities and good service. They are much favored by the general public.

PEOPLE'S HOTEL

Add: 500 Tianjin Rd

Tel.: 63517636

Means of communication: Public buses 20 and 37

JINJIANG STAR PUDONG HOTEL

Add: 3888 Pudong Rd, S

Tel.: 68700398

Means of communication: Public buses 574 and 581

SHANGHAI LUZHOU HOTEL

Add: 705 Pusan Road

Tel.: 58752188

Means of communication: Public buses 771 and 980

EVERBRIGHT HOLIDAY INN

Add: 1050 lane Changan Road

Tel.: 63170560

Means of communication: 95 and 113

SHANGHAI AOMEN HOTEL

Add: 4 Aomen Road

Tel.: 62666138

Means of communication; Public buses 113, 112 and 76

SHANGHAI LIANG YOU HOTEL

Add: 1455 South Suzhou Road

Tel.: 62533663

Means of communication: Public buses 64 and 16

JINJIANG STAR HOLIDAY INN

Add: 227 Hongmei Road

Tel.: 64518198

Means of communication: No 1 Subway Hongmei Road stop and public buses 50, 703 and 704

METROPOLITAN HOTEL TIANJIN BRANCH

Add: 293 Tianjin Road

Tel.: 63226651

Means of communication: Public buses 20, 21 and 37

METROPOLITAN HOTEL GREAT WORLD BRANCH

Add: 483 Yanan Rd, E

Tel.: 63869260

Means of communication: Public buses 71, 127 and 18

METROPOLITAN HOTEL XIANGRONG BRANCH

Add: 661 Zhejiang Rd, M

Tel.: 63514658

Means of communication: Public buses 64 and 19

TRAVELLING

Shanghai is China's largest city, as well as an important window and a leading port and airport on the Pacific coast and a hub of land communications. Shanghai's communication conditions are very favorable. The entry and exit from Shanghai and transportation by air, railway, highway, sea and inland river have developed rapidly. In the urban areas the Nanpu and Yangpu Bridges, the tunnels under Huangpu River, the expressway system (the Inner-ring Road, the South-North Viaduct, Yanan Road Viaduct, No 1 Subway and No 2 Subway under construction, the elevated Light-rail and the Outer-ring Road) has formed a major artery in Shanghai's traffic. The subways, taxis, public buses, mini-buses and ferries provide service to travelers day and night, reaching to every corner of the city. These are rendering great convenience to Shanghai citizens in their daily lives and domestic and foreign tourists in traveling and sightseeing

(I) ENTRY AND EXIT FROM SHANGHAI

Shanghai is China's important gate and window, as well as an important hub of communications by air, land and sea. Along with China's reform and opening to the outside world Shanghai has continually developed and made progress. Every year, there is an increasing number of domestic and overseas tourists coming to Shanghai for sightseeing, business and transit. Shanghai's traffic facilities and conditions have been improving and upgrading. The annual passenger and cargo transport volume of Shanghai Hongqiao Airport, Shanghai Port and Railway Station always ranks among the first of big cities on China's mainland. Following the completion and opening to traffic of Shanghai-Nanjing and Shanghai-Ningbo Freeways, the inland communications has been greatly improved. An express, convenient and three-dimensional communication network has been formed in urban Shanghai.

1. CIVIL AVIATION

Shanghai is one of China's leading airports, as well as an important aviation hub on the Pacific coast. Shanghai Hongqiao Airport connects directly or indirectly with important cities in the world. The annual passenger transport volume ranks second in the country. International routes reach big cities in 30 countries like Tokyo, Osaka, Nagasaki, Fukuoka, New York, Los Angeles, San Francisco, Toronto, Vancouver, Paris, etc. and domestic lines reach Hong Kong, Beijing, Guangzhou, Shen Zhen, Kunming, Chongqing, Wulumuqi, Xian, Guilin, Qingdao, Dalian, Shenyang, Haerbin, etc., covering almost the big and medium cities in the country. Hongqiao Airport dispatches planes on 300 air routes. About 40 domestic and overseas airlines have opened direct routes to Shanghai, while new routes and flights are increasing, making entry and exit by air more thoroughgoing.

HONGQIAO INTERNATIONAL AIRPORT

Hongqiao International Airport, located in the western part of Shanghai and 13 km from the People's Square in downtown, is the third largest international airport in the country and an aviation hub in east China. The airport has up-to-date navigation facilities, large lounges, spacious aircraft parking area. It has formed a multi-function and multi-level aviation service network.

Add: 2550 Hongqiao road

Tel.: 62688918

Means of communications: Public bus 925 and shuttle bus

PUDONG INTERNATIONAL AIRPORT

Pudong International Airport is located in Pudong New Area, 30 km from downtown Shanghai. The first phase of the airport was completed and put into operation at the end of 1999. It is equipped with world-grade advanced facilities. The second phase of the project will be completed in 2005. The project consists of a 4,000-m long runway, 80,000-sq.m. passenger building and 4 first-grade south-northward runways. Once completed, it will handle a yearly passenger transport volume of 70,000,000 person/times and a freight volume of 5,000,000 tons. It will lay a foundation for Shanghai's transport industry at the transit of the centuries.

Add: 100 No I Jiangzhenwei Road

Tel.: 58938800

Means of communications: Special bus line (Pudong

airport-Hongqiao Airport, Pudong Airport-Shanghai Railway Station and Pudong Airport-Civil Aviation bus stop at Shaanxi Road)

CIVIL AVIATION TICKET BOOKING OFFICE

China Eastern Airlines

Add: 200 Yanan Rd, W

Tel.: 62475953 (domestic), 62472255 (international)

Means of communications: Public buses 71, 127 and 57

Shanghai Airlines

Add: 212 Jiangning Road

Tel.: 62558888

Means of communications: Public buses 112, 23 and 24

Air China

Add: 600 Huashan Road

Tel.: 62692999

Means of communications: public buses 48 and 113

South China Airlines

Add: 2000 Zhongshan Rd, N

Tel.: 52912000

Means of communications: Public buses 69, 224, 68 and 112

Southwest Airlines

Add: 150 Maomin Rd, S

Tel.: 64333355

Means of communications: Public buses 17 24 and 96

Northwest Airlines

Add: 258 Weihai Road

Tel.: 62674233

Means of communications: Public buses 71, 49 and 127

North China Airlines

Add: 61 Nanjing Rd, E

Tel.: 63506030

Means of communications: Public buses 20, 37 and 55

Xinjiang Airlines

Add: 370 Changde Road

Tel.: 62474497

Means of communications: Public buses 15, 21 and 20

Shenzhen Airlines

Add: 504 Fanyu Road

Tel.: 62825275

Means of communications: Public buses 48, 806 and 572

Hainan Airlines

Add: 202 Hongda Building Hongqiao International Airport

Tel.: 63270259

Means of communications: Public bus 925 and shuttle bus

Yunnan Airlines

Add: 878 Jiangsu Road

Tel.: 62516996

Means of communications: Public buses 44, 62 and 96

Dragon Air

Add: 1376 Nanjing Rd, W

Tel.: 62797147

Means of communications: Public buses 20, 37 and 921

OVERSEAS AIRLINES SHANGHAI OFFICE

Untied Airlines

Add: 1376 Nanjing Rd, W

Tel.: 62798010

Means of communications: Public buses 20, 37 and 921

American Northwest Airlines

Add: 137 Nanjing Road, West

Tel.: 62798088

Means of communications: Public buses 20, 37 and 921

All Nippon Airways

Add: 1376 Nanjing Rd, W

Tel.: 62797000

Means of communications: Public buses 20, 37 and 921

Japan Airlines

Add: 205 Maomin Rd, S

Tel.: 64723000

Means of communications: Public buses 17, 24 and 96

Singapore Airlines

Add: 606-608 Karry Center 1515 Nanjing Rd, W

Tel.: 62891000

Means of communications: Public buses 20, 37 and 921

Asiana Airlines

Add: 2000 Yanan Rd, W

Tel.: 62194000

Means of communications: Public buses 831, 925 and 911

Thai Airways International

Add: 1376 Nanjing Rd, W

Tel.: 62797175

Means of communications: Public buses 20, 37 and 921

Dragon Air

Add: 1376 Nanjing Rd, W

Tel.: 62798128

Means of communications: Public buses 20, 37 and 921

Qantas Airways Limited

Add: 1376 Nanjing Road, West

Tel.: 62798128

Means of communications: Public buses 20, 37 and 921

Swiss Air

Add: 1376 Nanjing Rd, W

Tel.: 62797381

Means of communications: Public buses 20, 37 and 921

Air France

Add: 128 Nanjing Rd, W

Tel.: 63606688

Means of communications: Public buses 20, 37 and 921

Malaysia Airlines

Add: 1376 Nanjing Rd, W

Tel.: 62798607

Means of communications: Public buses 20, 37 and 921

Air Macau

Add: 65 Yanan Rd, W

Tel.: 62481110

Means of communications: Public buses 71, 127 and 925

Lufthansa

Add: 250 Huashan Road

Tel.: 62481100

Means of communications: 71, 127 and 48

2. RAILWAY

Shanghai's railway reaches 28 provinces and autonomous regions in the country and Russia, Korea, east Europe and northwest Europe abroad. Shanghai Railway Station dispatches every day 80 pairs of trains back and forth to big and medium cities in the country. With Shanghai as the center passenger trains running to cities at a distance about 1,000 km are dispatched in the evening and arrive in the morning. For the convenience of travelers, Shanghai has opened public bus and holiday lines. The public bus lines run between Meilong in Shanghai and Hangzhou in Zhejiang. Tourists need not to book tickets beforehand, but get the tickets on board. In this way, tourists can have more flexibility in arranging their travel. The holiday lines are specially arranged for tourists on holidays and at weekends, so that they can go sightseeing in nearby scenic spots on a short holiday.

Shanghai Railway Station

Shanghai Railway Station is a large-scale passenger terminal. The station has two exits, the north and the south, and the waiting rooms on an elevated level. In the station there is a train-boarding indicator system and 16 large and small air-conditioned waiting lounges. Outside the station are two squares, the south and the north. connecting respectively No 1 South Exit, No 2 South Exit and North Exit. There is a tunnel linking the subway. Around the squares there are many terminals of public buses.

Add: 303 Moling Road

Tel.: 63179090

Means of communications: Public buses 13, 41, 63, 64, 95, 104, 106, 109, 113, 114, 115, 117, 902, 903, 904, ZX502, 506, 507, 508, 592, No 3 Tunnel line, overnight lines 302, 305, 306, 308, 310, 315, 322, 324, 328 and 329

Ticket offices:

1. 230 Beijing Rd, E (for destinations south of Jinhua and north of the hangjiang River)
2. 121 Xizang Rd, S (for Nanjing, Tongling, Hangzhou and Ningbo)
   128 Yuyuan Road (for Nanjing, Tongling, Hangzhou and Ningbo)
   431 Changyang Road (for Nanjing, Tongling, Hangzhou and Ningbo)

The above ticket offices are for booking tickets 3 days before. Tickets for the day are available at the railway station.

Shanghai Railway West Station

Shanghai Railway West Station is a smaller station in Shanghai. From here the trains leave for Baotou, Qiqihaer, Yantai, Changchun and Hengyang and some of the trains to Guangzhou, Ningbo and Nanjing West Station.

Add: 1 Taopu Road

Tel.: 62549500

Means of communications: Public buses 106 and 129

Shanghai Railway Meilong Station

It is a special station for dispatching public bus lines to Hangzhou. It dispatches every day 4 trains to Hangzhou. It takes only Less than two hours to arrive at Hangzhou East Station. Passengers may get tickets on board. The station is connected to No 1 subway, much for the convenience of passengers in transfer.

Add: Meilong

Tel.: 63179090

Means of communications: No 1 Subway Hongmei Road stop

3. WATER TRANSPORT

Shanghai Passenger Terminal

Shanghai Port is China's leading port and one of 10 major ports in the world. International shipping can reach 400 ports in 160 countries and regions in the world. It is an important gate for entry and exit of Shanghai. It is also a hub of passenger water transport in East China. It is the only passenger terminal for sea and river transport. The terminal consists of three terminals at Shiliupu, Gongping Road and the International Passenger Terminal.

Shiliupu Passenger Terminal

Add: 111 Zhongshan Rd, E 2

Tel.: 63261261

Means of communications: Public buses 11, 22, 55, 65, 303, 307, 311, 313, 317 and 868

Gongping Road Terminal

Add: 60 Gongping Road

Tel.: 63261261

Means of communications: Public buses 13, 19, 22, 28, 37, 135, 145, 319 and 746

Ticket office:

Add: 1 Jinling Rd, E

Tel.: 63261261

Means of communications: Public buses 11, 22, 55, 65 and 126

The above ticket offices are for booking two days ahead. Tickets for the day are available at the terminals.

4. HIGHWAYS

The two freeways, Shanghai-Nanjing and Shanghai-Hangzhou, linking Shanghai are completed and opened to traffic; the Shanghai-Nanjing Freeway was completed on September 1996 and the Shanghai-Hangzhou Freeway, at the end of 1998. The Shanghai-Nanjing Freeway leaving Shanghai passes Suzhou, Wuxi, Changzhou, Zhenjiang and arrives in Nanjing with a total length of 274 km. The Shanghai-Hangzhou Freeway, 151-km long, is part of the Shanghai-Hangzhou-Ningbo Freeway, linking Shanghai, Hangzhou and Ningbo. These two freeways are part of the 320 State Highway, one of the 12 trunk lines in the country. They are equipped with first-grade facilities and the multi-media computer control system. Driving from Shanghai one will reach Suzhou, Wuxi, Changzhou, Nanjing and Hangzhou in 45, 75, 100, 160 and 90 minutes respectively. The time is much shortened compared with those in the past. The highway transport is much faster and more convenient between Shanghai and its neighboring cities.

(II) LOCAL COMMUNICATIONS

1. Subway

The subway is the fastest and most efficient means of communication in the city. At present, No 1 subway is in operation, starting from Xingzhuang to the Railway Station, with a total length of 21.51 km and 12 stops along the way. The stops are kept clean and neat, bright and elegantly quiet, full of the atmosphere of the times. Every stop has several entries and exits and distinctive signs giving directions to passengers. The first phase of No 2 subway was completed and opened to traffic at the end of 1999. No 2 subway will start from Hongqiao International Airport to Pudong.

Ticket price: 3-4 yuan (No 1 Subway)
Tel.: 63189188
Operation hours: 5:30-22:20 (to Railway Station), 5:30-22:00 (to Xinzhuang)

2. Special Tourist Lines

It is one of the projects of the municipal government for the convenience of citizens and tourists from other places in China in sightseeing in Shanghai. There are altogether 10 such special bus lines, each linking the different scenic spots along the route, reaching to different directions from Shanghai. There is music accompaniment on the way, guiding commentary on the scenic spots and offering entrance tickets with discount. The center of these buses is at Shanghai Stadium.

Add: of bus center: No 4 parking lot of Shanghai Stadium
Means of communications: No 1 Subway Shanghai Stadium stop and public buses 89, 42, 926 and 50

No I Bus Line: Shanghai Stadium - Scenic spots in Songjiang District

Tel.: 64265987
First bus: 6:30
Last bus: 17:00
Interval: 20-40 minutes
Bus tickets: Guilin Park - 2 yuan; Jiuliting - 4 yuan; Sheshan Drifting World - 8 yuan; State Forest Park - 10 yuan; Songjiang Square Pagoda and Pond of the Drunken Bai - 12 yuan

No 2 Bus Line: Shanghai Stadium - Scenic spots in Nanhui County

Tel.: 62701674
First bus: 6:30
Last bus: 19:15
Interval: 15 minutes
Bus tickets: Dapu Road - 2 yuan; Shiliupou - 4 yuan; Beicai - 6 yuan; Zhoupu - 8 yuan; Shaxiqi World and Hangtou - 8 yuan; Xin chang - 10 yuan; Wildlife Zoo and Huinan - 12 yuan

No 3 Bus Line: Shanghai Stadium - Scenic spots in Pudong New Area

Tel.: 64648536
First bus 7:30
Last bus: 16:50
Interval: 60 minutes
Bus tickets: People's Square - 2 yuan; Lujiazui Central Landscaped Ground, Oriental Pearl TV Tower, Riverside Boulevard, Jin Mao Tower, Shanghai Stock Exchange Building - 4 Yuan; Five-ox City, Garden of Celebrities - 6 yuan; Jinqiao Export Processing Zone, Zhangjiang Hi-tech Park Area, Sunqiao Modern Agricultural Park Area - 10 yuan; Huaxia Cultural Park - 10 yuan; Huaxia Tourist City and Huaxia Beach Touri Area - 12 yuan

No 4 Bus Line: Shanghai - Scenic spots in Qingpu County

Tel.: 64265991
First bus: 7:00
Last bus: 15:00
Interval: 30-60 minutes
Bus tickets: Shanghai Zoo - 2 yuan; Garden of Meandering Stream - 10 Yuan; Zhujiaqiao - 12 yuan; Water Sports Ground - 14 yuan; Baoguo Temple - 14 yuan; Fork Club - 16 yuan; Grand View Garden - 16 yuan

No 5 Bus Line: Shanghai Stadium-Scenic spots in Chongming County

Tel.: 64265989
First bus: 6:30
Last bus: 16:40
Interval: 40-90 minutes
Bus tickets: People's Square - 2 yuan; Baolong Hotel - 4 yuan; Wusong Wharf - 6 yuan; Xiayuan Hotel - 6 yuan; Baoyang Wharf - 8 yuan; Chongming Study Palace - 8 yuan; Chongming Dongping Forest Park - 12 yuan

No 6 Bus Line(A): Shanghai Stadium - Scenic spots in Jiading District

Tel.: 62465990

First bus: 6:30

Last bus: 17:00

Interval: 45 minutes

Bus tickets: Changfeng Park - 2 yuan; Zhenru Town - 4 yuan; Guji Garden - 6 yuan; Jiading Hotel, Dragons Meeting Pool, Confucius' Temple, Garden of Autumn Clouds, Shanghai Automobile Center - 10 yuan

No 6 Bus Line(B): Shanghai Stadium - Scenic spots in Jiading District(Anting)

Tel.: 63902262

First bus: 6:30

Last bus: 17:20

Interval: 30-35 minutes

Bus tickets: Changfeng Park - 2 yuan; Shanghai Jingdezhen Ceramics Art Center, Light Industrial and Textile Products Market - 4 Yuan; Jindian Ranch - 4 yuan; Imperial Club; Dreamland Amusement Park - 6 yuan; Meilihua Holiday Resort - 8 Yuan

No 7 Bus Line: Humanistic and Historic Sights

Tel.: 64265991

First bus: 6:30

Last bus: 18:00

Interval: 30 minutes

Bus tickets: Longhua Martyrs' Cemetery, Soong ching Ling's Former Residence, Shanghai Library, Shanghai Museum, Site of First National Congress of the Communist Party of China, Zhou Enlai"s Former Apartment, Dr Sun Yatsen's Former Residence - 3 yuan for each place

No 8 Bus Line: Overnight Sightseeing

Tel.: 64265989

First bus: 16:00

Last bus: 19:00

Interval: 50-60 minutes

Bus tickets: Jingan Temple, the Bund and Nanjing Road Pedestrian Walking street - 3 yuan for each place

No 9 Bus Line: Shanghai Stadium - Wuxi

Tel.: 64265986

First bus: 7:10

Last bus: 17:00

Dispatch hours: 8 shifts one day

Bus tickets: Wuxi Railway Station - 43 yuan

No 10 Bus Line: Downtown Shopping Tourist Line

Tel.: 64265987

First bus: 6:30

Last bus: 19:00

Interval: 10 minutes

Bus tickets: Xujiahui Commercial City, Huaihai Road Commercial Street, Nanjing Road Commercial Street, Sichuan Rd, N, Commercial Street, Lu Xun Park(Hongkou Stadium) - 3 yuan for each place

3. SIGHTSEEING BUS

Shanghai Jinjiang Sightseeing Bus is the first sightseeing bus line opened by Jinjiang Group. The bus line connects the major scenic spots in urban Shanghai. The bus fare is 18 yuan for the whole tour. Visitors may buy one ticket and get on or off the bus at any stop. This system is much appreciated by tourists. Later on, Dazhong Taxi Co. and Shanghai Tourist Taxi Co. also opened several bus lines reaching different major scenic spots in the city and the suburban counties. Such bus lines have rendered much convenience to visitors.

Shanghai Jinjiang Sightseeing Bus

Tour: Jinjiang Hotel (Gate 1)- People's Square - Oriental Pearl TV Tower (Gate 2) - Yaohan Nextage Commercial Building - Nanpu Bridge - Yuyuan Garden - the Bund - People's Square - Jinjiang Hotel (Gate 1)

For their convenience tourists may get on the bus at any one of the following stops:

Railway Station area: East China Hotel, Postal and Telegraph Building or Longmen Hotel

Caoyang area: Jinshajiang Hotel or Jiangsu Hotel

Tianshan area: Xianxia Hotel or Yuping Hotel
Hongqiao area: Friendship Co., Sanxiang Hotel or Rainbow Hotel
Time of the tour: 9:00-16:00
Interval: 45 minutes
Tickets are available at every stop
Group tickets are sold at 51 Guangdong Road
For individual tourist tickets are available on the bus
Tel.: 62701667

Dazhong Sightseeing Bus:

Tour: Xinjiang road (cross road of Xizang Rd, N) - Shanghai Railway Station - Shanghai Railway West Station - Guyi Garden in Nanxiang - Shanghai Universal Amusement Park
Time: 6:30 - 18:30 at Xinjiang Road; 8:00 - 21:00 at Shanghai Universal Amusement Park
Interval: 15 minutes

4. TAXIS

The taxi business has developed rapidly in recent years. At present, there are over 4,000 taxis running in the city. Taxis are available round the clock at the airport, railway station, wharves, hotels, major scenic areas and amusement centers. They are very convenient for travelers. The management of taxi service in Shanghai is standardized and service quality is good. Most of the taxis are Santana cars. Santana 2000-types are mainly in operation. Taxi fare for every km is marked on a sign on the window pane. There is a mileage meter on every car.

Qiangsheng Taxi Co.

Add: 920 Nanjing Rd, W
Tel.: 62580000
Tel. for complaint: 62581234

Dazhong Taxi Co.

Add: 1515 Zhongshan Rd, W
Tel: 62188888
Tel. for complaint: 62173350

Friendship Taxi Service Co.
(The three Taxi Co. combined to form Jinjiang Taxi Co.)
Add: 847 Yanan Rd, M
Tel: 62584584
Tel. for complaint: 62791279

Tourist Taxi Co.
Add: 16 Wuzhong Road
Tel: 62155555
Tel. for complaint: 64648888

Zhenhau Taxi Service Co.
Add: 147 Lingling Road
Tel: 62758800
Tel. for complaint: 64169898

5. PUBLIC BUSES IN URBAN AREAS

Along with the progress of times many new means of transportation have come into being, like the subway, the light-rail, taxis, and buses, which have provided a wide range for people to choose. However, public buses are still the first choice for the general public with their reasonable prices, extensive routes and long service hours. Since its reform public transportation has made big strides in rendering quick and convenient service. Many new lines have been added. Apart from regular buses there are night buses, air-conditioned buses, double-deckers, tunnel lines, and bridge lines. The bus fare is 1 yuan for regular buses, 1.2 yuan for tunnel and bridge lines and 2 yuan for air-conditioned buses.

6. FERRIES

In the past, the only means of transportation between the two banks of the Huangpu River was the ferry. With the building of 4 great bridges and 2 tunnels traffic has become much faster and more convenient. However, for bicycle riders, their choice is still the ferry. Tel. for complaint: 63200015

SURROUNDING AREAS

(I) ZHOUZHUANG

Zhouzhuang in Jiangsu Province is located 38 km from Suzhou and in the southwest of Kunshan City. It is like a shining pearl studded on the Dianshan Lake beside the Grand View Garden. It has a history of more than 900 years.

During the period of Spring and Autumn and the Warring States, Zhouzhuang was the fief of King Wu's younger son Yao and also named Yao City. In the Northern Song Dynasty (1086), the residence of Zhou Digong was made a temple, and the place was then named Zhou Zhuang. In the middle of the Yuan Dynasty, Shen Wansan, making use of the water transport in the Baiyan River in the north of Zhouzhuang Town, linking the Beijing-Hangzhou Grand Canal in the west and going to the sea by Liuhe River in the northeast, traded with foreign countries and became a millionaire. Zhouzhuang was thus developed into an important town south of the Changjiang River as a center for collecting and distributing grain, silk, porcelain and handicrafts.

Residents built their homes by the rivers and streets were formed alongside. Spanning on the rivers are 14 ancient bridges built in the Yuan, Ming and Qing Dynasties. Among these Fuan Bridge with a tower is the only one existing in China and the Double Bridge, well-known both at home and abroad. There are nearly 1,000 families living in the town. Architectures of the Ming and Qing Dynasties occupy 60% of all the buildings. There is the Zhang Hall built by the descendents of Xu Da of the Ming Dynasty featured by "Entering the front gate through a bridge and the boat sailing through the house" and the Shen Hall, built by the descendents of Shen Wansan with 5 arches and 7 connecting flats each with a courtyard in front. There is also the former residence of Ye Chulun (1887-1946, a member of the China Alliance, a bourgeois revolutionary party initiated by Dr Sun Yatsen), the Milou Chamber, where Liu Yazi (1886-1958), a poet and member of the China Alliance) and Chen Qubing (1974-1933, a poet and member of the China alliance) met and composed poetry and the rebuilt Song Dynasty architecture Chengxu Taoist Temple. Wu Guanzhong once wrote in his essay, "Huangshan Mountain collects the beauty of China's mountains and rivers, but

Zhouzhuang collects the beauty of China's water regions". People overseas call Zhouzhuang the "No 1 Water Region in China".

Shen Hall

The Shen Hall was built in the 7th year of Qing Emperor Qianlong's reign by the descendents of Shen Wansan, "No 1 rich family south of the Changjiang River" during the Yuan and Ming Dynasties. There are 5 gate arches and 7 connecting flats, each with a courtyard in front, and altogether over 100 rooms, occupying an area of 2,000 sq.m. It is typical of the residence south of the Changjiang River, with "sitting rooms in the front and halls at the back". There is a wharf in front of the building and a water gate, where the boats are anchored; in the middle section are lobbies, tea rooms, and main halls, where guests are received; on the sides are large and small halls, and back rooms, where live the families. The main hall, Songmao Hall, looks grand and magnificent, with a veranda in front and a screened corridor at the back. The hall is beautifully decorated, with carved beams and painted columns. The exquisitely carved brick gate arch facing the main hall is tall and looks imposing, one of the typical Suzhou-style brick carvings. In the hall is placed a statue of Shen Wansan looking true to life. Overhead is a horizontal plaque written with "Cherished with every success".

Zhang Hall

Zhang Hall is featured by "the sedan chair entering by the front gate and the boat sailing through the house", a unique feature of the water region and a great attraction for visitors. It was built by the descendents of the brother of Xu Da, of the Ming Dynasty. It was transferred to the Zhang family and popularly known as Zhang Hall. There are 6 connecting flats each with a courtyard in front and altogether 70 rooms, occupying an area of 1,800 sq.m. Ruojing River flows through the house. Over the river is a shed and the stream flows gently by your feet. On both sides of the stream are wing-rooms and through their windows one can see the landscaping in the backyard, appealing to visitors with its quiet beauty. The Yuyan Hall is the main hall, with a bright veranda, looking antique and simple, with thick round columns erected on nanmu drum-shape blocks, solid as stone and rarely found in China.

Double Bridge

The Double Bridge is the symbol of Zhouzhuang. It consists of the arched bridge, Shide Bridge, and the square-opening bridge, Yongan Bridge, spanning the South-North Shi River. The Double Bridge was built in the Ming Dynasty. The two bridges are entirely different in shape, the surface of one bridge is horizontal, while that of the other is vertical, but are connected; one has round openings, while the other, square. It looks like a key of the ancient times, thus it is popularly called the Key Bridge.

Chengxu Taoist Temple

Chengxu Taoist Temple is located in the western part of the town. It is also named the Holy Temple, It was first built in the Song Dynasty. Since the Ming Dynasty it began to extend in scale. There is a local saying, "Chengxu came first and then Zhouzhuang". Now existing are 3 connecting flats, still keeping the style of the Song Dynasty architecture. The temple is quiet and simple. There is the front gate, the Holy God Hall and the Doumu Hall (Doumu is a Taoist goddess, said to be the mother of the Big Dipper family). The foundation of the hall is built of gray stone and the wooden columns are supported on upturned plate-shape stone piers. The chamber and halls with upturned eaves and protruding roof corners all look magnificent. In the back of the temple stand the Wenchang Pavilion and Jade Emperor Hall. The whole structure of the temple appears to be increasing in height as the halls stand one above the other, imparting a feeling of flying like fairies. Zhang Leng, a poet of the Qing Dynasty praised the temple in his poem as "A land quiet and peaceful like the Penglai Fairyland".

Milou Hall

Milou Hall, built in the Qing Dynasty, was originally named Deji Restaurant. In the early '20s, famous poet Liu Yazi and Chen Qubin visited the restaurant 4 times, drank wine and composed poetry, publicizing modern culture and advocating democratic revolution. Later, their poems were collected and published in the "Collection of Milou Hall", which has circulated in the country. For this reason Milou Hall has been popularly well-known. The hall has been repaired many times; it still keeps its original style, standing by the river beside the bridge and attracting visitors with its charm.

Former Residence of Ye Chulun

The family of Ye Chulun, a senior member of the Chinese Nationalist Party, lived in Zhouzhuang for generations. The building at the back is 2-storied, with 3 rooms on the ground floor and 3 rooms on the first floor. Here are Mr Ye's living quarters. The wing-rooms on the south were Mr Ye's childhood studies. The courtyards in front and at the back of the building are landscaped beautifully. In the backyard there is a hundred-year-old jasmine tree.

Zhenfeng Water Kingdom Stone Arch

The arch stands at the border of the ancient town and the new area, opposite to the Quanfu Pagoda. The stone arch was built in 1891 in an antique architectural style, with stone pillars and supporting beams, upturned eaves and protruding corners. It is a magnificent structure.

Quanfu Temple

The temple was built in the Song Dynasty on the former residence of Zhou Digong; the town was thus named Zhou Zhuang. The ancient town developed around the temple to the present scale in the past 900 hundred years. The temple is also a well-known ancient monastery.

Wansan Pork Leg and Three-flavored Dumpling

Wansan pork leg and three-flavored glutinous rice dumpling are special delicacies of Zhouzhuang. It is soft, fat but not greasy, a little salty, sweet, and delicious. It is said that it was the main course for treating guests by the Shen Wansan family and also as a tribute to the emperor. The three-flavored dumpling is also called the gluten soup. The gluten dumpling is filled with chicken meat, shrimps, cooked pork, seasoned with scallion, ginger and yellow wine. It is cooked in chicken soup; the gluten skin is thin and the meat filling is tender, appealing to diner's palate. It is a snack, a dish and a soup at the same time.

Grandma Tea

It is known all over that Zhouzhuang people love tea. They are very meticulous about tea drinking. They prefer ancient tea sets, boil water in pottery, and use bamboo or twigs as firewood. They first pour a little boiling water over the tea, wait for a few minutes and then make tea with boiling water. In this way, the tea is ensured of its color, fragrance and flavor. Whether in town or countryside elderly women about 60-70 often gather together to drank tea, hence it is called "Grandma Tea".

RECOMMENDED TRAVEL SERVICE

SHANGHAI HUATING OVERSEAS TOURIST CO.

Add: F/4, 503 Wulumuqi Rd, N
Tel.: 62491234
Fax: 62485470,62482781
Post Code: 200040

SHANGHAI JINJIANG TOURS LTD.

Add: 191 Changle Road
Tel.: 64662828
Fax: 64662297
Post Code: 200020

SHANGHAI CYTS TOURS CORPORATION

Add: 2 Hengshan Road
Tel.: 64331826, 64331907
Fax: 64330507
Post Code: 200031

SHANGHAI CHINA INTERNATIONAL TRAVEL SERVICE CO., LTD

Add: CITS Building, 1277 Beijing Rd, W
Tel.: 62898899
Fax: 62894928
Post Code: 200040

SHANGHAI CHINA TRAVEL SERVICE

Add: 881 Yanan Rd, M
Tel.: 62478888, 62475770
Fax: 62475521
Post Code: 200040

(II) TONGLI

The ancient town of Tongli is situated by the Grand Canal, in the northeast of Wujiang city, 20 km from Suzhou and 90 km from Shanghai. It is a thousand-year-old town and a typical ancient town of the water regions. It is surrounded by 5 lakes and crisscrossed by 15 small rivers with a total length of 6 km, partitioned by 7 small dykes. Spanning the rivers are 49 stone bridges. Among these are 29 built from the Song Dynasty to the Qing Dynasty. Tongli abounds with cultural atmosphere and a gathering of literary men. There are many mansions and private gardens mainly built during the Ming and Qing Dynasties. Tongli Town is also known as "a gallery of ancient architecture". The town is known as 'every family facing the water and every household accessible by boat", a scene of an oriental Venice. The antique, peaceful, quiet and refined atmosphere in Tongli poses great attraction to visitors, bringing them back to nature.

Scenic Spots

Tuisi Garden (Garden of Retiring to Ponder)

The Tuisi Garden is known for its ingenuous plot in structure. The designer has broken through the convention of longitudinal layout of gardens and made the best of the site in arranging it horizontally from east to west. The main scenic building is the tastefully furnished Tuisi Thatched Hall built by a pool in the back garden. The garden occupies a small area but there is scenery at your every step. Since the garden is built by the water, it is also called the Waterside Garden.

The Twin Halls

The Jiayin Hall in Zhuxing Street and the Chongben Hall on the opposite bank of the river are popularly known as the Twin Halls. They are famous for the exquisite carvings in The buildings. There are over 200 pieces of carvings describing scenes in the Chinese classics "The Romance of the Three Kingdoms" and "The Romance of the West Chamber".

The Triple Bridges

Between the two halls on the T-shaped river span, three bridges were called the Taiping, Jili and Guangli. The local custom in wedding and birthday celebrations is to parade through the three bridges to ask for luck.

RECOMMENDED TRAVEL SERVICE

SHANGHAI HUATING OVERSEAS TOURIST CO.

Add: F/4, 503 Wulumuqi Rd, N
Tel.: 62491234
Fax: 62485470,62482781
Post Code: 200040

SHANGHAI JINJIANG TOURS LTD.

Add: 191 Changle Road
Tel.: 64662828
Fax: 64662297
Post Code: 200020

SHANGHAI CYTS TOURS CORPORATION

Add: 2 Hengshan Road
Tel.: 64331826, 64331907
Fax: 64330507
Post Code: 200031

SHANGHAI CHINA INTERNATIONAL TRAVEL SERVICE CO., LTD

Add: CITS Building, 1277 Beijing Rd, W
Tel.: 62898899
Fax: 62894928
Post Code: 200040

SHANGHAI CHINA TRAVEL SERVICE

Add: 881 Yanan Rd, M
Tel.: 62478888, 62475770
Fax: 62475521
Post Code: 200040

(III) SUZHOU

Suzhou is in the southeast part of Jiangsu Province, on the Changjiang River in the north, by the Taihu Lake in the west, neighboring Shanghai in the east. It is noted for its mild climate, beautiful scenery and abundant produce. Communications is very convenient. It has been known since ancient time together with Hangzhou as "the paradise on earth".

Since Taibo of the Zhou Dynasty (the founder of the Wu Kingdom) opened up Suzhou, it has up to now a history around 3,000 years. It has a total area of 8,488 sq.km., of which 70 sq.km. is the city proper. Its total population is over 6 million. With a long history, Suzhou is known for its cultural relics and historic sites. There is a large number of gardens. Hence, Suzhou is a famous historical and cultural city in China and a state-level tourist area. Suzhou gardens are well-known for their elegance and simplicity, delicacy and exquisiteness. It has been popular since ancient times as "Gardens South of the Changjiang River are the top in the world and Suzhou gardens are the top south of the Changjiang River". During the Ming and Qing Dynasties there were 200 private gardens in Suzhou. The gardens are usually small in area, generally less than 1 hectare; the largest is about 2 hectares. Most of them were built in downtown. In the gardening technique the designer ingeniously used the buildings, rockeries, ponds, vegetation to partition the garden into the principal and the secondary areas, alternating the large and small, the densely and sparsely furnished, and with the special technique of "borrowing scenery", to form scenic areas, each with its own unique feature. The whole Suzhou is a typical waterside city with "little bridges, flowing streams and families" found in every corner. Sightseeing in Suzhou makes one feel relaxed and joyous, as if he is amidst a beautiful painting scroll.

There are in Suzhou 419 cultural relic sites under state, provincial and municipal protection. Since the Spring and Autumn Period (770-476 B.C.) celebrities have come forth in Suzhou. On the historical stage of Suzhou many vivid historical dramas have found their place, such as Fuchai, Wu Zixu, Sun Wuzi, Chun Shenjun, Yan Zhenqing, Bai Yuyi, Sushi, Lin Zequ and Li Xiucheng have left their footprints here. Suzhou traditional arts and crafts and cultural articles have enjoyed a high reputation at home and overseas, like silk, Suzhou-style embroidery, jade carving, sanded-wood fans, writing brushes, ink-sticks, paper, ink-slabs, calligraphy, paintings and wood carving, each with its own characteristics.

TIGER HILL

The Tiger Hill, located in the northwestern suburb of Suzhou, is a well-known scenic area in the country. The whole area covers 17.5 hectares. The Tiger Hill is 36-m high covered by tall ancient trees. Around the hill are many scenic spots. On top of the hill is the Tiger Hill Pagoda. It is brick structure, 47.7-m tall, first built at the end of the Five Dynasties (907-960). Owing to reasons in the foundation the pagoda began to lean towards the northwest since 400 years ago. The leaning degree is now 2.47. It is the famous leaning pagoda in China and has been listed as one of the key cultural relics under state protection. The Tiger Hill has been a famous scenic area since ancient times. On the hill there are 18 scenic spots, such as the Broken Beam Hall, the Laughing Spring, the Sword Testing Rock, Zhenniang's Tomb, Thousand-men Rock, Twin Pavilions, 53 towering ancient trees, Quyan Pagoda, etc. Su Dongpo(1037-1101), a famous poet of the Northern Song Dynasty, once said, "It's a regret if you go to Suzhou and have not visited the Tiger Hill."

CANLANG PAVILION (GREEN WAVE PAVILION)

Canlang Pavilion, in Sanyuan Lane, Renmin Road, south Suzhou, is a famous garden with the longest history in Suzhou. It was built in the 4th Qingli year of the Song Dynasty (1044) by the poet Su Zimei. It is typical of the Song Dynasty gardening architecture known for its antique and quiet characteristic. The buildings are simple and unsophisticated, surrounded by ancients trees and densely planted bamboo. The pond outside the garden links with the pond inside, giving the garden a pastoral scene of wild delight. The arrangement of the garden is unique, different from all other gardens. On the walls in the buildings are carved stone portraits of 594 celebrities in the last 2000 years since the Wu State to the Qing Dynasty related with the history of Suzhou. There are also 200 stone tablets, precious relics of the area.

LIUYUAN GARDEN (LINGERING GARDEN)

Liuyuan Garden is in the northwest of Suzhou, occupying an area of about 3 hectares. The garden is featured for the compact and ingenious layout, especially in the arrangement of the spaces among buildings. The spaces were cleverly partitioned into several sections, each with its own special scenery. The middle section mainly consists of hills and ponds; the eastern section, chambers with overlapping eaves and rising one above the other and zigzag courtyards and winding corridors; the western section is natural scenery and the northern section, a pastoral landscape. The walls in the corridors are inlaid with 300 stone carvings of calligraphy by Su Dongbo and Mi Nei, known as the "Calligraphy Model of Liuyuan Garden". The middle section has a peaceful and serene surrounding with rockeries, plants, chambers and halls built around the ponds. Among the buildings in the eastern section there is the Nanmu Hall, typical of halls in south Changjiang River areas and the Mandarin Duck Hall. In the northwest corner of the garden is "Another Village" with maple trees on the hill and peach and willow trees at the foot of the hill, showing a scene of mountain village in the wilderness.

GARDEN OF MASTER FISHERMAN'S NET

The garden is the smallest in Suzhou. It is generally recognized as the best typical of small gardens. The garden covers only an area of 0.6 hectare. The designer made the best use of gardening technique to arrange the garden with compactness and delicacy, alternating pavilions, terraces, chambers and waterside pavilions and winding corridors, making the garden that strikes you as large, though small, with many scenes, though few. The workmanship is lucid, streamlined and clear-cut. The Chinese garden "Ming Xuan" in the

Metropolitan Art Museum in New York in the United States is a reproduction of the "Dianchun Yi" (Cottage of Heralding Spring) in this garden.

LION GROVE

Located on Yuanlin Road in northeast Suzhou, the garden is one of the famous gardens in Suzhou. It was built in the Yuan Dynasty by high monk Tianru. The garden is featured by its rockeries that look like lions of different shapes. The caves in the rockeries link with each other and extend winding around that look like a labyrinth. The rockeries are surrounded by long corridors and chambers and halls here and there. There are hills in the southeastern part and ponds in the northwestern part. The long corridors run to all directions, up and down, appearing and disappearing every now and then. On the walls of the corridors are inlaid with 67 stone tablets carved with calligraphy of the different styles of famous calligraphers Su, Huang, Mi and Cai of the Song Dynasty.

GARDEN OF THE HUMBLE ADMINISTRATOR

It is the largest garden in Suzhou, located in Dongbei Street in downtown Suzhou. It is not only one of the 4 famous classical gardens in Suzhou (namely, the Green Wave Pavilion, Lion Grove, Garden of Humble Administrator and Liuyuan Garden), it is also one of 4 famous classical gardens in China (namely, the Summer Palace, Summer Mountain Resort, Garden of the Humble Administrator and Liuyuan Garden). It tops all the gardens in Suzhou. It was first built in the Ming Dynasty (1506-1521). In the past 400 years, going through great changes and the hands of different masters, it still retains the original style of the Ming Dynasty. The garden is arranged with a pond as the center, with pavilions, chambers, halls and towers built around, corridors winding over water and ancient trees towering to the sky. With reflections on water, the scene presents a ingenuous and natural style. It is typical of classical gardens south of the Changjiang River.

HANSHAN TEMPLE (COLD HILL TEMPLE)

Hanshan Temple in Suzhou has become world-known with the

poem "Anchoring at Night by the Fengqiao Bridge" written by Tang Dynasty poet Zhang Ji, "The moon sets and crows crow in a frosty sky, the fisherman dozes off by his fishing light at the Feng Bridge; the bell in Hanshan Temple on the outskirts of Suzhou chimes, and arrives the passenger boat at midnight." The temple is located in Fengqiao Town, 5 km west of Suzhou city. It was first built in the Liang Dynasty and named Miaolipuming Monastery. Later, high monk Hanshan took charge of the temple and hence it was named Hanshan Temple. Historically, the temple has been one of the ten famous monasteries in China. There are many historic relics in the temple: the carved stone tablet of the poem by Zhang Ji, "Anchoring at Night by the Fengqiao Bridge", the stone statues of monks Hanshan and Shide, the remnants of carved tablets of calligraphy by Wen Zhenming and Tang Yan, famous calligraphers and painters of the Ming Dynasty.

PANMEN GATE

Panmen Gate is located in the southwest corner of Suzhou city. It is on the Grand Canal. In ancient days, there were water and land gates built on the city wall, the only ones in China. Nearby, are the Ruiguang Pagoda (Pagoda of Lucky Light), the Beamless Hall of the Ming Dynasty, Wumen Bridge of the Qing Dynasty. Now, the Panmen area has been built into a tourist attraction.

TIANPING HILL

The hill is well-known for its grotesque rocks, red maples, clear spring as the three "tops of scenery". The ancestors of Fan Zhongan, famous official in the Song dynasty, were buried here. There are the Temple of Loyalty and Heroism, Tianping Mountain Resort, Mansion of Worry First and Relief Later and the 270 maple trees planted by the ancestors of Fan Zhongan.

RECOMMENDED TOURS

One-day tour of Suzhou:

Garden of the Humble Administrator, Lion Grove, Suzhou Local Folk Custom Museum, Tiger Hill, Liuyuan Garden, West Garden, Hanshan Temple and Guanqian Street

Two-day tour of Suzhou:

1st day: Garden of the Humble Administrator, Lion Grove, Suzhou Local Folk Custom Museum, Tiger Hill, Liuyuan Garden, West Garden, Hanshan Temple and Guanqian Street

2nd day: Lingyan Hill, Tomb of Han Shizhong, the ancient town of Mudu and Tianping Hill

Three-day tour of Suzhou:

1st day: Garden of the Humble Administrator, Lion Grove, Suzhou Local Folk Custom Museum, Tiger Hill, Liuyuan Garden, West Garden, Hanshan Temple and Guanqian street

2nd day: Liangyan Hill, Tomb of Han Shizhong, the ancient town of Mudu and Tianping Hill

3rd day: Garden of Master Fisherman's Net, Canglang Pavilion, Suzhou Tablet Carvings Museum, three scenes on Panmen Gate, Tomb of Tang Yan and Mountain Resort on Stone Lake

RECOMMENDED TRAVEL SERVICE

SHANGHAI HUATING OVERSEAS TOURIST CO.

Add: F/4, 503 Wulumuqi Rd, N

Tel.: 62491234

Fax: 62485470,62482781

Post Code: 200040

SHANGHAI JINJIANG TOURS LTD.

Add: 191 Changle Road

Tel.: 64662828

Fax: 64662297

Post Code: 200020

SHANGHAI CYTS TOURS CORPORATION

Add: 2 Hengshan Road

Tel.: 64331826, 64331907

Fax: 64330507

Post Code: 200031

SHANGHAI CHINA INTERNATIONAL TRAVEL SERVICE CO., LTD

Add: CITS Building, 1277 Beijing Rd, W

Tel.: 62898899
Fax: 62894928
Post Code: 200040

SHANGHAI CHINA TRAVEL SERVICE
Add: 881 Yanan Rd, M
Tel.: 62478888, 62475770
Fax: 62475521
Post Code: 200040

(IV) WUXI

Wuxi is claimed by people as "a pearl on the Taihu Lake". It is a famous city south of the Changjiang River with a history of 3,000 years. It is a place of abundant produce, known as "a country of fish and rice"

Wuxi is located in the southern part of Jiangsu Province, neighboring Shanghai in the east, next to Nanjing in the west, on the Taihu Lake in the south and Changjiang River in the north. The Shanghai-Nanjing Railway and Shanghai-Nanjing Freeway transverse on its border from east to west. The Beijing-Hangzhou Canal cuts through it. It covers a total area of 4,650 sq.km. with a total population of 4,300,0000. Wuxi has a long history. The brilliant ancient Wu civilization began as early the last years of the Yin and Shang Dynasties. In the 5th year of the first emperor Gaozu of the Western Han Dynasty (202 B.C.), the tin mine in the Tin Mountain in Wuxi became exhausted, thus the city was named Wuxi, meaning "no tin".

Wuxi is full of talents passing down through the ages. It is a place with a great number of natural scenery and humanistic sights and has been known as "a famous scenic spot in the Wu Kingdom". The Taihu Lake scenic area is well-known at home and overseas. The Taihu Lake is one the three fresh lakes in China. It extends across both Jiangsu and Zhejiang Provinces. There are large and small islands on the lake and 72 peaks on the hills all around. The landscape is featured for its magnificence and serene beauty. The scenes change with the season and with morning and evening. The best scenery of the Taihu Lake is in Wuxi. Xihui Park, Turtle Islet Park, Liyuan

Garden, Meiyuan Garden, No 2 Fountain in the World, Jichang Garden have been attracting great numbers of tourists. The recently built Lingshan Mountain Giant Budda, Wuxi Central TV and Film Shooting Center are new favorable tourist attractions. Wuxi has such famous native products as the pork steak braised in thick sauce, fried gluten, Huishan oily short, Huishan clay figurine, Huiqun wine (also called No 2 Fountain wine), juicy peaches, and white bait from the Taihu Lake.

Wuxi is world-known for the beauty of its natural scenery, gardens typical in the south Changjiang River areas, and colorful humanistic sights.

TURTLE ISLET PARK

The best place to appreciate the scenery on the Taihu Lake is in the park. It is located on the lake in the west of Chongshan Hill. There is rock like the head of a turtle protruding into the lake, hence the name. Standing on the rock one can have a view of the vast expanse of water in the lake and the dim shapes of the 72 peaks in the distance. The building of the park started in 1918 and expanded in large scale in the '80s. The tourist area covers an area of 130 hectares. There are the Fairy Island on Taihu Lake, Scenic Spot of Juqu, Spring on Turtle Islet, Waves Rolling the Snow, Deer Greeting the Sunlight, and Quiet Beauty on Chong Hill. The park is built by the lake and on the slope of the hill, unique in its gardening art. The feature of the park is scenery on the Taihu Lake, supplemented by artificial decoration, appealing to visitors with unique beauty.

XIHUI PARK

Xihui Park combines the Xi and Hui Hills. It is said that a monk named Huichao once lived here and hence named Huishan Hill since the Tang Dynasty. There are 9 peaks on the hill, sprawling like a dragon. The main peak, Sanmao Peak, is 330 m high. Huishan Hill is known for its spring water. There are a dozen springs, such as the Huishan Spring, Longyan Spring and others. The Xishan Hill rises in the east of Huishan Hill, only 75-m above sea level. It is said that large quantity of tin was mined in the hill during the Zhou and Jin Dynasties, hence the name Xishan ("xi" in Chinese means "tin") On the top of the hill there is the Dragon Light Pagoda and Dragon Light Temple. Entering the park by the Guhua Gate, one can reach directly Huishan Temple, Jichang Garden and No 2 Fountain in the World. Huishan Temple is a famous monastery south of the Changjiang River, first built in the South and North Dynasties. When the Qing emperor Qianlong visited the Huishan Hill on his inspection tour of the south, he personally inscribed the horizontal board "Huishan Temple" hung above the temple gate. The temple always has large numbers of worshippers. The principal scenic spots are: Tang and Song Dynasty Buddhist scripture stele, Heavenly King Hall, Snow Flake Bridge, Sun and Moon Pond and Imperial Tablet Pavilion. Going east from the Guhua Gate you will find Jichang Garden. It was formerly a monks' dormitory and reconstructed into a park during the Ming Dynasty. The park is divided into two parts: the eastern part consists mainly of corridors along ponds; the western part, mainly of rockeries and trees. The Jichang Garden links with the nine peaks on Huishan Hill and Dragon Light Pagoda on Xishan Hill into one scenic area, a successful model of the gardening art of "borrowing scenery". On the Huishan Hill is the Huishan Spring, the No 2 Spring in the World. The spring was dug during the Tang Dynasty (766-777). The water is sweet and mellow. Lu Yu, a Tang Dynasty scholar, mentioned in his "Book of Teas" that the water in the world can be divided into 20 grades and the spring water of Huishan is the second in the world. Here we will find the No 2 Spring Pavilion, the Ripples and Billows Hall, Jinghui Hall, Guanyin Rock and Oyster Stone of the Ming Dynasty. The blind folk musician Ah Bing (officially named Hua Yanjun) composed his famous two-stringed fiddle piece "No 2 Spring Reflecting the Moon", which has made the spring known far and wide.

LIYUAN GARDEN

Liyuan Garden, located on the Lihu Lake, part of the Taihu Lake, also called Five-li Lake. The Lihu Lake and Liyuan Garden derived their names from Fan Li, an official of the Yue State by the end of the Spring and Autumn Period. When Fan Li Helped the Yue State to defeat the Wu State, he and Xi Shi, one of the four famous beauties in China, took a boat ride on the Five-li Lake. Later, people changed the name of the lake into Lihu Lake to commemorate this event. The Liyuan Garden partly consists of rockeries piled up with Taihu Lake stones and another part, a long corridor and a dyke along the lake. The garden faces the lake on three sides. Pavilions, corridors and dykes were built around the lake, all exquisitely and delicately designed and harmonious in colors. It is featured for its beautiful scenery and known as one the famous gardens south of the Changjiang River.

PLUM GARDEN

The Plum Garden is located on the southern slope of Hushan Hill on the western suburbs of Wuxi. Several thousands of plum trees were planted in the garden, thus it is called the Plum Garden. The feature of the garden is that the hill is covered by plum trees and plum trees are decorating the hill. Pavilions and pagodas are found on the hill alternating with each other. There are about 40 different species of plum trees in the garden; the famous ones being the Me Plum and Longyou Plum. Over a thousand sweet osmanthus trees were also planted there. The scenic spots are the Tianxi Terrace, Xiangxue Sea, Qingfen Chamber, Nianqu Pagoda, Chaohe Pavilion, Xiaoluo Float, and Huaran Cave. The best time for touring the Plum Garden is in early spring, when the plums are in full bloom.

GIANT BUDDHA ON LINGSHAN HILL

The Giant Buddha is on the Lesser Lingshan Hill in the south of Maji Hill in Wuxi. The site was the former historically famous Xiangfu Monastery. In preserving historic relics and carrying forth the Buddhist culture, while restoring the temple, a 80-m tall bronze statue of Sakyamuni was erected in the open air. The tallest Buddha statue in the world was completed at the end of 1996. The giant Buddha is on the Lesser Lingshan Hill, named by the high monk, Tang Xuanzhuang, thus it is called the Giant Buddha of Lingshan Hill. The Buddha statue is cast with tin and bronze and in the shape according to the record of the Buddha in the Buddhist scripture. The Buddha statue looks benign with smiles and looking kindly on all creatures in the world. He is holding in his right hand a "seal of wishes", representing the grant of happiness and bestow of blessings.

The sign on his chest represents solemnness and virtue. The whole statue is delicately shaped with a peaceful and relaxed look, displaying the kindness of Buddha. The giant statue stands on the hill by the Taihu lake. It is one of the Buddhist works in the most flourishing period of Buddhism in the recent 100 years and it is also a symbol of Wuxi - the pearl of Taihu Lake.

WUXI CENTRAL TV AND FILM MAKING CENTER

Wuxi Central TV and Film Making Center is the first of its kind in China for shooting films and TV films, combining the functions of film making and tourism. There are now the Tang Dynasty City, the City of the Three Kingdoms and City of the Heroes of the Marshes, together occupying an area of 106 hectares. The Tang City was built by the Central TV Station for shooting the TV film "Emperor Tang Ming Huang". There are nearly 100 scenic spots in the city, like the "Tang Palace", the "Chengxiang Pavilion", reproducing the flourishing period of the imperial palace and folk life styles. There, one can appreciate the prosperous scenes of the Tang Dynasty while learning something about the technique of film making. The City of the Three Kingdoms was built when the Central TV Station was shooting the TV film "Romance of the Three Kingdoms". There are several dozens of large-scale scenes, like the "Wu Imperial Palace", the "Seven-star Altar", producing 10 filming and tourist items, such as "Liu Bei on Marriage", "Arrow Shooting from Straw Boats", a race-course and a lake-side bathing ground. It is the largest scenic area in the filming city. The City of the Heroes of the Marshes covers an area of 36 hectares at the foot of a hill and by the lake. There is a vast expanse of water surface for filming. Settings, consisting of palaces, ministers' mansions, mountain villages and folk residences, courts and prisons, monasteries and ancestral temples, markets and stores, restaurants and inns, lakes and marshes, and the Mountain Fortress of Liangshan Heroes.

RECOMMENDED TOURS

One-day tour of Wuxi:

Xihui Park, Turtle Islet Park, Liyuan Garden, Plum Garden, No 2 Spring in the World and Jichang Garden

Two-day tour of Wuxi:

1st day: Xihui Park, Turtle Islet Park, Liyuan Garden, Plum Garden, No 2 Spring in the World and Jichang Garden

2nd day: Tang City, City of the Three Kingdoms, City of Heroes of the Marshes and Giant Buddha on Lingshan Hill

RECOMMENDED TRAVEL SERVICE

SHANGHAI HUATING OVERSEAS TOURIST CO.

Add: F/4, 503 Wulumuqi Rd, N

Tel.: 62491234

Fax: 62485470,62482781

Post Code: 200040

SHANGHAI JINJIANG TOURS LTD.

Add: 191 Changle Road

Tel.: 64662828

Fax: 64662297

Post Code: 200020

SHANGHAI CYTS TOURS CORPORATION

Add: 2 Hengshan Road

Tel.: 64331826, 64331907

Fax: 64330507

Post Code: 200031

SHANGHAI CHINA INTERNATIONAL TRAVEL SERVICE CO., LTD

Add: CITS Building, 1277 Beijing Rd, W

Tel.: 62898899

Fax: 62894928

Post Code: 200040

SHANGHAI CHINA TRAVEL SERVICE

Add: 881 Yanan Rd, M

Tel.: 62478888, 62475770

Fax: 62475521

Post Code: 200040

(V) NANJING

Nanjing, named in ancient days Jingling, located downstream of the Changjiang River, beside the mountain and by the river, is one of China's great ancient capitals. From 472 B.C. during the Spring and Autumn Period, when Fan Yi, a minister in the Yue State, had the city built up to now, it has undergone 2,400 years of stormy changes. In history, more than 10 dynasties have built their capitals here, hence it is known as the "capital of 10 dynasties". Nanjing is the capital of Jiangsu Province. It has a total area of 5,698 sq.km. and a population of about 6 million. It has a mild climate, with four distinct seasons. The average annual temperature is 15.4℃. The city is surrounded by mountains and water and popularly known as a "green shade".

Stormy changes in history have brought forth the national spirit, colorful culture and brilliant civilization, leaving a great number of historical traces here. Nanjing is abundant in tourist resources. Famous scenic areas are such as Dr Sun Yatsen's Mausoleum, the Ming Tomb, Xuanwu Lake, Mochou Lake, Yuhua Terrace, the Drum Tower, and Qixia Mountain. Famous native products are the round sausage, sweet osmanthus duck, brocade, Yuhua tea, sugared porridge and lotus root, sugared taro, seasoned dried bean curd and eight-flavored bean curd.

DR SUN YATSEN'S MAUSOLEUM

The mausoleum is the tomb of Dr Sun Yatsen, the forerunner of China's great Democratic Revolution. It is located on the southern slope of Purple Gold Mountain in Nanjing. The architecture is magnificent and imposing. The mausoleum covers an area of over 80,000 sq.m., 73-m high, 158 m from the sea level. There are 392 steps, divided by 8 terraces, leading to the tomb. It was designed in the shape of a bell. The main structures are: the archway, tomb passage, tomb gate, tablet pavilion, sacrificial hall and tomb chamber. At the entrance to the tomb there is a tall granite tablet carved and inlaid with gold with the characters "Universal Fraternity" written by Dr Sun Yatsen. On the overhead door frame are four characters inscribed by Dr Sun Yatsen, "Righteousness in Heaven and Earth". In the hall is a marble statue of Dr Sun Yatsen in sitting posture, 4.6-m tall, looking vivid and lifelike. On the walls around the statue are bas-relieves describing his revolutionary achievements. On the two screen walls beside the statue are carved the script of Dr Sun Yatsen's last works "Program of Building the Country". The tomb chamber is of dome-shaped, with a diameter of 18 m and a height of 11 m. In the middle is the tomb vault, above which is a marble statue of Dr Sun Yatsen in lying posture. Underground is the remains of Dr Sun Yatsen.

MING TOMB (XIAO LING)

It is the tomb of the founder of the Ming Dynasty, Zhu Yuanzhang. It is located on the southern slope of the Purple Gold Mountain. The tomb was built in the 9th year of Hongwu of the Ming Dynasty (1376). The remaining relics are the Horse Dismounting Lane, Great Golden Gate, Square City, Sacred Passage, Stone Beasts, Stone Figures, Stone Pillars, Tablet Hall and Treasure City. It is one of the existing largest ancient tombs of emperors with a history of 600 years. The Square City is a tablet pavilion, located between Weiqiao Bridge and Dr Sun Yatsen's Mausoleum. It was erected by Ming Emperor Chengzu, Zhu Di, in praising his father, Zhu Yuanzhang's merits, named "Tablet of Sacred Merits of the Great Ming Xiao Ling". The top of the pavilion had been destroyed and only the four walls remain. In the pavilion is a stone tablet inscribed by Zhu Di, describing in details the merits of the first emperor of the Ming Dynasty. The sacred passage is 1,800-m long. The middle section is the passage of stone elephants with 12 pairs of beasts arranged on both sides. At the back is a pair of ornamental columns with carved dragons on their tops, looking magnificent and dignified. In the northern section of the sacred passage are arranged on both sides 4 pairs of officials dressed in mandarine robes and generals in armors. All the stone beasts and figurines are huge in shape. They are the masterpieces of stone sculpture of the Ming Dynasty.

SCENERY ON THE QINHUAI RIVER

The Qinhuai River is a tributary of the Changjiang River with a total length of 110 km. It is the main river course in Nanjing. The area around the Qinhuai River and Confucius' Temple was already a prosperous place as early as the Six Dynasties. Generations of aristocrats used to live on the banks of the river. It was also a place gathered with scholars and literary men. It became more prosperous during the Ming and Qing Dynasties, when the place was crowded with rich merchants, brothels, painted pleasure-boats and where the beauties south of the Changjiang River were found. In the '80s, Nanjing municipal government spent a large sum of money to rebuild and restore the scenic area. The Qinhuai River has again become a famous tourist attraction in China. It is not only known for its beautiful scenery but also for its many historic sites, featured by the characteristics of an ancient capital. Tourists can take a boat-ride on the river or visit scenic spots on shore. Principal tourists attractions are: Confucius' Temple, Former Residence of Li Xiangjun, a famous songstress of the Ming Dynasty, Egret Islet Park, Zhanyuan Garden and Zhonghua Gate Fortress. The Dacheng Hall in the Confucius' Temple was built in the 1st year of Jingyou of the Song Dynasty (1034). It was the principal hall for offering sacrifices to Confucius. Zhanyuan Garden was ingeniously designed and known as one of famous classical gardens in China. In the garden is found the Historical Museum of the Taiping Heavenly Kingdom, the only one in China. The Egret Islet Park is a classical garden arranged with landscapes of hills, water, and woods. The fortress on Zhonghua Gate was built in the Ming Dynasty. The Meixiang Chamber is the former residence of a famous Ming Dynasty songstress Li Xiangjun, "one of the eight great beauties on Qinhuai River". The place is quiet and exquisitely arranged with a beautiful atmosphere. Along the Qinhuai River are found historic sites, gardens, painted pleasure-boats, markets, halls and local residents' houses, which have formed a tourist attraction that appeals to visitors with great interest and charm.

XUANWU LAKE

The Xuanwu Lake is located outside of Xuanwu Gate, with a water surface of 444 hectares and a circumference of 15 km. In the old days it served as a place for drilling the navy and also a pleasure resort for emperors and senior officials. It was turned into a park in

1909. There are 5 islets on the lake, called Islets of Liang, Huang, Ling, Cui and Ying, connected by bridges and dykes. The Xuanwu Lake is a famous lake in the city. The green ripples in the lake, long winding dykes, willows on the shore, five islets dotting the lake, pavilions, hills in the misty distance and an ancient pagoda together form a picturesque scene. In summer and autumn, on a stretch of green water, float the pink lotus blossoms with fragrance permeating the air. It is really an enchanting scene!

QINGLIANG HILL (COOL HILL)

The Qingliang Hill is located at the west end of Guangzhou Road in Nanjing, on the north side of Qingliang Gate. The hill is 100-m high, covering an area of 4 km. There is the Qingliang Park on the hill. The park is precipitous in topography but luxuriant with trees. Principal historic relics are the Qingliang Pavilion, Chongzheng Academy, Saoye Hall, Zhuma Slope, and Cuiwei Garden. Qingliang Temple is on the southern slope of Qingliang Hill. There is only the remaining 5-room single-story house, with red walls and black tiles. On the board above the door is written "Ancient Qingliang Temple". Saoye Hall, on the western slope of the hill, is a 3-room two-story building of wood structure with upturned eaves. Chongzheng Academy , on the slope of the hill to the east of Qingliang Temple, was built during the Ming Dynasty. To its east are the Zhuma Slope and the Cuiwei Garden.

DRUM TOWER

The Drum Tower is found in the eastern corner of the Drum Square in Nanjing. It was built in the Ming Dynasty (1382). In the old days it was used for giving the time. The tower was built on top of a high mound. The structure consists of two parts. The lower level is of a watch-tower shape, with dark red exterior walls and three arched doors inside in the front and the back, and four side-halls. The upper level is a wood and brick structure with 3 stories and upturned eaves, surrounded by 12 red pillars. The whole architecture gives an imposing air and magnificent view. The Drum Tower is now made into a park. Visitors can climb to the top and have a bird's-eye view of the city. In 1995 a new bell, weighing 5 tons, was hung on a dragon-shape beam, on the north side of the tower. The bell is called the Bell of Peace, ready for visitors to strike.

QIXIA MOUNTAIN

Qixia Mountain, located on the outskirts 22 km from Nanjing city, was called Sheshan Mountain in the old days. There are three peaks on the mountain; the eastern peak that looks like a dragon is called the Dragon Hill, the western peak that looks like a tiger is called the Tiger Hill; the main peak is the Fengxiang Peak. The mountain is 286 m above sea level. The western side of the mountain is called the Maple Ridge. In late autumn the mountain slope is covered by maple leaves, a charming scene of crimson. It is the main attraction to visitors. There are many historic relics and grotesque rocks on Qixia Mountain. It is a popular scenic area well-known far and wide. Qixia Temple was first built in the South Qi Dynasty (489). It is known as one of 4 great temples in China beside the Lingyan Temple in Changqing, Shandong Province, Yuquan Temple in Jingshan, Hubei Province and Guoqing Temple in Tiantai Shan, Zhejiang Province. The main existing structures are the Mountain Gate, Pilu Hall, Shecui Chamber, and Scripture Chamber. It is the largest temple in Nanjing.

YUHUA TERRACE (RAIN FLOWER TERRACE)

Yuhua Terrace, located outside of Zhonghua Gate, is said that during the Liang Dynasty a high monk named Yunguang preached Buddhism here. The god in heaven was moved and flowers fell like rain, hence the name "rain flower". It has been listed as one of the "18 scenes of Nanjing", a popular tourist attraction. During the Guomintang days, the terrace became the principal execution ground in Nanjing. Thousands of Communists and patriotic personnages gave up their lives here. After liberation, it was converted into the largest revolutionary martyrs' cemetery and a base for educating young people in revolutionary tradition. It is a famous tourist area combining revolutionary education with sightseeing.

MOCHOU LAKE (NO-WORRY LAKE)

The lake, located outside of Shuixi Gate, has a total area of land and water of 40 km, with a circumference of 5 km. It has gained its name from a girl named Mochou, a historical figure. In ancient days it was famed as "No 1 famous lake south of the Changjiang river". There are such scenic spots in the garden as Shengqi Chamber, Yujin Hall, Lotus Hall, and tombs of Guangdong army martyrs.

RECOMMENDED TOURS

One-day tour of Nanjing:

Dr Sun Yatsen's Mausoleum, Ming Tomb, President's Mansion, Yuhua Terrace, Mochou Lake and Drum Tower

Two-day tour of Nanjing:

1sr day: Qinhuai River scenery, Xuanwu Lake, Yuhua Terrace, President's Mansion, Mochou Lake and Drum Tower

2nd day: Dr Sun Yatsen's Mausoleum, Ming Tomb and Qingliang Hill

RECOMMENDED TRAVEL SERVICE

SHANGHAI HUATING OVERSEAS TOURIST CO.

Add: F/4, 503 Wulumuqi Rd, N

Tel.: 62491234

Fax: 62485470,62482781

Post Code: 200040

SHANGHAI JINJIANG TOURS LTD.

Add: 191 Changle Road

Tel.: 64662828

Fax: 64662297

Post Code: 200020

SHANGHAI CYTS TOURS CORPORATION

Add: 2 Hengshan Road

Tel.: 64331826, 64331907

Fax: 64330507

Post Code: 200031

SHANGHAI CHINA INTERNATIONAL TRAVEL SERVICE CO., LTD

Add: CITS Building, 1277 Beijing Rd, W

Tel.: 62898899

Fax: 62894928
Post Code: 200040

SHANGHAI CHINA TRAVEL SERVICE
Add: 881 Yanan Rd, M
Tel.: 62478888, 62475770
Fax: 62475521
Post Code: 200040

(VI) HANGZHOU

Hangzhou is the capital of Zhejiang Province. It has been listed by the State Council as a famous historical, cultural city and a key tourist city in the country. It has a total area of 6,596 sq.km. (683 sq.km. in the urban area) and a population of 6 million (1.64 million in the city).

Hangzhou is one of China's ancient capitals. During the period of the Five Dynasties and Ten Kingdoms, Wu Yue State made it its capital. During the Song Dynasty it became one of the leading commercial ports in the country. Great men of letters, Bai Juyi of the Tang Dynasty and Su Dongbo of the Song Dynasty, had been senior officials in Hangzhou and contributed much effort in dredging the West Lake. Since the Southern Song Dynasty established its capital here, it had become the most popular city in China. In the 13th century, famous Italian tourist Marco Polo visited Hangzhou several times and praised it as "a heavenly city".

Hangzhou has a topography of a plain, slanting from southwest towards the northeast. In its southwest there is the last part of the Tianmu Mountain Range called Tianzhu Mountain. The northeastern area is a plain with rivers crisscrossing it; it is the southern end of the Hangjia Lake Plain. The West Lake is in the western corner of the city. It was originally a bay of the Qiantang River. The Treasure Hill in the north and Wushan Hill in the south used to encircle the bay and, later, the mouth of the bay was blocked by the mud and sand brought down by the Qiantang River and a lake was formed. The famous Beijing-Hangzhou Canal finds its terminal here.

The West lake in Hangzhou is a state-level tourist area. With its beautiful natural scenery, many historical relics and scenic spots and brilliant historical culture, it has been world-known. Popular scenic spots are: 10 scenic spots on the West Lake, Dragon Well, Lingyin Temple, Six Harmonies Pagoda, Tiger Spring, Yue Fei Temple, Yunqi Vale, Jade Spring, Yellow Dragon Cave, Misty Clouds Cave, North Peak, South Peak, Jade Emperor Hill, Treasure Hill, Phoenix Hill, and Wushan Hill. Hangzhou is also popular for its special, native products, like the Dragon Well tea, Hangzhou dried chrysanthemum, West Lake water shield, Tianzhu Hill chopsticks, West Lake silk parasols, Wangxingji fans and Zhang Xiaoquan scissors.

WEST LAKE SCENIC AREA

The West Lake, is encircled on three sides by mountain ranges and facing the city on one side. As it is in the western part of Hangzhou, it has been known since the Song Dynasty as the West Lake. The landscape on the lake is beautiful and enchanting. The lake covers an area of 5.6 sq.km. with a circumference of 15 km. The Suti Dyke and Baiti Dyke partition the lake into five parts: the Outer Lake, Inner Lake, Yue Lake, Xili Lake and Little South Lake. The 10 scenic spots on the West Lake have been well-known since the Song Dynasty: namely, Three Pools Reflecting the Moon, Spring on Suti Dyke, Autumn Moon on Lake Terrace, Orioles in the Willows, Gold Fish in Flower Mound Park, Lotus Blossoms in Zigzag Courtyards, Last Snow on Broken Bridge, Twin Peaks Towering into the Clouds, Evening Bell in Nanping, and Sun Set on Leifeng Pagoda. In recent years 10 new scenic spots have been added: Tiger Spring, Dragon Well Tea, Bamboo Paths in Yunqi Vale, Sweet Osmanthus Blossoms in Manglong, Nine Winding Streams, Wind on Wushan Hill, Flying Clouds on Jade Emperor Hill, Sunset Glow on Treasure Hill, Green Stream Encircling Ruandun and Luxuriant Green in Yellow Dragon Cave. The double ten scenic spots have endowed much poetic lyricism and artistic concept to the West Lake. There are flowers blossoming in all four seasons and scenes differ in each season and in the morning and evening, attracting visitors with its beauty and charm. The great writer Su Dongbo of the Song Dynasty once praised the scenery, "Water reflections are beautiful on fine days, but misty hills in the rain are also wonderful; Comparing the West Lake with Xizi, the beauty, it is equally beautiful whether heavily or lightly made up."

YUE FEI TEMPLE

Yue Fei Temple, located by the West Lake at the foot of Qixia Hill, was first built in the Southern Song Dynasty (1221) to commemorate the national hero Yue Fei. Visitors to the temple enter first through the majestic-looking front gate of a two-storied structure with overlapping eaves. Next, they will come to a courtyard with a passage paved with gray stone slabs leading to the tomb and flanked by ancient tall trees. In the main hall a plaque is overhanging above inscribed with four characters by Ye Jianying "A devote heart under heaven". In the middle of the hall sits Yue Fei's statue in purple robe and shoulderless armor, displaying the air of a general. On the walls are written by Hong Zhu in the Ming Dynasty four big characters "Serve my country with loyalty". Above the statue hangs a horizontal plaque inscribed in Yue Fei's hand script "Return our Land". On the two sides are hung two horizontal plaques, each respectively with the characters of "Hot blood and loyal heart" and "Noble spirit lasts forever". At the back of the hall, on the two sides are huge carved murals, describing the scene when Yue Fei's mother punctured on Yue Fei's back the four characters, "Serve my Country with Loyalty", showing his heroic spirit and determination of protecting his country. On the west side of the main hall is a courtyard. At its entrance is the Cypress Pavilion of Loyalty, in which are 8 stocks of withered cypress. On both sides of the courtyard are tablet corridors; on one of them is carved with the poems written by Yue Fei and memorials to the emperor in his handwriting. On the other side are poems written by famous scholars and poets in the past dynasties paying respect to Yue Fei. In the middle of the courtyard is a stone bridge called Loyalty Bridge. Beyond the bridge is the tomb chamber. On the side by the wall are four cast iron statues in kneeling posture. These are the images of the traitors kneeling there to be spit on and cursed by generations of people and passed down in history in infamy.

PAGODA OF SIX HARMONIES

The name of the pagoda indicates the combination of heaven, earth and the four corners of the world. It is located on the Yuelun Hill by the side of the Qiantang River in the south of Hangzhou city. It was first built in the Northern Song Dynasty (970). It was then the capital of the Wu Yue State. The king had the pagoda built to subdue the tides in the Qiantang River. The present pagoda was rebuilt in the Southern Song Dynasty (1153). In the 25th year of Qing Emperor Guangxu's reign (1899), the pagoda was rebuilt into a 13-storied wooden-frame structure with eaves on the exterior. In recent years, it has been repaired several times. In 1961, it was listed as a key cultural relic under state protection. The pagoda is a precious legacy of China's ancient architecture. It is 59.89 m high, in octagonal shape, with 13 stories on the exterior and 7 stories in the interior. The body of the pagoda is narrowing upward at every story. On the upturned eaves are hung 108 iron bells. Inside the pagoda, every two stories make up one flight with winding staircases. On the walls are carved Buddha statue pedestals, human figures and flowers, birds and animals of exquisite workmanship. From the top of the pagoda visitors can have a full view of the beautiful scenery on the Qiantang river.

LINGYIN TEMPLE

Lingyin Temple is on the slope of the Lingyin Hill in the northwest of the West lake, by the Cold Spring and facing the Flying-here Peak. In the Eastern Jin Dynasty an Indian monk named Huili, on seeing the peak, exclaimed. "This is the little peak on the Vulture Mountain of the Tianzhu Mountain Range. When did it fly here? When the Buddha is here, the celestial spirits are hiding in it." He then had a temple built facing the peak and named it Lingyin Temple ("ling" in Chinese means "spirit" and "yin" means "hidden"). The temple has a history of 1,600 years. The first hall in the temple is the Heavenly King Hall with a horizontal plaque above head with the characters "Monastery in the Clouds" inscribed by Qing Emperor Kangxi. In the middle of the hall is the statue of Buddha Maitreya with a bared bosom. At its back is the Boddhisatva Skanda with a solemn look and holding a devil subduing staff. The statue is carved out of a single piece of camphor wood, a cultural relic of the Southern Song Dynasty. The main hall in the temple is 33.6 m high, grand in scale and magnificent in appearance. In the middle of the hall is the statue of Sakyamuni, 9.1 m tall, carved from the model of famous sculpture of the Chan Sect in the Tang Dynasty, made up of 14 pieces of camphor wood. The halls, pavilions, scripture stella, stone pagodas and Buddha statues are precious cultural relics and serve as a valuable reference for the study of the history of Buddhism, architectural art and sculptural art. The Flying-here Peak facing the temple is the principal scenic spot. The Song poet Su Dongbo once said in his poem, "I can stay anywhere amidst hills and streams, but the best place I like is the Flying-here Peak." The peak is 168 m above sea level and composed of lime stone. Having been eroded by underground water throughout the years many strange and changeable caves have been formed. It is not only popular for its beautiful scenery but also famous for the art of ancient caves in south China. In the Green Wood Cave, Milky Jade Cave, Deep Water Dragon Cave and Sun Shooting Cave and on the precipitous slopes of the peak along the winding stream are over 330 stone sculptured statues from the Five Dynasties to the Song and Yuan Dynasties. The most interesting and attractive one is the smiling Buddha Maitreya with a bared bosom. It is the largest statue among the caves in the Flying-here Peak. It is a typical work of art of the Song Dynasty with a high artistic value.

TIGER SPRING

The spring is found at the foot of Daci Hill in the southwest of the West Lake and known as "No 3 Spring in the World". The water in the spring tastes sweet and mellow and together with the Dragon Well Tea are called the "two tops" of the West lake. It is said that during the Tang Dynasty, a monk named Xingkong was told in his dream at night, "Tomorrow two tigers will move the Lad Spring from the Southern Peak." The next day, there were really two tigers digging the ground and making a hole. From the hole was gushing out spring. The water in the spring is good for health. Going up the mountain path beside the Tiger Spring one will find a stone sculpture of "Dreaming of the Tiger" with the half reclining statue of Monk Xingkong with a benign face and closed eyes and two tigers beside him, all looking lifelike and with bold and soft lines in alternating workmanship. Beside the Tiger Spring tea house is the Jizu Pagoda Courtyard, where the high monk Jigong of the Song Dynasty was buried. On the back wall of the hall are several stone carvings, describing the stories of Jigong.

DRAGON WELL

Dragon Well is on the Phoenix Hill in the west of the West Lake. The well is a round pool and does not dry up even in draught. The ancients said that the spring was connected to the sea and there was a dragon in the spring, hence it is called the Dragon Well. About 500 m from the well is the Dragon Well Temple. The Dragon Well is one of the great famous springs in Hangzhou. The water from the spring is pure and mellow. The Dragon Well tea is world-famous. The tea is divided into 4 categories according to the places of tea growing, namely, the Lion Peak, Dragon Well, Yunqi Vale and Tiger Spring, among which the best is the Lion Peak Dragon Well tea, green in color, nice in shape, fragrant and mellow in taste. These four categories are known as the "four tops" of tea.

RECOMMENDED TOURS

One-day tour of the north line: Lingyin Temple, Tea Museum, Yue Fei Temple, Jade Spring, Yellow Dragon Cave, Treasure Hill, and Purple Cloud Cave

One-day tour of the lake: Autumn Moon on the Terrace, Three Pools Reflecting the Moon, Mid-lake Pavilion, Zhongshan Park, Xiling Seal Academy, Provincial Museum, Lotus Blossom in Courtyard and Famous Stones south of the Changjiang River

One-day tour of the south line: Silk Museum, Jingci Temple, Zhang Taiyan Memorial Hall, Tomb of Zhang Changshui, Prince's Bay Park, Watching Gold Fish at Flower Mound, Tiger Spring, Pagoda of Six Harmonies and City of the Song Dynasty

One-day tour of essence: Three Pools Reflecting the Moon, Watching Gold Fish at Flower Mound, Yue Fei Temple, Lingyin Temple, Dragon Well, Tiger Spring, Pagoda of Six Harmonies and City of the Song Dynasty

RECOMMENDED TRAVEL SERVICE

SHANGHAI HUATING OVERSEAS TOURIST CO.

Add: F/4, 503 Wulumuqi Rd, N

Tel.: 62491234

Fax: 62485470,62482781

Post Code: 200040

SHANGHAI JINJIANG TOURS LTD.

Add: 191 Changle Road
Tel.: 64662828
Fax: 64662297
Post Code: 200020

SHANGHAI CYTS TOURS CORPORATION

Add: 2 Hengshan Road
Tel.: 64331826, 64331907
Fax: 64330507
Post Code: 200031

SHANGHAI CHINA INTERNATIONAL TRAVEL SERVICE CO., LTD

Add: CITS Building, 1277 Beijing Rd, W
Tel.: 62898899
Fax: 62894928
Post Code: 200040

SHANGHAI CHINA TRAVEL SERVICE

Add: 881 Yanan Rd, M
Tel.: 62478888, 62475770
Fax: 62475521
Post Code: 200040

(VII) SHAOXING

Shaoxing, once the capital of the Yue State during the Spring and Autumn Period, has a history of 2,400 years. It is a famous historical, cultural city in China.

Shaoxing covers an area of 8,023 sq.km., with a population of 4.30 million. It has a mild climate with four distinct seasons. In Shaoxing, lakes and ponds are found everywhere. Crisscrossing rivers are dotted by black awning-boats sailing in them and spanned by stone bridges. It is a typical scene of a watery region and a famous city south of the Changjiang River in China. Shaoxing is abundant in tourist resources. There is the Huiji Hill provincial-level holiday resort and 6 provincial-level scenic areas. Popular tourist attractions are: the Dayu's Tomb, Lanting Pavilion, East Lake, Keyan Crag, Giant Buddha Temple, Lu Xun's Former Residence, Former Residence of Zhou Enlai, Shenyuan Garden, and Green Vine Academy. The best known product in Shaoxing is Shaoxing wine. The Jiafan brand has been commended in wine appraisal meetings as a famous wine in China. There are many wine shops in the city, full of local flavor. Visitors passing by on smelling the fragrance of wine are tempted to have a drink. Besides, there are Yue Kiln porcelain, Shaoxing fragrant cake, Shaoxing fermented bean curd and pork stewed with dried preserved vegetable.

EAST LAKE

The East Lake, located in the eastern suburbs, 3 km from Shaoxing city, is one of the great lakes in Zhejiang Province. The area of the lake is not very big and is known as "a potted landscape". It lies against a small rocky hill and at the foot of the hill there is a cave. Visitors can take a boat and sail into the cave; there they can see a wonderful view. Since the Han Dynasty people have quarried the hill for rocks. Through a thousand years' quarry a cavity was formed inside the hill and a deep cave took shape with precipices on all sides, rising about 50-60 m high. The deepest part of water in the cave is 20 m. Looking up above head, one can see the sky through a narrow opening, from which light pours into the dark cave, making visitors on the boat feel as if they are at the bottom of a well. In this scenic area there is Taogong Cave, Pavilion of Listening to the Waterfall, Pavilion of Drinking from the Stream, Cave of Fairy Peach and Taoshe Academy.

LANTING PAVILION

The pavilion is in the southwestern part of Shaoxing, 13 km from the city. The antique and graceful garden has been made known by the "Preface to the Lanting Collection of Poems" by famous calligrapher Wang Xizhi. In 353, in the Eastern Jin Dynasty, great calligrapher Wang Xizhi and his friends Xie An, Sun Chao, relatives and others, all together 42 people, gathered at Lanting Pavilion to hold a ceremony to drive away bad luck according to the traditional custom, and composed poetry over a cup of wine. Wang Xizhi collected all the poems and compiled into "A Collection of Poems", for which he wrote a preface, that is the famous "Preface to the Lanting Collection of Poems". In the garden there are the Goose Pool Tablet, Pavilion of Floating Wine Cup, Youjun Ancestral Temple, Ink Pool and Pavilion of Imperial Tablet. In front of the Pavilion of Floating Wine Cup is a little winding steam. Water flows gently in it, thus it is called the winding stream. Youjun Ancestral Temple is the ancestral hall for Wang Xizhi. In the temple there are many carved tablets and in the middle is hung the portrait of Wang Xizhi. On both sides of the portrait are couplets, saying "Travelling among mountains and rivers all my life, there is no precedence in the ages by sitting here." In the temple there is a pool called the "Ink Pool". It is said that Wang Xizhi used to dip his brush in the pool for writing and gradually the pool was turned black by the ink.

FORMER RESIDENCE OF LU SHUN

Lu Shun Memorial Hall is located at the entrance of Duchang Lane in the south of Shaoxing city. The memorial hall consists of the former residence of Lu Shun, the Herb Garden, Sanwei School and an exhibition hall of the life story of Lu Shun. The whole compound is a courtyard building, typical of the architecture south of the Changjiang River. It was built in the Qing Dynasty (1796-1820). The Herb Garden is at the back of the residence. It was formerly the vegetable garden of the Zhou Family. It was also the playground of Lu Shun in his childhood. 100 m from the residence and beyond a stone bridge is the Sanwei School, where Lu Shun studied in his youth. In the middle of the study there is a horizontal plaque written with the characters "Sanwei School" and below a painting of pine and deer. In the study there is a square table and wooden chairs. The exhibition hall of the life story of Lu Shun is in the east of the residence. Above the gate are inscribed six characters painted in gold "Lu Shun Memorial Hall in Shaoxing" written by Guo Moruo. There are spacious halls for introduction and exhibits. In the middle is a courtyard surrounded by corridors. A large number of articles, pictures, manuscripts, letters, models, magazines and fine art works are on display, following the main trend of the development of Lu Shun's thinking, vividly describing the life story of Lu Shun.

DAYU HILL

It is said that Dayu was a king in the Xia Dynasty 4,000 years ago. He was a hero in harnessing the rivers. This is the place where Dayu was buried and for commemorating him. Dayu Hill consists of Dayu's tomb, Dayu ancestral temple and Dayu Temple. The main architecture is the Dayu Temple, built in 545. The main hall is 24 m high and inside there is a 6-m tall statue of Dayu.

BARKING HILL

The hill was originally called the "Dog's Hill". During the Spring and Autumn and the Warring States Periods the King of Yue State Goujian kept dogs here. The hill was called "Barking Hill" because of the barking of the dogs. The hill is known for its rocky scenery.

FORMER RESIDENCE OF ZHOU ENLAI'S ANCESTORS

Zhou Enlai's ancestors' former residence was also called "Hundred-year Old Hall", built during the Ming Dynasty. It is now an exhibition hall, displaying cultural relics of the time when Zhou Enlai was engaged in anti-Japanese activities here.

RECOMMENDED TOURS

One-day tour of Shaoxing:
Morning: East lake, Dayu Tomb, Lu Shun Memorial Hall and Xianheng Wine Shop
Afternoon: Lanting Pavilion, Former Residence of Qiujin and Former Residence of Zhou Enlai

RECOMMENDED TRAVEL SERVICE

SHANGHAI HUATING OVERSEAS TOURIST CO.

Add: F/4, 503 Wulumuqi Rd, N
Tel.: 62491234
Fax: 62485470,62482781
Post Code: 200040

SHANGHAI JINJIANG TOURS LTD.

Add: 191 Changle Road

Tel.: 64662828

Fax: 64662297

Post Code: 200020

SHANGHAI CYTS TOURS CORPORATION

Add: 2 Hengshan Road

Tel.: 64331826, 64331907

Fax: 64330507

Post Code: 200031

SHANGHAI CHINA INTERNATIONAL TRAVEL SERVICE CO., LTD

Add: CITS Building, 1277 Beijing Rd, W

Tel.: 62898899

Fax: 62894928

Post Code: 200040

SHANGHAI CHINA TRAVEL SERVICE

Add: 881 Yanan Rd, M

Tel.: 62478888, 62475770

Fax: 62475521

Post Code: 200040

(VIII) NINGBO

Ningbo, called "Yong" in short, is situated on the East Sea. It is a famous historical, cultural city and also an opened coastal port. It covers an area of 9,360 sq.km. with a population of 5 million. It has a mild climate with four distinct seasons and an average temperature of 16℃.

Ningbo has a long history. As early as 7,000 years ago our industrious and wise ancestors lived and worked on this piece of fertile land and created the brilliant Hemudu culture. During the Ming Dynasty, the name Ningbo was derived from the saying, "When the sea is stable, the waves are calm." ("Bo" in Chinese means "wave" and "Ning" means "calm"; "Ningbo" means "calm wave".) Since the Tang and Song Dynasties, Ningbo has been a well-known port city for traffic, trade and cultural exchanges with foreign countries and regarded as the starting point of the "silk road on the sea". It was opened as a treaty port after the Opium War. After the founding of New China, especially since China's reform and opening to the outside world, the state has listed Ningbo as a key region for investment. In 1995, Ningbo Port ranked the 4th place in its handling capacity among all the coastal ports in China.

Ningbo is rich in tourist resources. There are many tourist areas and relic sites of the Hemudu culture, such as the Tianyi Chamber, Baoguo Temple, ancient kiln on Shanglin Lake, Ayuwang Temple, Xuedou Hill scenic area in Xikou, Fenghua, and Beichang Port area. Famous arts and crafts and native products are the bone and wood inlaid work, Ningbo-style furniture, red and gold wood carving, gold and silver colored embroidery, gold clay and colored paint. These are done with meticulous choice of raw material and exquisite workmanship; thus they are well-known in the country and abroad.

TIANYI CHAMBER

Tianyi Chamber, located in the western part of the city, was built in the Ming Dynasty (1566). It was formerly the book storehouse of general Fanqin. He derived the name "Tianyi" from the words "Tianyi produces water" in the calligraphy model tablet of the "Record of Tianyi Pond on Longhu Mountain", implying the meaning of "controlling fire with water". Tianyi Chamber has a rich collection of books. It is the most ancient book storehouse of a large scale. It is not only well-known for its collection of books but also for the novel design of architecture and gardening art. The storehouse is a 6-room, two-storied building. In front of the building there is a pond with a pavilion on it and ancient trees and bamboos all around and rockeries in the shape of nine lions and one elephant, all looking vivid and lifelike. Behind Tianyi Chamber is the Junjing Chamber, on which gray brick walls are inlaid with 80 large and small stone tablets, known as the "Table Forest of Mingzhou". Now, Tianyi Chamber has a collection of more than 300,000 volumes of precious ancient books. They are valuable references for the study of the Chinese history, especially the history of the Ming Dynasty.

BAOGUO TEMPLE

The temple, located in Hongtang Town, was built in the Northern

Song Dynasty. It is the best kept of Northern Song Dynasty wood architecture with a history of more than 970 years. The grand hall looks magnificent and imposing. All the different parts in the whole wood structure were tightly riveted together in the column supports without using a single nail. The workmanship is exquisite indeed! The exterior of the grand hall looks magnificent and elaborate in structure, expressing a rich national style. The temple has a high value for the study of China's ancient architectural art. It is a state-level key cultural relic under state protection.

TIANTONGCHAN TEMPLE

The temple, located on the slope of Taibai Mountain, 25 km east of Ningbo city, is the second of the five mountains of Buddhist Chan Sect. It was built in the West Jin Dynasty (300) with a history of 1,600 years. The architecture is grand in scale and magnificent in workmanship. The Buddha statues are huge, rarely found in China. There are 20 groups of ancient buildings with over 730 halls, chambers, pavilions, and rooms, occupying a total area of 58,000 sq.m. The halls are on the mountain slope rising one above the other, from the Six Harmonies Pagoda in front of the temple, to the Heavenly King Hall, the Buddha Hall, the Preaching Hall to the Arhats Hall. The temple is surrounded by a mountain range and towering ancient trees. In the temple are kept carved tablets of the script by emperors Shunzhi, Kangxi and Yongzheng of the Qing Dynasty and the stone carvings of the portraits of the 18 arhats by monk painter Zhuchan.

YUWANG TEMPLE

The temple, located on the Yuwang Hill below the highest peak of the Taibai Mountain, 16 km east of the city, was built in the Western Jin Dynasty (282). It is one of the Buddhist "five mountains". The temple is known for its keeping of the Buddhist treasure "genuine bone relic of Sakyamuni". The temple is grand in scale. It consists of 600 structures, such as the mountain gate, bell tower, heavenly king hall, grand Buddha hall, bone relic chamber, Buddhist scripture storeroom, preaching hall, Huankui chamber, abbot's room and many side rooms. It covers a total area of 11,700 sq.m. It is famous Buddhist shrine south of the Changjiang River. The buildings, paintings, sculpture, garden, calligraphy and carved tablets representing China's ancient cultural and art relics are all well preserved.

EAST QIAN LAKE

The lake is the largest fresh water lake in Zhejiang Province and popularly known as "the beauty of the West lake and the vastness of the Taihu Lake". It covers an area of 22 sq.km., filled in by 72 streams. It is full of historical relics and beautiful natural landscape. Historical relics are the rocky cave of the Southern Song Dynasty called the "Puduo Dongtian" and Temple of Wang Anshi. It is said that the site of the angling by Taogong was the place where Fan Yi and Xishi lived in retreat. There is a poem describing it, "Here is an angling rock for Taogong, a swarm of egrets fly among the misty hills and lake; the angler catches live fish and leaves alone the right or wrong of Wu Yue." The lake is surrounded by mountains and glitters under sunlight in a vast expanse of ripples. Many hotels, amusement parks and water sports grounds are found by the lake side. The lake is abundant in fresh fish that appeal to the palate of visitors.

SCENIC AREA IN XUEDOUSHAN HILL IN XIKOU

The scenic area, located 35 km southwest of the city, is a state-level scenic area. It consists of three scenic areas of Xikou Town, Xuedou Hill and Tingxia Lake. In Xikou Town are found the former residence of Chiang Kai Shek and his son Chiang Jingguo called Fenggao House and a little villa, Yutai Salt Store, Wenchang Chamber, Wuling Gate, Water Bridge, Angling Terrace, Wuling Scenic Spot, tomb passage of Chiang Kai Shek's mother and Wushan Temple. In the Xuedou Hill is the Meitreya Buddha shrine, the Xuedou Temple, Thousand-feet Rock Waterfall, Miaogao Terrace and Imperial Script Pavilion. Below the pavilion are the Gold Turtle Pond and Sanyin Pool. Here people will find grotesque peaks and beautiful valleys, clear streams and splashing waterfalls and also traces left by historical celebrities. It is a famous summer resort.

BEICHANG PORT

It is deep water harbor, known as "a great port in the east". The main water channel is 50-m deep and unfreezing all the year round. It is accessible for 150 thousand-ton ships and for 200 thousand-ton ships at high tide. Along the deep water coastline are built 12 berths for 25 thousand-ton to 150 thousand-ton ships. Its yearly handling capacity is 40 million tons.

RECOMMENDED TOURS

One-day tour of Ningbo city:

Tianyi Chamber, Tianfeng Pagoda, Drum Tower, Seven-Pagoda Temple, City God Temple, Shaobao Hill (including the historic site of ancient coast defense at Zhenhai Mouth) or Baoguo Temple

Two-day tour of Xuedou Hill scenic area:

Wuling Gate, former residence of Chiang's family (Fenggao House) and a little villa, Wenchang Chamber, tomb passage of Chiang's mother, Thousand-feet Rock, Miaogao Terrace, Xuedou Temple and Sanyin Pool

One-day tour of Tiantong Temple and Ayuwang Temple:

Tiantong Temple, Tiantong Forest Park, Ayuwang Temple and Pagoda of Five-Buddha Subduing the Python

One-day tour of East Qian Lake:

King Yue E Temple, Children's City, Butterfly Art Museum, Little Putuo Mountain, Erling Pagoda, Temple of Wang Anshi and Sha Menghai Painting Studio

One-day tour of Historical Site of Yue Kiln at Shanglin Lake and Wulei Hill:

Historical Site of Yue Kiln, Display Hall, Wulei Hill

One-day tour of Hemudu historical site and Baoguo Temple:

Hemudu historical site, ancient ferry crossing, Baoguo Temple

RECOMMENDED TRAVEL SERVICE

SHANGHAI HUATING OVERSEAS TOURIST CO.

Add: F/4, 503 Wulumuqi Rd, N

Tel.: 62491234

Fax: 62485470,62482781

Post Code: 200040

SHANGHAI JINJIANG TOURS LTD.

Add: 191 Changle Road
Tel.: 64662828
Fax: 64662297
Post Code: 200020

SHANGHAI CYTS TOURS CORPORATION

Add: 2 Hengshan Road
Tel.: 64331826, 64331907
Fax: 64330507
Post Code: 200031

SHANGHAI CHINA INTERNATIONAL TRAVEL SERVICE CO., LTD

Add: CITS Building, 1277 Beijing Rd, W
Tel.: 62898899
Fax: 62894928
Post Code: 200040

SHANGHAI CHINA TRAVEL SERVICE

Add: 881 Yanan Rd, M
Tel.: 62478888, 62475770
Fax: 62475521
Post Code: 200040

SERVICE

(I) CONSULTANT SERVICE FOR TOURISTS AND TOURIST SUPERVISORY ORGANIZATIONS

SHANGHAI TOURIST CONSULTANT SERVICE COUNTERS

Location	Tel.	Service hours
Hongqiao Airport	62688899-56750	10:00-21:30
Subway People's Square stop	64381693	8:00-19:00

SHANGHAI MUNICIPAL TOURISM ADMINISTRATION

Shanghai Municipal Tourism Administrative Commission 64391818

Shanghai Municipal People's Government Foreign Affairs Office 62565900

Shanghai Municipal People's Government Overseas Chinese Affairs Office 62490880

Shanghai Municipal People's Government Taiwan Affairs Office 62758877

Shanghai Municipal Public Security Bureau Administration of Entry-Exit for Foreigners 63576666

Shanghai Municipal International Travel Service Association 64391818-2415

Shanghai Municipal Domestic Travel Service Association 63809610

Shanghai Municipal Taxi Association 63681055

FOR TOURISTS' COMPLAINTS

Shanghai Municipal Tourism Administrative Commission 64391818-2501

Shanghai Municipal Tourist Quality Supervisory Office 64391818-5001

Shanghai Civil Aviation East China Administration 62688899

Shanghai Hongqiao International Airport 62688899

Shanghai Port Passenger Transport Service Corp. 63260050

Shanghai Railway Administration 56221862

Shanghai Municipal Public Transportation Administration 63232150

(II) TELEPHONES COMMONLY USED

Tourist quality supervision	64393615
DDD directory inquiries	114
IDD directory inquiries	116
Police alarm	110
Fire alarm	119
Ambulance	120
Weather	121
Time inquiry	117
Aviation service	63261261
Railway information	63179090
Airport information	62688919
Express mail	185
Postcode information	184

(III) BUSINESS DIRECTORY

1. EXHIBITION CENTERS AND CONVENTION FACILITIES

Shanghai is an important port for foreign trade in China. It has trade relations with over 160 countries. As an international metropolis, it has paid much attention to develop facilities for international conventions and exhibitions, sponsor all kinds of international, cultural and sports activities and hold international expositions. At present, Shanghai is developing into a city capable of being a center for holding international conventions and exhibitions. Every year in the past, it had held several dozens of large and small international conventions and exhibitions.

SHANGHAI INTERNATIONAL CONVENTION CENTER

Shanghai International Convention Center, located on Riverside Promenade in Pudong, has a total floor space of 110,000 sq.m. and modernized meeting halls and rooms, including a 4,300 sq.m.-multi-functional hall (with a seating capacity of 3,000 people as a banquet hall and 4,000 people as a convention hall and also available for holding exhibitions), a 3,600-sq.m. news center (exhibition hall), a 800-seat meeting hall and two 200-seat meeting rooms, and 30 meeting rooms for 100 and 50 people. It was the meeting place for the '99 Fortune Global Forum of 500 Tops.

Add: 2727 Riverside Avenue, Pudong

Tel.: 50370000

Means of communications: Public buses 81, 82, 870, 871, 872, Tunnel lines 3, 4, 5 and 6

SHANGHAI INTERNATIONAL EXHIBITION CENTER

Shanghai International Exhibition Center is located in Hongqiao Economic Development Zone, next to Shanghai International Trade Center and several designated foreign-service star-rated hotels. It provides the site for exhibitions and facilities for arranging exhibitions, including show counters. It is also equipped with a business center, providing communication, translation, interpretation and typing service. It is a principal site for holding large-scale international exhibitions.

Add: 88 Loushanguan Road

Tel.: 62755800

Means of communications: Public buses 127, 57, 911 and 925

SHANGHAI INTERNATIONAL TRADE CENTER

Shanghai International Trade Center, a Sino-Japanese joint venture, is located in Hongqiao Economic Development Zone. It occupies an area of 126,410 sq.m. in 37 stories. It provides, besides offices, exhibitions halls, meeting rooms, Chinese and Western restaurants, a clinic and an outdoor parking lot. The international convention halls provide simultaneous interpretation.

Add: 2200 Yanan Rd, W

Tel.: 62757212

Means of communications: Public buses 127, 57, 911 and 925

SHANGHAI EXHIBITION CENTER

Shanghai Exhibition Center is located on Yanan Road in downtown Shanghai. It is a large-scale multi-functional organization, occupying an area of 93,000 sq.m. There is a central hall with a seating capacity of 2,000 people, a banquet hall able to accommodate 50 tables of diners. There is also a east hall, a west hall and a movie house. Large-scale domestic and overseas general or specialized industrial, scientific and cultural exhibitions and meetings are often held here.

Add: 1000 Yanan Rd, M

Tel.: 62790279

Means of communications: Public buses 127, 71, 921, 37 and 48

SHANGHAI INTERNATIONAL EXPOSITION CENTER

Shanghai International Exposition Center is being built in the landscaped area of Pudong New Area. Once completed, it will become the largest exposition center in Asia-Pacific area. It is a joint venture, invested and managed by 3 big exposition companies in Europe, namely, the Hanover, Dusseldorf and Munich. The indoor exhibition hall will cover an area of 200,000 sq.m. and an outdoor exhibition ground, 50,000 sq.m. It will be equipped with a convention center and a parking lot with several thousand parking lanes. It will be a first-rate international exhibition center.

Add: Pudong

SHANG MART

Shang Mart located in Hongqiao Economic Development Zone, provides a first-rate exhibition place complete in facilities and business services. It is the principal site for holding different kinds of large-scale domestic and foreign exhibitions.

Add: 2299 Yanan Rd, W

Tel.: 62366888

Means of communications: Public buses 127, 57, 911 and 925

2. EXPRESS MAIL

POSTAL EXPRESS MAIL

Add: 250 North Suzhou Road

Tel.: 63252070-1337

SINO-FOREIGN TRANSPORT- DUNHAO INTERNATIONAL EXPRESS AIRMAIL CO.,LTD.

Add: 303 Jinian Road

Tel.: 65362900

UNITED PARCEL POSTAL SERVICE

Add: Rm 304A, 65 Yanan Rd, W

Tel.: 62486060

SHANGHAI ORIENTAL WANBANG EXPRESS MAIL

Add: 1200 Zhongshan Rd, N

Tel.: 65601111

SINO-FOREIGN TRANSPORT- TIANDI EXPRESS MAIL CO.,LTD.

Add: 777 Hangxin Road

Tel.: 64211111

(IV) FOREIGN CONSULATES-GENERAL IN SHANGHAI

Foreign visitors may seek help from the consulates in the following cases:

1. Loss of passports or visas
2. Arrangement for travelling visas for the next stop
3. Inquiry for Information about the country concerned
4. Contact with relatives or friends in case of emergency
5. Need for finding a doctor who speaks the same language
6. Inquiry for information about posted documents about goods
7. Inquiry for information regarding laws

BRITISH CONSULATE-GENERAL IN SHANGHAI

Add: Rm 301 Shanghai Center, 1376 Nanjing Rd, W

Tel.: 62797650

Means of communications: Public buses 20, 37, 921 and 40

FRENCH CONSULATE-GENERAL IN SHANGHAI

Add: 21A 1375 Huaihai Rd, M

Tel.: 64377414

Means of communications: Public buses 126, 926 and 911

ITALIAN CONSULATE-GENERAL IN SHANGHAI

Add: 11A 1375 Huaihai Rd, M

Tel.: 64716980

Means of communications: Public buses 126, 926 and 911

AUSTRALIAN CONSULATE-GENERAL IN SHANGHAI

Add: 17 Fuxing Rd, W

Tel.: 64334604

Means of communications: Public buses 48, 96 and 44

CANADIAN CONSULATE-GENERAL IN SHANGHAI

Add: Rm 604 Shanghai Center, 1376 Nanjing Rd, W

Tel.: 62798400

Means of communications: Public buses 20, 37, 921 and 40

IRAN CONSULATE-GENERAL IN SHANGHAI

Add: 296 Xinhua Road

Tel.: 62814666

Means of communications: Public buses 48 and 831

JAPANESE CONSULATE-GENERAL IN SHANGHAI

Add: 8 Wanshan Road

Tel.: 62780788

Means of communications: Public buses 911, 926 and 126

RUSSIAN CONSULATE-GENERAL IN SHANGHAI

Add: 20 Huangpu Road

Tel.: 63937547

Means of communications: Public buses 22, 37, 921 and 934

GERMAN CONSULATE-GENERAL IN SHANGHAI

Add: 181 Yongfu Road

Tel.: 64336953

Means of communications: Public buses 96 and 93

AMERICAN CONSULATE-GENERAL IN SHANGHAI

Add: 1469 Huaihai Rd, M

Tel.: 64336880

Means of communications: Public buses 911, 926 and 126

FINNIC CONSULATE-GENERAL IN SHANGHAI

Add: 7A 1375 Huaihai Rd, M

Tel.: 64740068

Means of communications: Public buses 911, 926 and 126

SINGAPORE CONSULATE-GENERAL IN SHANGHAI

Add: 400 Wulumuqi Rd, M

Tel.: 64370776

Means of communications: Public buses 911, 926 and 126

INDIAN CONSULATE-GENERAL IN SHANGHAI

Add: Rm 1008, 2200 Yanan Rd, W

Tel.: 62758886

Means of communications: Public buses 71, 925, 127 and 911

KOREAN CONSULATE-GENERAL IN SHANGHAI

Add: Fl/4, 2200 Yanan Rd, W

Tel.: 62196417

Means of communications: Public buses 71, 925, 127 and 911

MEXICAN CONSULATE-GENERAL IN SHANGHAI

Add: Fl/9, 1375 Huaihai Rd, M

Tel.: 64379585

Means of communications: Public buses 911, 926 and 126

NEW ZEALAND CONSULATE-GENERAL IN SHANGHAI

Add: Fl/15, 1375 Huaihai Rd, M

Tel.: 64711108

Means of communications: Public buses 911, 926 and 126

CUBAN CONSULATE-GENERAL IN SHANGHAI

Add: Fl/5, No 55 Loushanguan Road

Tel.: 62753078

Means of communications: Public buses 71, 48, 127 and 57

DUTCH CONSULATE-GENERAL IN SHANGHAI

Add: 88 Xianxia Road

Tel.: 62099076

Means of communications: Public buses 71, 127 and 911

ISRAEL CONSULATE-GENERAL IN SHANGHAI

Add: Rm 703, No 55 Loushanguan Road

Tel.: 62098008

Means of communications: Public buses 71, 48, 127 and 57

DANISH CONSULATE-GENERAL IN SHANGHAI

Add: Rm 701, 2200 Yanan Rd, W

Tel.: 62090500

Means of communications: Public buses 71, 925, 127 and 911

BRAZILIAN CONSULATE-GENERAL IN SHANGHAI

Add: 10B 1375 Huaihai Rd, M

Tel.: 64370110

Means of communications: Public buses 911, 926 and 126

CZECH CONSULATE-GENERAL IN SHANGHAI

Add: 12B 1375 Huaihai Rd, M

Tel.: 64712420

Means of communications: Public buses 911, 926 and 126

SWEDISH CONSULATE-GENERAL IN SHANGHAI

Add: 6A 1375 Huaihai Rd, M

Tel.: 64741311

Means of communications: Public buses 911, 926 and 126

SPANISH CONSULATE-GENERAL IN SHANGHAI

Add: 12 Zhongshan Rd, E 1

Tel.: 63234265

Means of communications: Public buses 37, 22 and 55

EGYPTIAN CONSULATE-GENERAL IN SHANGHAI

Add: Fl/19 1375 Huaihai Rd, M

Tel.: 64331020

Means of communications: Public buses 911, 926 and 126

A HANDBOOK
FOR "HELP YOURSELF"
SHANGHAI TOURS
SHANGHAI MUNICIPAL TOURISM
ADMINISTRATIVE COMMISSION

上海科学技术出版社出版、发行

（上海瑞金二路 450 号　邮政编码 200020）

新华书店上海发行所经销

深圳中华商务联合印刷有限公司印刷

开本 889×1194　1/40　印张 7.7　字数 120 千

2000 年 7 月第 1 版　2000 年 7 月第 1 次印刷

ISBN 7-5323-5589-6/K·53

印数 1–3,500　　定价：23.00 元

9,00